An Instrument of Revival

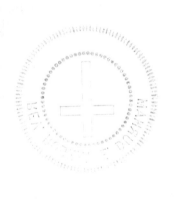

Brynmor Pierce Jones

M.A. (Wales)
B.D. (London)
Diploma in Education (Cardiff)

An Instrument of Revival

The Complete Life of Evan Roberts
(1878-1951)

BRIDGE PUBLISHING
South Plainfield, NJ

An Instrument of Revival by Brynmor Pierce Jones
ISBN 0-88270-667-5
Library of Congress Catalog Card #95-75539
Copyright ©1995 by Bridge Publishing

Published by:
Bridge Publishing Inc.
2500 Hamilton Blvd.
South Plainfield, NJ 07080

To the officers and faithful members of the five little Gwent churches which were under my pastoral care sometime during the period 1965-1995.

Contents

Foreword

I welcome the opportunity to write this foreword to the story of Evan Roberts, who, under God, became a leading figure in the 1904 Welsh revival. One of my grandfathers witnessed the 1904 revival, and I can remember, as a boy, sitting with my cousin underneath my grandmother's large kitchen table (she had 12 children) listening to him recounting to the family the stories of the revival, and of Evan Roberts in particular.

I was intrigued then—and still am—as to what kind of a man was Evan Roberts. What motivated him? What kind of family did he come from? What was his educational background? Did he ever marry? What was he like prior to the revival, and what effect did the great move of God that shook the principality have upon him personally? These and many other questions are answered for us in this book.

It was Horatius Bonar, the great Scottish preacher, who having witnessed the 1839-42 awakening in Scotland said, "The stories of revivals form the true history of the church *and to observe the means and instruments by which God has carried out his work cannot fail to be profitable and quickening"* (italics mine).

I like too his profile of the kind of person God uses to initiate a revival. He says there are nine outstanding characteristics: deep earnestness, a desperate desire to see God work most powerfully, great faith, great patience, a willingness to expend energy and labor fearlessly, determination, deep spirituality, and fervency in prayer. Evan Roberts, as Brynmor Jones so clearly shows, had all of these characteristics.

But as with most people whom God uses, alongside the positive characteristics are human flaws and shortcomings. I am glad the author draws attention to these. Indeed it would be sad if they were overlooked, for it would give the impression that God uses only perfect people. It must be a source of encouragement for us that whilst God desires perfection of character (and we ought always to long for it ourselves), He will not hold back His blessings from us even when perfection is not present, providing our desire is toward Him.

There can be little doubt that one of the greatest challenges facing the Church today is the concept of revival. Some ignore the subject altogether, claiming the work of the Church is to get on with the task of preaching the Gospel, and not to concern ourselves about something that is a sovereign act of God. Some are confident we are on the verge of a worldwide revival, while others speak more carefully and guardedly on the subject.

My own view is that many are wishing for a revival but do not want it deeply enough to pay the price in fervent, believing intercession and prayer. And generally speaking, we are far too easily intoxicated by our successes and thus less dependent on the Holy Spirit than we ought to be. The key word for the life of the Church nowadays seems to be "organize," rather than "agonize."

This is why any literature that reminds us of past revivals is especially welcome at this time. Biographies have a different effect on us than any other type of literature. They reach out invisible hands, draw us into the pages and seem to say: "Look at what God did in the life of this person. Could He not do an equally great work, albeit different, given your own abandonment and dedication?"

My own longing for revival, and for a deeper walk with God, has been quickened by reading this book. I hope yours will be also.

Selwyn Hughes

Crusade for World Revival
Waverly Abbey House
Farnham, Surrey.
September, 1993

Author's Preface and Introduction

It is difficult to introduce to readers a man who said over and over that he wished to remain out of sight. This anointed "messenger and watchman" founded no new church, initiated no new movement, taught no new theology and appointed no successors. He accepted that he was only a channel of the Father, an instrument of the Holy Spirit, a bondservant of the Lord Christ. History will see him as a man appointed by God to apply truths which would surely awaken the churches.

During the revival itself, he was living proof that God uses that which is base and foolish in order to accomplish His purposes. Here was a lad who left school at twelve, laboured in coal mines for twelve years, undertook part-time study and a brief pre-college course. Here was a twenty-six-year-old man who had no pastoral or evangelistic experience but did have a pure faith and a burning passion for souls. As Eifion Evans wrote long ago, he was always in, "The School of the Spirit." Through this dedicated soul, God willed to display His glory.

Though this book does not gloss over flaws in an unmatured temperament, nor the errors of judgment when under pressure, nor the periodic collapses, it does demonstrate that this young man was never far from the God who rescued David from his "pit," Elijah from his "juniper tree," Jeremiah from his "fire in the bones" and the Apostle Paul from his "thorns" and his heavy yoke.

The second part of this book deals with a previously unknown phase of counselling and spiritual teaching at a time when Evan Roberts was thrust into great spiritual battles once more. There were sacred rooms in "Cartref," Toller Road, Leicester, where the man from the revival stood before the Lord, pleading daily for Wales and the world. In this book, Evan Roberts the sufferer, spiritual teacher and prayer warrior, stands alongside Evan Roberts the missioner and the inspirer—or catalyst—of revival.

****

Although the framework of this revival story has already been set up in two companion volumes and in Eifion Evans's older book (see Suggested Readings), it seems advisable to answer two preliminary questions in this Preface: 1. Was Wales and its neighbours in a prepared state for revival? 2. In what way did this national awakening or revival take shape and spread so widely?

In many ways, the word "awakening" is the more accurate when picturing the first stages of the great Holy Spirit event in 1904-1905. A survey of the religious journals covering the last years of the nineteenth century would prove that the churches were socially, culturally, and educationally active, but spiritually inert and asleep. There were scores of singing festivals, preaching festivals, poetry circles, choral festivals, sacred concerts, competitive meetings and public lectures sponsored by each denomination. One could attend such events—along with the Missionary Exhibitions and the Temperance Crusade Meetings—all year-round.

However, the closest one could get to spiritual activity

on weekdays in English chapels was the "Christian Endeavour," which was then still very new. Similarly, in Welsh chapels the only spiritual activity was in the "seiat" gathering. Each denomination was actively involved in political debates, in community politics or in matters denominational, all of which diverted the best minds away from urgently needed mission work. There were few who found time to cultivate the spiritual graces—fewer still who were interested in personal holiness, personal witness and discipleship.

In the last few years of the nineteenth century, a small number of revival prayer meetings sprang up all over Europe, North America, Australia, and many other places. People began to cry that something had to be done about the lost, especially those who sat in the pews with their families but then went out of the service without hearing an invitation or a challenge to repent and believe. The resounding success of the Salvation Army, the Forward Movement, and the first Torrey-Alexander mission caused many churches to sit up and get more decisive. So the Twentieth Century Fund and the Twentieth Century Mission were launched with open-air work, visiting work, and student teams of witness.

The results of these, however, were so small that one leader wrote, "This may not be the best method but we have a real need of revived churches." There was a new spirit of prayer and self-examination stirred up by a "Free Church" president who cried, "Awake to love and self-sacrifice and to cooperation with the Holy Spirit and insight into God's will," and by a very aged dean of "St. David's" who wrote, "The chief need of my dear country and dear nation at present is a spirit of revival through a special outpouring of the Holy Ghost."

The last six months before the awakening in November 1904, were marked by almost desperate seeking after the blessing. Very soon there were small churches where the

Spirit had already come down and one could hear sins confessed, hidden enmities ended, and a great outburst of prayer and impromptu praise. A typical manifestation was at Ponciau near Wrexham, in June 1904, where two guest preachers at a Festival found themselves surrounded by people who where longing to confess and fully yield. One young minister predicted that a cleansing revival was coming to purify every part of God's temple.

Things looked promising but the regular services were still very routine and formal. People seemed to be able to discuss the great doctrines intellectually but never feel the impact on their hearts. One minister said, "They discuss the Atonement without claiming it; they discuss "assurance" without desiring it, and they discuss the work of the Holy Spirit without seeking to experience Him." The Rev. Charles Davies of Cardiff said that the churches refused to take some doctrines seriously. Scholars such as R. Ellis and Vyrnwy Morgan and D. M. Philipps could see that there was a serious lack of power in the preaching because sermons were too objective and cool and because the preachers were not trained to preach for the salvation of souls.

It is hardly surprising that the 1904 revival had to begin with the ministers before it reached the elders and members and the young people. In 1899, W. S. Jones, a successful Welsh minister serving the First Welsh Baptist Church, Scranton, Pennsylvania, began to be convinced by Dwight L. Moody's teaching on consecration and total commitment. Then he had a vision leading to an experience of a thrilling new life which he longed to share with other ministers. There came a second experience—of the holiness and majesty of God—which he also proclaimed with authority. The consequence was a great outburst of repentance and reconciliation and rededication at Scranton and in later pastorates at Carmarthen and Tonypandy. It soon became evident that God had chosen him to be the first receiver and transmitter of Holy Spirit baptism. Around him there gathered a group of young pastors such as Keri Evans,   W. W. Lewis and D. Saunders who sought the same experience. One of these men deeply influenced the young Pastor Joseph Jenkins of Newquay who wrestled with God over his spiritual needs. Afterwards, he set up "Conventions for the Deepening of Spiritual Life." At the second and third of these, the flames of revival were kindled and various revival missions were begun.

Meanwhile, other ministers in South East Wales had decided to seek the help of Dr. F. B. Meyer at the first Keswick Convention in Wales, which was held in August 1903. All their hesitations about receiving the Holy Spirit in a new way were laid to rest. About a dozen or more ministers came home rededicated and rejoicing. Their churches were puzzled at first but gradually their leaders and members also sought some kind of new blessing. All over Wales there were groups not just longing for revival but expecting it and inwardly prepared for it.

Finally, we come to the 1904 summer convention at Blaenannerch near Newquay in Dyfed, where a young student called Evan was utterly broken and remoulded as God's chosen instrument. Other cleansed and surrendered men had returned to churches all over Wales. This is the chief reason why the revival broke out simultaneously in November 1904 in Glamorganshire, Clwyd and Dyfed. It was speedily realised that this revival was a direct work of the Holy Spirit. It had to move along denominational channels at first, and it was also subject to geographical and language barriers, but it was one great revival and it spread over the borders in England and Ireland, and then the countries of Northern Europe. The Holy Spirit awoke a sleeping Church not only in Loughor, Rhos, Newquay, and Aberdare, but in London and Leeds, Pennsylvania and Patagonia, and in the mission fields of North India—in fact, wherever the wind of the Spirit blew.

The companion volumes to this book, will show how the great revival flames leapt up in scores of communities never visited by any "revivalist." Nevertheless, it is also true that the Lord used Evan Roberts in such significant and dramatic and enduring ways that the full story of his ministries must be placed at the centre of events.

Acknowledgments

Thanks are due to the ministers who indicated where rare tape-recorded and other materials could be found. Thanks also to Mr. Meurig Thomas of Rhos, Llandyssul, who has taken great pains to provide photographic records, also Rev. N. Carr of *The Overcomer Testimony*.

I have benefited from the advice of the Rev. J Elwyn Davies (EMW. Wales), and of Mr. David Davies (Swansea Bible College). All of us are indebted to the Rev. Selwyn Hughes of the "Crusade for World Revival" for his helpful foreword.

The copy-editing work was done by my patient wife and especially by my son, Colin, who gave it meticulous attention. Then the final task of publishing was taken up by Ray Stanbury and Guy Morrell, who came to my rescue at God's appointed time.

While this book and its two companion volumes (see "Editor's Note") were just sketches and workbooks, I was laid low with a severe heart attack. Thanks be to a gracious Lord who has given me this opportunity to complete the story of God's revival work in those far-off days.

Editor's Note

This is a general readers' edition, and as such does not contain footnotes referring to research sources, many of which are virtually inaccessible. A list of suggested additional reading is at the end of this book and, as a help to non-Welsh readers, there is also a selected biographical index and information about some of the people related to the Evan Roberts story. For those interested in further study, full documentation and a detailed bibliography is incorporated in a library edition of this book.

There are two companion volumes to this book. One is *Voices From the Revival* (Pub. Spring 1995, E. P. W. Bridgend), which is a compilation of 144 eyewitness accounts. The other is *Revival and Reaction* (Pub. late 1995, Mellen Press, Lampeter). In some places, this book parallels those books and so there are some shared paragraphs, especially in the first part of it.

1

Schoolboy and Collier Lad

A hundred years ago, on the east bank of the River Loughor in South Wales, there was a marshy meadow encircled by thickets. It was called the island because its coarse grass, thin rushes and mud pools were covered by floodwaters when storms filled the river or when a high tide flowed through the two bridges. It was the perfect playground for the agile boys of Bwlchymynydd. On the narrow strip of beach, they wrestled and boxed, fished with peeled sticks, or skimmed small stones across to the Llanelli side.

Among the boys who played there in 1888 was a tall, slender lad with wavy, slightly auburn hair. With him was a stockier lad—his brother Dan. As always, they boxed and wrestled while a friend held the ring. That tall lad, Evan John, would one day be God's "special messenger"; the stocky lad would become a minister of the gospel. The "referee," Dai Grenfell, would one day be a well-known political leader.

Sometimes Evan John would leave his playmates and spend the day deep in a book or perhaps minding his baby sister, but the village lads knew he was no sissy or wimp. It was Evan who had rescued Dan when he became wedged upside down in the well which was used by Bwlchymynydd folk. It was Evan who had dragged that same rash brother out of the treacherous pools in the River Llwchwr.

Another village boy, Jenkin Evans, who played with them on the island would not have been alive if it were not for Evan's courage. Jenkin had been dared by the others to wade across a swiftly rising creek connected with the river. He had floundered in a soft-bottomed stretch and was sinking and crying out when Evan plunged in to save him. It is said that young Evan John uttered a prayer of faith, because he knew very well that he was no swimmer.

Evan John was not a skilled fighter, yet everyone in Loughor had heard how he had thrashed the school bully who had been persecuting the smaller boys. After that incident, even the youngest children knew they could always get help from Evan. In the BBC's special Jubilee interview in 1954, Grenfell described him as,"The most affectionate and easy going of all the youngsters I knew when I was a little scrap."

During those six or seven years in school, Evan met the rather timid Sidney Evans who would become his closest friend. All the older lads attended the National School in Upper Loughor. In its cold, echoing hall, schoolmaster Harris did his duty with the three Rs, but he put his heart into his history lessons and into life-studies such as personal hygiene and personal relationships. In a letter written twenty years later, Evan reminded his old teacher about his many talks about being upright and honourable. When Evan's name eventually became a household word, visitors came to Loughor to talk to Mr. Harris. He told them that Evan had been a quick reader and a disciplined worker but he wasn't particularly precocious or brilliant.

Like most other lads, Evan knew that for him there would be only three choices in life: the shop counter, the workshops in the forges, or the underground where his father and brother worked. The long shadow of the Broadoak

Colliery was cast far across Loughor's streets, just as the fiery sparks of the tinworks fell upon nearby Gorseinon.

Like most schoolboys who lived in Bwlchymynydd, a mile north of Loughor proper, Evan would often do errands for the people who lived along his lane. His neighbours were charmed by his ready smile and his courtesy. The mother of Mrs. Jessie Davies was a close neighbour, but Jessie said that Evan Roberts's parents kept mostly to themselves. The Robertses' home was called "Island House" because it faced the meadow. It had eight small rooms which were just capable of holding Henry and Hannah Roberts and their five daughters and three sons. Its square lines were softened by the shrubs in the front lawn and by a tree which Evan had planted. It had a good cottage garden which the eleven-year-old lad was already strong enough to dig and plant. Hannah and the girls kept the house spotless, and took pride in putting good food into the children's mouths and good clothes on their bodies.

Their home was one of those wonderful Welsh cottages where there were two shelves of good books and a harmonium for family entertainment. Dad's well-read Bible, from which he memorised hundreds of verses, mother's well-worn hymnbook and a study Bible for each child, so that they could prepare for the Sunday school examinations, were there as well. On Sundays the family would walk a mile and back, two or three times, to the Moriah Chapel where Henry and Hannah had taken Evan John to be baptised a few weeks after his birth on June 8, 1878.

Henry Roberts was a serious, orderly, self-disciplined man who had saved enough money to become a homeowner. After he courted and married Hannah, the daughter of a village blacksmith, he had taken a job at Derwen Lydan (Broadoak) Colliery and had been entered on the membership roll (his name is spelt Hendryd) of Moriah Calvinist Methodist Church. He served his church faithfully for forty years.

Hannah was greatly honoured for her practical kindness and, above all, for her love of God's house and God's Word.

Like many, they had their ups and downs. Hannah was so ill after one childbirth that Evan had to take over the minding of the new baby sister while the girls managed the house. Then Henry sustained a serious leg injury and he was forced to take Evan out of school and bring him into the colliery to help him maintain the pumps.

Evan's brief morning of childhood was over as he put on the tough clothing of a collier lad, collected his personal lamp at the pithead and went down into the depths. As his mother watched him go to join his father and brother, she may have felt a little saddened. No vision or voice had yet shown her what God had in mind for her boys. Many Welsh mothers in those days dreamed their sons would become preachers, but an even greater joy was reserved for Hannah.

The first job given to the new recruits in a pit was that of "doorboy." This entailed opening and shutting the ventilation doors and all other gates whenever the next journey of drams was passing through. It was a cheerless job, sitting there in near darkness and hearing strange sounds until the shine of lamps and the rumble of heavy wheels broke into a boy's daydreams. Evan once had a narrow escape when a runaway dram slid back down the slope and almost pinned him to the harsh wall. Some men already believed that the hand of God was in this. The unusual lad always had a Bible with him, and as each collier passed by his door Evan would offer him a text and ask him to think about it during any slack moment he might have. At the end of the shift, as each man walked wearily towards the pit bottom, this remarkable boy would ask him, "What truth did you find in that text?" When Evan was promoted to help an older man cut coal, he took his Bible there and found a niche where he could keep it for use. This is the origin of that true story of how, when Evan was not on shift, there was an explosion and fire in the headings and, afterwards, they found this Bible marred and scorched but still usable (it can still be seen).

4

The colliers learned to respect young Roberts as a good worker but they soon found that he would not listen to their usual vulgar jokes, nor use their kind of language, nor could he get excited about their sports and amusements. At times he seemed totally distant. They did not know that in his first three years as a miner, Evan had crossed a threshold into a larger place where his mind and soul found room to expand. His name appears in the church roll for the first time in 1893-94 after he had been instructed by the elders in a preparation class.

At some point during that important period, Evan experienced his first spiritual crisis. Something was preached there which made him feel guilty before God and in great need of forgiveness. He confessed his sins and put his trust in God's grace. Filled with a new certainty, he made a solemn vow that he would be a useful member and would serve the Master. It was not easy for a lad to work a whole shift underground and come home to bathe and eat, then walk a mile to Moriah. But he kept his vow to put chapel first.

It was during one of the weeknight meetings that the second crisis came. Words were said that profoundly affected Evan's spiritual life. A godly deacon exhorted people to come to the means of grace more regularly. He reminded them that when Thomas was absent from the upper room, he had missed that vital moment when the Lord came and breathed His Spirit into the others. At once the impressionable young lad vowed that he would never be absent from such meetings and that he would also wait and pray faithfully for the coming of the Holy Spirit. If only his private diary had survived, more would be known about his developing grasp of the truth and his deepening spiritual desires. Grenfell testified that Evan had no dogmatic beliefs: "I would rather call it an idealistic element, elevated and ethical and of the highest purity." His father was thrilled when the earnest lad joined him in local crusades on behalf of strict temperance. His mother was not an idealist but she greatly loved this son and tried to understand his emotional and spiritual needs, even his need to be alone.

In that study where he had knelt and made his vow to do some service for his Lord, Evan taught himself to play the violin, the mandolin and the harmonium. He believed that God would use these skills some day. Just as his father had done, Evan spent hours memorising key passages of scripture, using a shorthand Bible. He pored over *Ellicott's Commentaries* and his *Cruden's Concordance,* and made his own notes.

When he had a little pocket money, Evan bought leather-bound editions of the religious classics and also of Christian novels, such as J. H. Ingraham's *Prince of the House of David* or C. R. Sheldon's *In His Steps,* which deeply influenced him. The subtitle, "What Would Jesus Do?" seemed to urge him to ask himself a very disturbing question, "What have I done for Jesus' sake?" In his sixteenth year an unexpected opportunity was given him.

It came from the colliery management. This fact amazed even those workmen who knew he was highly regarded as a skilled, energetic coal cutter and an able spokesman on their behalf when matters of welfare were being discussed. The under-manager of the Broadoak, a decent and a religious man, was also the superintendent of a "ragged school" for children. Mr. Samuel Thomas, the owner, had set it up in the colliery works office. Knowing something about Evan's abilities, the under-manager recruited him as his helper and secretary.

A few months later, the mine owner himself appointed Evan to teach music, mathematics and moral values to the workers'children. He put his heart and soul into lifting them out of a state of ignorance and dull apathy, not because he upheld any educational philosophy or political ideology, but because he loved children. Several years later, that same love would be shown to the young people of the district.

In 1895 Samuel Thomas decided that the works office was not good enough and that land must be set aside for building a schoolroom near the workmen's cottages. He asked seventeen-year-old Evan if he would superintend its construction. Although he was young, he organised things well and made his helpers so keen that they set aside much of their savings for the project. The colliery was on short time so men had hours available for trenching, bricklaying, laying a path and setting up special railings. Soon the little community had its new schoolroom which also served as a place of worship. Evan felt led to present this little sanctuary, called Pisgah, with a Bible, which is still kept there in a place of honour.

For three years, life was full to the brim with activities and new plans, especially when Evan was given even more responsibility in the school chapel and in the parent chapel. He had no time for the sporting interests of other young men. Neither would he join that interesting world of courting couples. It was the pleasant custom in those days for young men and women who attended various chapels to walk between Gorseinon Cross and the Loughor Stone for an hour or so after Sunday evening service. This was an approved way to meet and chat with potential partners who would later on make "appoints." Evan was never seen on that parade; he was more likely to be in an after-church discussion group. In due course he had the permission of the officers of Moriah to start up a weeknight debating circle, mainly for serious-minded young men like himself. Despite his great love of music, he never seems to have joined a chapel choir.

This happy, fruitful period came to an abrupt end in 1897-98 because Broadoak colliery fell on hard times. A costly explosion came at a time when collieries were competing for a share of a shrinking market. Instead of short time there were stoppages and disputes and strikes which did even more damage. There was a kind of unwritten law in those days that when men had to be paid off, the single men would go first and the married men last. The bachelors would go on their travels to the pits in other valleys or try their hand at some different trade. At first Evan was on temporary jobs in Maesteg, Blaengarw and possibly the Rhondda. He could go home on weekends and carry on some of his spiritual work. But one year later (1898) he was given work in Mountain Ash, to the north of Cardiff, and it became necessary to resign from his work in Moriah and Pisgah. What a bitter blow that must have been; yet, as so often happens, the Lord was closing these doors in time to open a great door of opportunity for His chosen servant. The three years spent in other valleys did him a world of good.

2

The Candidate for the Ministry

here are many paths by which the Lord leads His servants into full-time ministry. Although Evan Roberts had showed early signs of spiritual maturity and of ability to communicate, there was no sign of a call to preach until he came to Mountain Ash. When the young miner attended Bethlehem for the first time, carrying with him the customary letter of commendation, he was welcomed by Mr. Jones, the minister who had baptised Evan John as an infant in 1878. After the revival had begun, this pastor felt that he had been an instrument of Evan Roberts's conversion or reconsecration. Certainly the minister and officers put Evan Roberts to good use. He was involved in the Christian Endeavour branch and learned a great deal from its training methods. He was also asked to give papers on various subjects, which was excellent practice.

Once he had found out about Evan Roberts's growing reputation as a man of prayer and vision, the minister encouraged him even more. The story of Evan Roberts's scorched Bible was going the rounds, especially that part which purported that the one leaf that was only partly scorched was the page on which is recorded Solomon's prayer for his nation and the coming of fire down from heaven (2 Chron. 7:1). "Was this a sign of things to come?" they wondered.

Other stories were circulated about Evan Roberts's supposed mysticism. People saw his lips moving and could hear deep sighs coming from his bosom as he stood stock-still by the roadside, but they could hear no words. No one had seen him kneeling in prayer, not even in a chapel meeting. People also knew that he often meditated and studied so long during the day that he missed his evening meal. He seemed to forget both the clock and his whereabouts. A Christian man who lodged in the same house as Evan Roberts had this to say: "We usually had a reading and prayer together before we put out the lamp. Then I could hear Evan calling and groaning in the spirit. I could not understand what was his message to God again, and some holy fear kept me from asking."

During this period at Mountain Ash, there were two incidents which pointed Evan Roberts in a new direction. The first was a visit to Cardiff where he had arranged to consult Dr. Williams, the phrenologist. In those days there were many practitioners of a pseudo-science that measured the cranium, deduced certain patterns, and suggested the kind of work people were fitted for. After he had done all this to the young miner, Dr. Williams told him, "You ought to be a public speaker or a preacher."

The second incident convinced Evan Roberts far more. He had travelled to Builth Wells for some kind of conference or inter-church prayer meeting. He was suddenly moved to pray and did so with such power that people's hearts were melted. After that meeting, a local minister came to him and said, "Look here, young man, you have talents for the pulpit. Do not abuse them. It is a matter for prayer. You, my friend, must pray over it. PRAY!"

Doubtless Evan did pray over it, but there was an idol

in his heart that had to be cast out. This was powerful ambition or *drive* to become a successful Welsh "bard"—a role which then had considerable status in Wales. Already, during his teenage years and his time at Mountain Ash, he had written a number of poems cast in the form of parables. Several had been accepted by editors of local newspapers. Others were put in for competitive meetings after he returned to Loughor and Pontardulais where he won several prizes. This urge to write poetry was to be transformed one day into a spiritual *drive*. (He told one friend, "My Muse has never been idle.") But at this particular crossroads in his life, God showed him a different path to take and a new challenge to be faced.

Evan Roberts returned to Loughor in 1900 and showed at once that he was ready for new spiritual tasks. Before long he called together a band of youths, some of whom had been his pupils in the "ragged school" and others members of a debating circle. All these young men agreed to take part in a new venture which was not unlike the Christian Endeavour. It was to meet at Pisgah and was to be called the "Cylch Gweddi" (Prayer Circle). Its aim was to train each member to take part in public worship and service and it was ruled from the start that "No one is to lead the meeting, but each one is to take part as moved by the Spirit." Was this a foretaste of 1905?

Evan soon realised that some men would have difficulties, so he wrote out some short pattern prayers for them and also made a list of the Bible portions they could use in public worship. On a free Saturday, when he was not on shift, he would take this unusual kind of youth group along the riverside paths. They would argue vigorously about some problem or other until they came to a quiet place where they could sit and pray. One day a tactless person described these walks as spending an idle afternoon, and Evan Roberts replied with a crushing rebuke, "Not at all; we must be holier after this." In God's plan, these men were ready for more blessing when revival came.

Workmen on the same shift as Evan had long been used to his habit of reading the Bible by the light of his Davey lamp whenever there was a short break in the arduous work. No one gave him hard times when he knelt in the coal dust to read and pray, but they exchanged puzzled looks when he seemed to become absolutely still and far away from them. Their wives and children had also seen Evan standing in a trance-like state by the roadside, as if communing with the Unseen. His family knew that he sometimes spent the whole night in prayer, but only his mother knew of the unique experiences he now enjoyed.

She wrote, "A remarkable thing happened to our Evan one Sunday. As was his custom, he had attended the services and was very tired. There was something peculiar about him. At first he did not seem willing to talk much, but he later told me that he had been face to face with God."

The members of Moriah were deeply impressed by the way that Evan Roberts came alive in the chapel prayer meeting and in that peculiarly Welsh form of discussion group, called "Y seiat." His favourite topics were George Mueller on "Absolute Faith" and "Answers to Prayer"; John Bunyan on "Pilgrimage"; and Williams Pantycelyn on "Spiritual Longings." After the meeting he would walk home with a friend and stay up half the night to talk and pray about revival. There is a story that certain deacons were a bit concerned about this and went to see Evan John, who told them firmly, "But the Spirit moved me."

In 1902 the senior deacons met him and asked him whether he was being called by God to the ministry. At that very moment Evan was being tested. Certain people told him that he had a great aptitude for literature and music, and that he could become a bard rather than a preacher or a missioner.

One day he was reading aloud a hymn about receiving

the Holy Spirit. He felt that the Lord was commanding him to be obedient even unto death and he decided to go to his parents and say to them, "I will do my best and the consequences will be God's. It would be terrible for me, when I go to the judgment seat, for Christ to tell me, 'You could have preached for me, but you refused.'" As soon as he had yielded, the tension left him and he was given a fresh experience of the Lord's nearness. Now he knew what he had to do.

The first step was to write to a friend named W. H. Morgan who was versed in these matters. He told him about his longing to tell people about God's love, and about his fear that any academic studies would shatter him because he had so little schooling. His first plan was to learn a craft and become self-supporting like St. Paul, so that he could then travel far and wide. Such a thing was common enough in the early days of Nonconformist preaching. Because of this plan he left the colliery and became an apprentice to his blacksmith uncle at the forge in Fforest, Pontardulais in 1902.

For fifteen months he worked at the forge from 8.00 a.m. to 8.00 p.m., from Monday to Saturday, leaving only a little time for study. While the forgemaster and other apprentices chatted with farmers and colliery craftsmen in the glow of the fires, Evan would try to sit in the shadows and pick up his Bible, which always lay within his reach. By the end of 1903 he already knew that he would have to abandon his first plan and turn his back on the apprenticeship. Because of his mother's strict code, she made her family offer compensation to her brother for the cancellation of the training.

After receiving a letter full of advice from W. H. Morgan, Evan consulted the minister and elders about ways and means to do preparatory study. His name was passed on to the district meeting where he was advised to go to Newcastle Emlyn School and there prepare himself for matriculation as the means of entrance to Trefecca College. The next step was the trial sermon which was preached at Moriah in the presence of his family and friends. His chosen themes that day were "Christ's Rights Over Us" and "The Need to Follow and Obey." At the church meeting which followed, the members were asked if they would support his case to go for training. A few wondered if Evan could cope, but the minister ended the discussion by calling for the members to vote if they felt that the Lord had truly called Evan Roberts. Thus the first hurdle was crossed.

The next months would have been a testing time for any candidate because they were all required to preach twice at each of twelve churches. Each church sent its report and all were favourable. The only sermon title that has been preserved was "Jeremiah's Call and Jeremiah's Doubts." In another address, he set forth his own desire to live a life which would have a positive influence on others. This motivation came out clearly in the final interview with two senior ministers. First, the Rev. William Jenkins examined every aspect of his temperament and spiritual experience. Then the Rev. Davies of Pontardulais examined his motives. Davies asked, "What has prompted you to enter the ministry? Is it a desire to be in the respectable office of minister?"

Roberts answered, "My motive is a passionate desire for the privilege of proclaiming Christ to the lost."

One effect of all these tests was to make Evan very concerned about his own spiritual needs. Writing once more to W. H. Morgan, he said, "I have prayed that the Lord will baptise you and me with the Holy Spirit." He confided to another friend that he had been forced to learn a heavenly secret, "Ask and it shall be given unto you. Practise entire, definite faith in God's promise of the Spirit." In His wisdom and mercy, the Lord now gave him one of those visions which came to him in a time of difficult choice.

He reported, "I was frightened that night, but never since. So great was my shivering that I rocked the bed. My brother

Dan, being awakened, took hold of me thinking I was ill. After that experience I was awakened every night at one o'clock. From that time I was taken up into divine fellowship. About five o'clock I was allowed to sleep on till nine. It was too divine to say anything about. I cannot describe it but I felt it. It changed my whole nature."

When he preached at Moriah in December 1903, he told them, "I have reached out my hand and touched the flame. Now I am burning and waiting for a sign." This was the very year when all over Wales, leaders of every denomination were calling for revival. (See *The King's Champions,* Ch. 2, p23 ff.) But from this point until the summer of 1904, Evan had to buckle down to the studies prescribed for the entrance examination, which was to be taken at Pontrhydyfen in August. He made constant use of the commentaries of Cruden and Ellicott, but also mastered the textbooks written by Thomas Charles and Dr. Angus.

It is almost impossible for modern students to imagine how much basic knowledge of ethics and doctrine an intelligent chapel member could pick up in the many debating societies. He could acquire detailed biblical knowledge through the Sunday school exams and the catechisms; he could learn the principles of worship and evangelism by example. Candidates for the ministry would often attend the preaching festivals in every chapel and hear the best expositors and the princely preachers whose manners and methods they were encouraged to imitate. As yet the pulpit of Moriah had hardly been touched by "higher criticism" and the kind of theology which was so soon to sweep from the continent into Wales. (See *The King's Champions,* Ch. 10.) Moriah Church was committed to Calvinist doctrine and Evan had a thorough grasp of "man, sin and salvation."

There were echoes of these doctrines and of the preaching style in Evan Roberts's pre-revival sermon which

D. M. Phillips included in his biography. One can almost hear the great rolling sentences and the bursts of passion, combined with careful logic. The presentation of the "Rights of the Saviour" led to an awful picture of how men and women rejected the divine claims. Then Evan cried out, "Will you reject and thus endure the bitter wrath of God? Will you accept and have entry to that eternal state where Jesus will be the theme of everlasting wonder and unceasing praise?" Already at this stage, Evan Roberts was evangelist enough to state his conviction that "the Saviour has sufficient grace to rescue the most desperate sinner."

After the season of preaching festivals, there remained the final bout of study and discussion during July and August, 1904. Sidney Evans heard his friend praying for help to pass the examination without delay, but he also heard him praying that he should be empowered to become an evangelist as soon as possible. As these two strong desires began to battle in his mind, he became dry and depressed and lost that glad communion and mystic experience, just as he feared. Sidney Evans said they often put aside their books and talked about the state of Wales, and that Evan loved to recite, "If my people . . . will humble themselves and pray. . . ." (2 Chron. 7:14.) He needed a new encouragement from the Lord.

About the encouragement he received, Evan wrote, "I was troubled in my soul by thinking of the failure of Christianity. Such a failure. I prayed and prayed but nothing seemed to give me any relief. One night, after I had been in great distress praying about this, I went to sleep. At nine o'clock I was awakened out of my sleep and found myself with unspeakable joy and awe, in the very presence of Almighty God. For the space of four hours I was privileged to speak with Him as a man speaks with his friend. I saw things in a different light. I knew God was going to work in the land."

On 14 August, Sidney and Evan were informed that they passed the entrance examination and that fees would be paid. For a month they were both engaged in breaking off ties with church life and Evan felt that God was not coming to him in the mornings any more. However, he seemed to have fully accepted that he needed the kind of knowledge that a college course could give before he could serve the Lord. One month later he was on his way by train to Carmarthen and northwards to Newcastle Emlyn, deep in the heart of rural Wales.

On 13 September 1904, Evan Roberts and other young men entered the doors of a compact little stone building known locally as the Emlyn Grammar School. It still stands at the eastern entrance of the little market town, but it can easily be missed by anyone who drives in. Not far away was another old house, called "Ty Llwyd," where two Christian ladies provided meals and beds for students. There was not a great deal of entertainment in the town, except on market days. The curving main street, with chapels at each end, sloped gently down to an imposing bridge over the River Teifi. The town had a somewhat leisurely train service by which some student preachers could travel farther afield. The people usually depended on "wagonnettes" which could be hired to take parties out to those preaching and singing festivals which were bright spots in chapel-goers lives.

In due course, Evan and Sidney attended the Bethel Chapel and all its meetings. Members were impressed by these serious young men and Mr. J. J. Morgan, the biographer of its famous minister Evan Phillips, recorded the testimony of eyewitnesses that there was a real challenge in Evan's voice and that nothing could stop him when he was on fire. He was soon noticed by the aged Pastor Evan Phillips who had so often called upon his people to seek after God.

Sometimes the students would be invited to the Phillips's house, called "Sunnyside," and Evan loved to sit with the aged minister who had seen the 1859 revival and longed for a new outpouring. Evan trusted him enough to disclose his first dreams, such as that of Satan's face sneering at him in the midst of some garden shrubs. The wise pastor rightly dismissed these as products of overwrought imagination, yet he recognised the true visions which called the young man to his ordained task.

During these student suppers, Rachel and Ann Phillips did their best to draw out "Roberts bach," even when he puzzled them. At times the company in the drawing room was very pleasant and Evan would smile gently at the jokes and tales. One thing he did really well—he could compose little proverbs which the listeners thought good enough to note and repeat. Here are two examples: "The Christian life is not a grave but a garden though there may be some weeds in it." "You can always smile at the world when God smiles on your soul."

The one member of the Phillips family who was uncomfortable was John Phillips. As a tutor he was upset by Evan's restlessness, his strange actions and his claims that he was under the Spirit's command when he missed a class or forgot a study period or failed to finish an essay. Years after the revival, John admitted that he had failed entirely to see that many of these acts and words were the first signs that the hand of the Lord was upon an anointed student. But other teachers were also annoyed and puzzled by Evan's attitude to the courses of study which he had once tried so hard to enter. They could see that he had the ability to succeed. D. M. Phillips discovered that Evan Roberts had begun to feel a new conflict between desires to study and longings to witness.

Phillips wrote, "When engaged with his school books, he was possessed with some strange unaccountable feeling. Owing to this, he was sometimes a burden and a terror to himself. The strange thing in connection with this experience was that to take hold of the Bible gave him peace. His experience in school was repeated at home. He would open a book, only to find it flaming in his hands. He would at once kneel in prayer, seeking deliverance. When he had the Bible in his hand, the commotion ceased at once. This experience increased daily until the awe that possessed him made it impossible to battle on."

Friends advised him to blot out from his mind any force that constrained him to opt out of school. One or two even went so far as to introduce him to Dr. Hughes, an American specialist, who told them that Evan was suffering from religious mania. However, time would show that this mysterious conflict within Evan was not a mental or emotional problem, but was spiritually connected in some way with those powerful movings of the Spirit which had already begun in West Wales. The hour of decision was coming; the hour of God was about to strike; and Evan Roberts was feeling within himself the first great stirrings of the Holy Spirit.

3

Changed, Consecrated, and Commissioned

oth Eifion Evans's general survey and the many personal testimonies recorded in *Voices From the Revival,* show that just at the time when Evan Roberts was taking steps to enter ministerial training at Newcastle Emlyn, the whole of the South Cardiganshire region was in a state of ferment. Some of the churches were filled with a new energy and vision. At Newquay, the Rev. Joseph Jenkins and others, filled with longings to receive holiness and power, had set up district conventions for the deepening of spiritual life. Preachers such as W. W. Lewis and D. Saunders had shown them the way to be cleansed, baptised with the Spirit and filled with joy and assurance. As these conventions moved southwards towards Blaenannerch and Cardigan, the students from the Newcastle Emlyn School had begun to attend.

Meanwhile, teams of young people from Newquay and Aberaeron had begun to surge out into the villages which fill that quadrant bounded by the Aberaeron - Cardigan coast road on the west and the Lampeter - Llandyssul - Carmarthen road on the east. Students could hardly resist their bold testimonies and their calls to full surrender. Finally the local ministers arranged a gospel mission and invited that rugged evangelist, Seth Joshua. His mission began at Newcastle Emlyn just after Evan Roberts joined the school. People noticed that the new student from Loughor sat through every meeting as though he were entranced.

One evening his closest friend, Sidney Evans, came back with the others from Cardigan all aglow and eager to tell how they had surrendered their lives to the Lord and now wanted to be witnesses for Him. At first Evan Roberts showed no sign of profound change. A few days later, after a bout of flu, he fell into a deep depression. He could not even pray in the church meeting, even though he had rushed down on the Tuesday evening, as if he were compelled to attend. Evan said that on that terrible night: "I could look at the Cross without feeling. I wept for the hardness of my heart, but I could not weep for Christ."

The following morning he wrote to a friend, "I am like a flint. I feel as if someone has swept me clean of every feeling."

When he met up with the sympathetic Magdalen Phillips, he burst into tears and asked her to pray for him. About this, he wrote: "Both of us were blessed the same day. I received something about half-past-three and I asked Mag if she had been praying for me at that time. She told me, 'I have been praying for you all day, Roberts bach.' When returning on Wednesday night the young women from Newquay tried to influence me, but nothing touched me. They said, 'We can do nothing for you.' 'No,' said I, 'I have only to wait for the fire. I have built the altar and laid the wood in order and prepared the offering. I have only to wait for the fire.'"

One of the tutors noticed that at the Wednesday evening meeting the new student from Loughor had been praying with strong cries of supplication to heaven, and that he was uttering the single word "Oh!" many times, as if his heart was melting. Surely that melting had to happen before the soul of Evan Roberts could be poured out into a new mould. Only a few hours remained before God answered that "Oh!" And another "Oh!" had been answered as well, because for some time Seth Joshua had been beseeching the Lord to take "another Elisha" from his daily work and then "mantle him with power."

They all travelled to Blaenannerch that day, the students sharing a wagon with Mr. Joshua, the people from Newquay riding down. As their wagonette drew near to the chapel they sang: "It is coming; it is coming; the power of the Holy Ghost. I receive it; I receive it; the power of the Holy Ghost."

The first service was at 7.00 a.m., and Mr. Joshua was quiet until he began to pray for the "bending." Afterwards, they all went to a minister's house for breakfast before the 9.00 a.m. prayer meeting. Evan was quiet, solemn and so tense that one little incident upset him again. As he was refusing some food, a voice spoke within his troubled heart, saying, "What if God is offering me the Spirit and I am not ready to receive Him, when others would be ready to accept were they offered?"

In such a mood, he went back to the chapel and sat in a side pew on the right hand, not with the ministerial students but with his Newquay friends. Two of the ministers looked at him and dismissed him as a neurotic type. Even the chapel pastor, M. P. Morgan, was annoyed when he heard a disturbance and saw that this young man seemed to be making an exhibition of himself. A few realised that Evan had come to a crisis point and was responding at last to Seth Joshua's words, "Bend us; Bend us." The chairman, who could see other young people also weeping and trembling, could do nothing to ease Evan Roberts's pain.

Weeks later, at the request of the journalist W. T. Stead and a minister named Thomas Francis, Evan described this unforgettable experience of the "Living Energy" which had invaded his soul, burst all his bonds, and overwhelmed him.

What boiled my bosom was the verse, "For God commendeth His love." I fell on my knees with my arms outstretched on the seat before me. The perspiration poured down my face and my tears streamed quickly until I thought the blood came out. Mrs. Davies of Mona, Newquay, came to wipe my face, and Magdalen Phillips stood on my right and Maud Davies on my left. I cried, "Bend Me, Bend Me, Bend Me....OH! OH! OH!" Mrs. Davies said, "O wonderful grace." "Yes," said I, "O wonderful grace." It was God commending His love that bent me, and I not seeing anything to commend. After I was "bended," a wave of peace and joy filled my bosom.

When Evan Roberts gave his testimony at the afternoon service, he spoke of this experience as if it were a kind of conversion or new birth, as well as an act of surrender. He told everyone how he had been set free once and for all, from all doubt and fear and guilt. Now he was ready to become God's messenger, as soon as the Lord would open the way for him. He wrote these lines expressing the great and blessed change:

> My heart was ever like a stone,
>   My tongue still as the grave.
> But from another world there shone
>   A light my soul to save.
> Now I am singing all day long
>   The praises of His blood.
> No other theme awakes my song
>   Like Calvary's crimson flood.
> I feel the presence of His hand,
>   Bending my sinful heart.
> Henceforth no power can command
>   My soul from Him to part.

The new mood of joyous confidence seemed to permeate his conversations and even his letters. A church leader at Newcastle Emlyn said that Evan Roberts was acting like a particle of radium or like a consuming fire which "took away sleep, cleared the channels of tears and sped the wheels of prayer throughout this district."

A letter, sent to his mother and brother, assured them that now he felt courageous for Christ and joyful in Christ. Another letter to his friends at Loughor spoke of the radiance which was soon going to flood Wales with light. Perhaps he was thinking of that vision he had of the sun rising behind a candle and making its light look so pale. He took this as a sign that whatever blessings had already come were but a feeble glow if compared with the glory yet to come. He lived in a spirit of hope, yet he was also intensely serious. When he stepped into a pulpit he was solemn and earnest because he saw souls in danger of the final judgment, if he did not warn them.

Once he had had a vision about Satan mocking and obstructing his future work. Now, as the fire spread through his whole being, he confided to his friends that: "The devil is doing his worst these days. He attacks me with all his resources and also ploughs up my past life." During this self-examination, he made every effort to pay off unsettled debts and return borrowed books.

Evan had an amazing experience one moonlit evening in the garden of Ty Llwyd. It was all the more convincing because it was shared with Sidney Evans, a modest man who kept quiet about it. Mr. Evans eventually told the full story to a BBC interviewer during the Golden Jubilee of the revival: "I saw him looking at the moon and I said to him, 'What are you looking for? What are you doing here? This is a strange place. What are you seeing?' Then there was seen a kind of arm stretching out from the moon in the direction of earth. I saw something of the sort. I do not usually get visions, but I saw it also. We both had a vision that night. The explanation I would like to give to that vision would be that we had been praying for one hundred thousand, and that the vision had been given in answer to it."

Evan Roberts had not received exact guidance yet, and Sidney Evans called this time a "Seeking experience when the Holy Spirit had taken over control of the instrument, but one still had to apply and make use of the instrument. It was a seeking time and a wearying time, though peace possessed his soul." A Pembrokeshire minister saw how tense he was in the pulpit and was told that the young preacher was already very anxious to go out and catch a "big net full of fish."

In this state of high tension, Evan rebuked the Phillips sisters for disobeying the Spirit when prompted to take part in a service. He told a Newquay friend that nothing could be done until they had learned the meaning of Matthew 28:18—ALL POWER. He confessed to a Llanelli friend that he felt that God had taken hold of him and pressed him down to earth, but that he still had to wait for the Master's leading.

Many bands of young people were already visiting the villages and rural chapels in order to "make churches alive," as they informed a minister's conference. Now it was the turn of Evan Roberts, Sidney Evans and some young ladies to plan a mission. They were prepared to give time, money and talent for this work, but Evan had warned them, "We can do nothing without the Holy Spirit." When they felt they needed guidance, Evan wrote down four questions in shorthand and placed them on two small Bibles in the Lord's presence. They came back in fear and trembling to that room to collect God's answers, but there were none. Then a voice spoke to Evan: *"You asked who should go and where and when and how. First you should have asked God, 'Shall we go?'"* The good Lord permitted them to go ahead, but they had learned a vital lesson for missioners.

Their first meetings at Blaenannerch and near Newquay were so successful, that one night the student members walked a dozen miles to Newcastle Emlyn in a rainstorm which they hardly noticed. Their landladies were even more worried when the young men stayed up half the night, praising the Lord.

In the third week of their mission, when they were visiting villages on the Pembrokeshire side of the River Teifi, they ran into trouble. In one village there was both a preaching festival and a singing festival, so they asked if they could hold a special meeting for the young people. This was refused and someone told them sourly that he would drive them home in his pony and trap. People began to whisper that there was something improper and scandalous about this business of young men and women going out into the countryside all day and coming back long after nightfall. Even in Newcastle Emlyn, where many knew the young men, there were chapel people who murmured, "Why is it only these three students feel they are obeying the Spirit?"

When Evan Roberts wrote next to his family and his prayer partners, he asked them to pray right through the next mission:

> I know that prejudice will be strong against the movement. Therefore we must be armed with the Holy Spirit. Amongst many there will be levity and this calls on us to be very watchful with our movements and our words, and remember to keep our eyes from wantonness. There will be another class who will come out of curiosity and possibly to scoff. Therefore what will be necessary for us is to be strong in prayer. Oh that we could all feel we can do nothing without the Holy Spirit and, in that feeling, fall in lowliness before God with a broken heart, beseeching him to show us His face, especially at Capel y Drindod. It would be awful for us without God.

He need not have worried because the Lord blessed and safeguarded this band for months after Evan left them. When they dared to hold an open-air service in Cardigan Fair, they felt an evil, hostile atmosphere there. But they found also that "all the devils in Gehenna are under marching orders. Their kingdom is brought to the dust."

Evan Roberts came under personal attack as a lunatic at worst and eccentric at best. He didn't help matters by jumping to his feet in the middle of a meeting and accusing the people of not being in earnest. Some of his actions really worried his fellow workers, but if they had seen his letters to his "kid sister," their fears would have been laid to rest. He told her about his studies, advised her about her own study problems and then showed her how to obtain full assurance that all her sins had been forgiven. Part of that letter was a set of sensible guidelines on how to set up a family altar in Island House. Sane enough, surely.

In the last days of October, Evan Roberts was led to his final commissioning. It was not entirely unexpected since he was already in touch with the Rev. Thomas Francis about bringing a mission team to Loughor and was already engaged in prayer and fasting before that weekend, which changed everything. One evening in Capel y Drindod he rose suddenly and called out fervently, "Jesus is not being glorified here as He should because men are showing themselves too much." After this outburst, he began to pray in such a manner that it seemed to burn into the hearts of the congregation. A certain Mrs. Davies began to sing hymns in honour of the Lord Jesus, and the entire congregation responded with two hours of weeping and praising which "filled the chapel with heavenly sound." This was not mission but revival and Evan announced that more wonderful things would happen soon.

Evan was persuaded to go back to his lodging but could

not go to sleep because "the room was full of the Holy Spirit. The outpouring was so overpowering that I had to shout and plead with God to stay His hand." At 3.00 a.m. he and Sidney were crying for lost souls; at 4.00 a.m. they were weeping at the foot of the Cross; at 5.00 a.m. their hostesses came to the room and rebuked them. Surely this was the long-awaited filling with the Holy Spirit which preceded his final call to be a witness.

On the next Sunday morning, the Rev. Evan Phillips entered his pulpit and announced his text, "Father, Glorify Thy Son." The two Phillips girls saw Evan's face shining and they could hear him saying: "Oh dear! This place is full of the presence of the Holy Spirit. I felt it coming over me like a breeze." Later on that day, there was a young people's prayer meeting where he repeated over and over, "Glorify Thy Son." At the tea table he was sighing deeply and he refused to go with the rest to a singing practice. They were now seriously concerned about him.

Yet in the evening service, Evan seemed to be in an exalted state and he seemed to react like quicksilver to the readings and the prayers. But when Evan Phillips read out his text, "Father, the hour is come," Evan seemed to lose contact with his surroundings and heard the service as if afar off. With his whole body shaking and his sight also wavering, he seemed to see the people of Loughor and then the young men sitting in rows in the Pisgah schoolroom. Then there was a voice speaking inwardly, *"Go and speak to these people."* He confessed to Mr. Phillips, and Mr. Stead later on, that he could not keep up his resistance when that voice kept saying, *"YOU MUST GO!"* At length he said, "If it is Thy will, I will go." Then the whole chapel seemed filled with light so dazzling that, "I could faintly see the minister in the pulpit; but between him and me, the glory as of the light of the sun in heaven."

Before he took the final step of leaving Newcastle

Emlyn, Evan went out to see his pastor and ask him whether he thought that this was a deceiving vision from Satan who might want him taken away from the missions. The godly Evan Phillips discerned this was a true calling and that this was definitely the voice of the Holy Spirit. Roberts returned quietly to the house and prayed openly, "Lord, I am willing to shed my blood for Thy Son." The others were silent with astonishment as he told them, before he went to his lodgings, that he had to go home the next day because of the vision and the voice calling him. One of them wrote, "We were not at all willing for him to go for there was so much charm in his company and such divine fervour." But at ten o'clock on Monday morning, October 31, Evan began the most exciting journey of his life.

4

The Altar, the Sacrifice, and the Flame

hat strange thoughts must have passed through the mind of Evan Roberts as he sat in the compartment of the slow country train. He was travelling homewards just when fellow students were returning to college from weekend engagements. He had once planned to take a mission team to Loughor, but now he was alone and facing the unknown. He had spent all his money on team evangelism; he had no grant or wages and no convenient inheritance to lean on. He had no sponsors, no organisation, no publicity experts and no supporting group. Even before he was halfway home, he penned an appeal to Florrie Evans of Newquay, "Could you have a meeting to pray on our behalf for the Lord Jesus' sake. The Spirit has given me an earnest of a blessed future among our young people in Moriah." One assumes that this "earnest" was a dream in which he was told how many would answer the first call. That was his support—the God of visions.

Aware that he had left the team mission which he had inspired and planned, Evan scribbled another letter to Nellie Evans to describe the divine command which he dared not disobey. Then he asked that the whole group would go to the throne of grace and pray for him. One can almost see his head bowed over this letter which he wrote in pencil as the train chugged towards Pencader. A few miles later, as the train descended the wooded ravines towards the town of Carmarthen, he decided that he would have to start his witness at once. People standing on the platform at the junction must have been a little surprised as a complete stranger spoke publicly about his faith and then warned them, "Perhaps we shall not meet again until we meet in the Judgment." Certainly no one could have imagined that all Wales would be meeting him soon.

Evan Roberts's sudden return to Island House took everyone by surprise, especially Mary who had just received a long, rambling letter in which he spoke mainly about students, work and team mission. Yet there was a little hint of his intentions even in that letter:

> I wish it were practicable to come with these meetings to Loughor. I had intended to write to Moriah's Young Men's Prayer Meeting, as to how to prepare for and receive this great blessing. I am waiting to see what the near future may bring to me.

Evan's mother believed that he had called in on his way back from some preaching engagement. The rest were puzzled and uneasy, especially after he announced the purpose of his coming. His brother Daniel was the first to feel the change. He testified to the *Efengylydd* readers (vol. 17), that his brother's letter had set him free from his doubts about the Atonement and had given him courage to take part in the "seiat" devotions. He had begun to share Evan's longings for revival but he was sorely tested and cast down. After a medical, Dan had been warned that his eyesight was rapidly failing. He had to miss work and the future looked dark. Mary Roberts was with him in the room when Evan turned to his brother and said, "Dan, you shall have your sight. The Lord Himself has need of you." When Dan went back to the specialist he was told that his sight was now safe, but no one knew how this had happened. The family and close friends acknowledged then that God had given Evan a new authority. Yet even they could never have guessed that in a few days time they would all be caught up in the great winds of revival.

Evan knew he would have to talk with each of the Moriah officers who would hesitate to let a student, absent without permission and still unqualified, conduct any meetings. As he repeated the story of how God had compelled him to come home and gather helpers and win all who would obey the Spirit, these men could not gainsay him. A niece of Mr. Jones, the pastor, testified that her uncle was won over when Evan Roberts cried, "God has called me to this in Wales. God is alive in Wales. We are going to have a meeting in every place."

The next minister to be totally convinced was the Rev. Thomas Francis who wrote:

> At midday on Wednesday, November 2nd, there hurried towards me someone who at first sight looked like Evan John Roberts. I could not believe my eyes, but it was he. Yet not the same. He had been a reserved, very aloof boy who was very independent of spirit. Now he was a new man, so supple and flexible. Every muscle and sinew was thrilling with new life abundant and his face was like a June sun.

As he listened to the story of the "bending" and the commission, Mr. Francis felt the first stirrings of Holy Spirit renewal which brought him into personal blessing a few days later. One by one the churches agreed to hear the young man—Moriah, Libanus, Pisgah, Bethel, Brynteg. Already the district was beginning to talk about Evan's message and its effects.

Yet it was a very small-scale beginning. The first after-meeting gave him the little consecrated band that God had promised him. These workers witnessed to the gypsies on Kingsbridge Common and went out in wagons to witness to nearby villages (see *Voices From the Revival*, Ch. 2.) During the second and third meetings, Evan Roberts spelled out for these firstfruits the four preconditions for God-sent revival: everyone must avoid doubtful things, confess secret sin, confess the Lord Jesus publicly, and pledge full obedience to the Holy Spirit. His recommendations were followed by intense prayer and discussion in chapel meetings and in many homes.

According to many eyewitnesses, Evan used to speak more like an elder brother than an evangelist. He would walk up and down the aisles and stop where he sensed there was a need. Then he would ask directly, "How do you feel now?" or "Are you ready to stand up now and confess Christ?" These early meetings were a means of preparing the dedicated young people to contact and counsel people and to act as intercessors. It was as if Evan was fulfilling the words of his pre-revival poem.

> *Send the Spirit, blessed Jesus*
> *Into every waiting heart.*
> *Lest the fear of man oppress us,*
> *Thine own strength, O Lord, impart.*
> *May we speak Thy words for ever;*
> *Grant us eloquence and grace,*
> *To attract souls without number,*
> *Now, to see Thy smiling face.*

Evan was convinced that the fast-growing group needed to be filled with the Holy Spirit if they were to be channels of revival. He believed that "revival comes from a knowledge of the Holy Spirit and a way of co-working which enables Him to work in revival power" (*War on the Saints,* First Edition, p.30). All through that first week, the ministers and church elders watched in amazement as the preparation meetings bore fruit. Evan was so ecstatic that he hardly ever went home until midnight, after striving in prayer with earnest young people who were seeking the Spirit. They cried aloud for Him to come down, and He came.

At a Thursday evening "seiat," Evan felt that he should teach children how to pray a new prayer, "Send the Spirit to Moriah for Jesus Christ's sake." When they were asked to say this prayer every night and morning, they all shouted, "I will!" ("Mi wnaf!") In the closing meetings of the week he was able to call on the young people to testify what full surrender to Christ meant.

In the midst of this joyous time, Evan was under severe testing. He seemed to hear a voice saying, *"You are not needed here. Why you, when there are ministers here who could do this work?"* There were times of anguish, but they were outweighed by the hours when his heart was brimming over with joy. He wrote, "This is a jolly time. I am contented and perfectly happy." Gleefully he watched one staid deacon coming up to embrace him and another standing on a bench and clapping. On another occasion he met Mr. Francis in the street and said, "We have all heard it said about joy coursing and tingling through our fingertips. Now it's literally true."

In letters sent to the prayer groups in West Wales, Evan Roberts told them how he himself felt that he had received the filling of the Spirit and how he had preached to the whole congregation on the text, "Be not drunk with wine but be filled with the Spirit" (Ephesians 5:18). He explained the four points in greater detail:

1. Confess all known sin.
2. Search out all secret and doubtful things.
3. Confess the Lord Jesus openly.
4. Pledge your word that you will fully obey the Spirit.

The response to that message on the last night of the "week of preparation" was final proof that the revival flood had come. There is no doubt that the great awakening of the community took place between November 6th and 13th. It centred upon seven chapels in Loughor and Gorseinon. There were such amazing scenes that Evan was urged not to go back to his school studies but to send for more helpers. The stories of those wonderful days will be found in the books of Evans, Matthews, and Stewart (see "Suggested Readings"), and presented by many eyewitnesses in *Voices From the Revival*. In this biography, we look at the events and scenes through Evan Roberts's eyes.

Sunday Morning
"Everyone present uttered this prayer, 'Send the Spirit now for Jesus Christ's sake.' It was a chain prayer and its effect was wonderful. As the prayer went around, one of the young men was filled with the Spirit. We repeated the prayer with this addition, 'Send the Spirit now more powerfully for Jesus Christ's sake.'"

Sunday Evening (After Midnight)
"I led in prayer; then, from seat to seat, I felt the place being filled. Before the prayer had gone halfway round the room, I heard some brother weeping and sobbing, saying, 'Oh dear! Oh dear!' Others began to break and to lie on the ground crying for mercy or saying, 'No more, Lord Jesus, or we die.'"

Monday Evening

"After the service continued to twelve o clock, I said I was not satisfied with it, and that we must get the blessing, even if it were necessary to stay down till daybreak. I said we should have to strive with heaven. Then the people came down from the gallery and sat close to one another. 'Now,' said I, 'We must believe that the Spirit will come, not hope He will come but firmly believe that He *WILL* come.' Then I read the promises of God and pointed out how definite they were (remember I am doing all this under the guidance of the Holy Spirit). After this, the Spirit said that everyone was not to confess or sing or give experiences but pray and believe and wait. The people were sitting and only closed their eyes. The prayer began with me, then went from seat to seat, boys and girls, young men and maidens. Some asking in silence and some asking aloud; some coldly and some warmly; some formally and some in tears; some with difficulty and some adding to it."

On the first morning of that miraculous week, people stood in groups in Gorseinon's High Street and the main question on their lips was, "How do you feel now? Don't you feel odd?" Their minds were filled with pictures of the Sunday services where, in each chapel, scores of people seemed to be overwhelmed. The scenes were repeated each day and Evan's joy knew no bounds. The Rev. Mathry Morgan of Llanon came in one night and saw the revivalist "almost dancing with joy over one who was praying fervently and who was actually laughing while he was praying, having become conscious that these pleas were prevailing. Mr. Roberts showed lively signs of exultant joy, in sympathy with him. Glory to God for a happy religion."

It was remarkable that so inexperienced a messenger perceived the dangers in this overexcited atmosphere. He did not want a revival ritual, with crowd chants and repeated prayer phrases. He told a friend how he taught gatherings to pray serially, but as individuals not groups:

1.   Send the Spirit now.
2.   Send the Spirit powerfully now.
3.   Send the Spirit more powerfully now.
4.   Send the Spirit still more powerfully now for Jesus Christ's sake.

As the tide swept in through towns and villages, Evan Roberts realised that all denominational barriers had broken down and that "young people from the Baptists and Independents come to these meetings, and I cannot stop them. I should like it very much if the Spirit would descend on other denominations." The age barrier broke down and even the sex barrier broke down. Throughout the nineteenth century women were banned from any public role in church life, but now they were set free to pray and praise openly. Evan took the ancient Pentecostal promise literally, "Upon my maidservants I will pour my Spirit" (Joel 2:29). Soon he would insist that national and racial barriers should go also.

It was now high time for Evan Roberts to go back to college and make his peace with the tutors, but local ministers begged him to remain and to send for Sidney Evans and the Newquay girls. The old painful problem came back, "I want to pursue my studies but I also want to work for my Friend and Redeemer." When Sidney Evans visited, Evan showed him a sheaf of urgent requests to go to various Welsh towns, requests he had to refuse. Sidney felt he had to join his friend, so he went back to college and promised to bring Evan's luggage back with him. A decision had been made which led both men into a far wider work. They understood each other perfectly and rejoiced to see the fulfilment of the "Vision of the Hand Outstretched."

Among all the joys of that week there was a special thrill

awaiting him at home. He knew that his brother Dan was now ready for whatever the Lord called him to do. He took part in revival services in the Aberdare and Rhondda districts and in the valleys to the north of Swansea where the testimony of a working man had great effect. Although much younger than the others, his sister Mary was also ready to obey the Spirit at all costs. Another sister who had been noted for a peevish nature and sharp tongue, had been totally transformed. Now the time had come when the Lord would bless his sadly puzzled mother. She went to several revival meetings and once stayed until 3.00 a.m. but then walked out. Her son followed her out, as if to shut the door, and he said to her, "Are you going home now?" She pointed out rather sharply that everyone in the village was asleep because they would have to go to work at 5.00 a.m. But when she went to bed, she grieved over her words and could not rest until Evan came into her room at 5.00 a.m. and she and her son prayed together. Tudor Rees told the sequel:

> One day, after having spent some time on his knees in his tiny room, he went out to his mother. Placing his hand upon her shoulder, he said with a tremor in his voice and a strange light in his eyes, "Mother, you have been a Christian a good many years, and a good Christian mother you have been. But Mother, there is one thing more that you need." Mrs. Roberts, astonished and visibly affected, looked into her son's face and wistfully queried what this one thing was. He answered, "Mam, the one thing more that you need is the baptism of the Holy Ghost." So unexpected was the message and so strangely it was uttered that the mother said little, if anything, to her son about what he spoke. She told a family friend, Mr. T. Rees, "For eight days I pondered his words over in my heart, mentioned the incident to nobody, and prayed that He would baptise me with His Holy Spirit. Day after day I uttered that petition, but the the eighth day, the fire descended and my joy knew no

heavens seemed as brass and there was no answer. On bounds. Oh what a change has come over me, and not only me but the whole family since then."

No one commented on the father's reaction to all this but he was a deeply religious man. One can easily imagine them gathered together at the family altar and then pouring out their souls in united prayer .

There was a price to be paid for the astonishing success of the first revival mission. It became national news that was read at hundreds of breakfast tables. Pressmen came in from all directions and some of these were openly scornful at first. Stories of his visions and voices laid him wide open to attack but Evan expected that. He told his prayer partners: "I have to say strange things. I have to open my mouth and speak out. I am bound to speak the truth, be the cost what it may."

After a while, the reporters were far too impressed to say anything critical. A few of them were converted. Their glowing reports drew hundreds down to the revival meetings. On rare occasions they obtained interviews and asked many questions about his role. If at times they asked what the unusual behaviour of the congregations meant, he would say, "The Spirit is at work. Just accept it."

One of the reporters said there were rumours that a revival committee was being formed, but Evan retorted at once, "They wish to direct me and my companions as they would a travelling show. I shall never submit. The only director is the Holy Spirit. What have these men given up for the Gospel? They want to preside, but God is a far better leader. Let them now preach for 'Yr Enw' (the Name) instead of for 'Yr Elw' (profit or gain)."

Evan would not usually speak of his boyhood experiences of God nor about the times of waiting and struggling to anyone. But he did tell Brinley Evans of the *Llanelly Mercury* about the divine guidance he had received:

> I am here in obedience to the command of God who
> sent me here. God is working in this, and the prophecy
> of Joel is about to be fulfilled. I am in the hands of God
> and He will direct me what to do and where to go.

It was not long before someone complained that he was
practising obedience to the Spirit in such a literal way that he
would not control any prayers and praises in meetings. No one
could foresee that this was going to be the pattern of the
revival for months. As Sidney Evans remarked, "Each move
that Evan made was a puzzle to men but known to God."

Journalists who had already covered the missions of
Torrey, Alexander and others were amazed at the complete
lack of advertisements and announcements. Others wondered
why there were no choirs and no special ceremonies. But the
chief cause of surprise was the revivalist's tremendous energy.
Evan told them: "It is a wonderful life. I am so blessed that I
could walk on air. Tired? Not once. God has made me strong
and manly. I can face thousands. My body is full of electricity
day and night and I have no sleep before I am back in meetings
again." It is a known fact that he ate and slept little during
the first two months.

One day another journalist asked the cheerful, confident
young man to reveal the secret of his way of life. Evan Roberts
answered, "I will go where the Spirit takes me. I've given
everything up. I am awaiting the Master's commands." That
is always a bold thing to say because our Lord takes us at our
word and will put our obedience to the test. Within days, he
was called away from Loughor to completely new fields. This
new ministry did not begin with the kind of vision which once
sent Philip from Samaria to a deserted road. It was just a letter
of request from a chapel in Trecynon, not very far from the
colliery village where he had first felt the call of God. The
Head of the Church, preeminent in all things, was now sending
His messenger into the mining districts which sorely needed
new life.

5

Whirlwind in the Valleys

welve miles north of the city of Cardiff, the busy market town of Pontypridd lay astride the narrow entrance to the main valley roads. One road entered the Dare Valley where several villages housed hundreds of colliers. At its head lay Aberdare and its five satellite villages. These towns were the next to feel the mysterious power of Evan Roberts's ministry. Unlike later campaigns this one was not visited by scores of curious outsiders. Most of the meetings were conducted in the Welsh language, which left most reporters in the cold. Evan Roberts was not even called to be a missioner, but was asked to be a substitute preacher at Bryn Seion Chapel. When the officers learned that the booked preacher had cancelled, someone who had read about the blessing at Loughor suggested that they should invite the young student. No one was told that he would also bring two earnest young ladies to sing and testify. Stranger things were to happen.

When the faithful few turned up for the morning service, the first thing they saw were two girls standing in their pulpit. They heard them praying and pleading that the people would surrender to the leadings of the Holy Spirit. As this strange service began, one of the girls gave her testimony in song but suddenly burst into tears. The other girl did the same while the congregation stared perplexedly. Some wondered why the invited preacher had not opened his mouth. Then they saw that he too was weeping and pleading with God as he knelt in the pulpit.

Suddenly a chapel member fell to her knees, and her friends heard her confessing all her sins publicly. After that shock there was a wave of sorrow and another wave of joy. Women knelt in pews, men lay down in the aisles and a few stood there speaking joyfully about the blessing they had now received. There was still no Bible reading or address and the church organist stayed idle while the people sang hymns unaccompanied. Somehow, people forgot to go home for their Sunday dinner, a thing almost unheard of in South Wales in those days. Sunday school was cancelled and the evening service became a continuous prayer meeting.

On Monday morning the housewives in the shops and their husbands in the pits spoke in excited whispers about this strange event. The "team" was invited to stay overnight because they wanted to continue their witness. The Aberdare branch of a Rationalist Society soon began to talk about "unbalance," "unseemliness," "hysteria," etc. Meanwhile, some of the chapel leaders met quietly and decided to make preparations for a week of revival meetings.

Ebenezer Chapel opened its doors very early on Monday evening but no collier dreamed of going until he was bathed, fed and clothed in his chapel suit. So a small and rather self-conscious congregation faced the girl singers as they began a time of prayer and praise which they called "warming the atmosphere." As more people arrived they were amazed to see Evan Roberts coming in with them and just walking up and down the aisle. Soon he was swinging his arms, clapping his hands, jumping up and down at times, and always smiling warmly at each new arrival just as if he loved them. At this Monday service he spoke about Christ's love and Christ's light. His hour-long address was more like a personal testimony than a sermon. The meeting went on well into the night and some of the workmen snatched only two hours of sleep before going back to the colliery. As they walked home, people were repeating the striking things that Evan Roberts had said,

> Religion should be the happiest thing in life. Our fathers were gloomy and melancholy as though religion were a severe trial to the flesh. What they had missed was the joy of the Lord. They got themselves into a groove; we must get out of it.
>
> Some people wonder why we laugh and are happy at meetings. Well! Who would be happy except those who have love in their hearts. . . . Look at this from the father's point of view. Would a father be offended when his children laughed? No! Certainly not. But we are children in our Father's house, happy and joyous. Our Father will not be offended.

The first outsiders who hastened to the town didn't quite know what to make of this young man, who beamed at the people constantly and who never lifted his voice to a preachers shout. He was a puzzle to the average chapel member who expected thunder and lightning from the pulpit. Many Welsh homes had bedroom pictures of the fiery-eyed preachers of old, such as John Elias and Christmas Evans. So people expected a severe face and a dignified manner and certainly no habit of roaming about the chapel. One can picture their faces when in Pontypridd Chapel, some presiding minister read out the names of thirty-three converts, and the revivalist threw his arms around the surprised clergyman and shouted ecstatically, "Is this not glorious?" No one could resist Evan's infectious joy for long. It was a mixture of youthful cheerfulness with thankfulness to an all-loving God, and a great excitement as so many accepted Christ and stood up with radiant faces.

The last night of this visit to Aberdare was like a pageant of praise, prayer and testimony. The formerly closed frontiers of age, sex, language and social background were crossed time and again. At length, Evan Roberts stood up in the big seat, a pew usually reserved for the deacons. Then he opened his New Testament and slowly and emphatically read the thirteenth chapter of First Corinthians. In a quiet and solemn voice he emphasised the words, "If I have not love I am nothing—nothing—NOTHING," and then he sat down. That was all, but it was enough.

There was another moment of high drama when a man who belonged to a local circle of agnostics tried to interrupt Evans exhortations. He wanted to ask a question, he said, and he pushed forward towards the pulpit, but never got there. The Holy Spirit overpowered the man; he collapsed and had to be helped; he cried out for mercy and pardon. Soon there was a great outburst of joyful singing over a repentant rebel.

Four times during the mission to Aberdare and nearby Mountain Ash, Evan Roberts left the pulpit to deal with men and women in great spiritual distress who were either out of sight in a distant balcony or were actually outside in the graveyard or porch. The most striking incident was in an Aberdare chapel where a prodigal son was coming home, never more to roam. The incident was noted by Mr. T. Williams in a Welsh language memoir:

> When the breath of the Almighty had filled the hall, behold Evan Roberts hastening in himself, like a doctor hastening to the sick. Without even casting his eyes across the meeting, and without any pause, he was directing his steps straight to the left-hand wall at the top end of the chapel, and then falling to his knees alongside a young married man who was pleading earnestly. The young revivalist kept a clear circle round

the praying one, lest anyone should disturb or impede his winning the battle. We saw him often pulling a handkerchief from his pocket to dry the man's sweat drops. How quickly his eyes had perceived the battle and how soon he had rushed to that place and become inflamed with love for him.

The burden of his prayer was a plea to God to give the man the victory over Satan and strength to break out. Then the young man prayed, "Take the mud from my clothes for I have been in the gutter. Take the sin stain from my flesh; divorce me from secret iniquity." This was a complete confession of sin.

The revivalist at once knew what steps to take to fight this battle; he knew what spiritual treatment was needed in this terrible struggle. He stood above the pleader like a mother over a sick baby, and poured out the oil and wine of comforting prayers, brief testimonies and deep counsels. He had perceived the inner hardness of the battle going on in this soul. "Dear people," he said with a loud cry, "Here's a terrible battle and here's prayer which will conquer the fiends and buffet Satan. Pray on, people. PRAY! PRAY!" It was easy to see, as you looked at his face, that for a few moments he feared this battle and did not know how to turn it to advantage. His face betrayed the terrible anxiety felt towards the end of a birth.

This discerning of souls in conflict was accepted as one more sign that Evan Roberts was being led continually by the Spirit. Some called it telepathy but his closest friends knew that this strange empathy with lost and lonely souls was linked in some way with his prayer life and with his holy desires to share in the concerns of his Lord. D. M. Phillips understood better than any that, in private devotions as in public prayer, his friend's close communion with God had been the true source of this awareness that others were calling upon the Lord. It was like a three-way radio link:

For some time he would listen attentively as though
he could hear the prayers, and then he would come to
himself again and converse with us. This is a mystery
that cannot be explained on natural grounds. It seems
to me that by soaring near to God, some communion
with spirits is possible. By ascending to the tops of
God's mountains in prayer, spirits in some way perceive
one another and have communion which they cannot
have but through prayer.

People soon began to notice other remarkable effects of
his belief in specific Holy Spirit guidance. The young man
who had told reporters, "I will go where the Spirit takes me,"
could not be tied down to one building or even one meeting.
He was not invited, but directed to any meeting that was
clearly under the governance of the Holy Spirit. The doctors
lectured him for going out bareheaded from the superheated
chapels into chilly streets on winter evenings. But he would
obey only the commands of the Spirit and gave his friends
many an anxious hour.

Another thing which visitors could not understand was
why he allowed so many people to sing or speak and why
he didn't control meetings. Those who asked were told, "It
is the Spirit alone who is leading us." When certain chapel
members moaned that he had not turned up at their revival
preparation meetings, he would say: "Don't wait for me. Wait
for the Spirit. Someone tells me they are breaking their hearts
for me not going. Will they also break their hearts for the
Spirit?"

What mattered most was that the Spirit had promised that
He would enter and abide. Journalists such as W. T. Stead
marvelled that the crowd inside the chapel and those outside
the chapel seemed to know by instinct when it was time to
swallow up prayer in praise or to cut off the songs of praise
in order to hear some quiet, humble prayer. They didn't even
need to hear what Evan or anyone else was commanding.

This was surely the seal of the Spirit, they felt.

There were other sincere worshippers who asked in great perplexity, "What has happened to the Scripture readings and why has the service ended without a sermon?" W. T. Stead mentioned this oft-repeated lament when he asked Evan Roberts about his methods. Evan's reply showed a clear understanding of the needs of his own nation which was so well taught by a number of gifted expositors that it would not benefit from someone who was basically an evangelist/exhorter: "Why should I teach when the Spirit is teaching? What need have these people to be told they are sinners? What they need is salvation. Do they not know it? It is not knowledge they lack but decision."

This refusal to teach could be justified in the special circumstances of Welsh Nonconformity where thousands of uncommitted people had at some time passed through the catechism and scripture examinations. But it would be quite invalid as a guideline for present day missioners who know the biblical illiteracy of the unreached multitudes and the equally terrible doctrinal ignorance of the churched.

After Evan Roberts had moved on and handed over leadership to his brother Dan, who had just arrived with messages from Loughor, the mighty revival flamed through Aberdare for another four months. It could not be extinguished by the all-out attack in the *Aberdare Leader*. Indeed, the removal of Evan to another valley made nonsense of their charge that the revival depended on his hypnotic skills and magnetism. Exactly the same wonderful things happened when local pastors of revived churches took over the task of reaching every village.

****

Officially, Evan Roberts was only to address a special meeting during the semiannual conference of the South

Wales Women's Temperance Union. But certain young people had heard of revival and had longed for such revival. Now they were able to meet the man whom God had anointed. God had answered their fervent prayers.

For the first time, Evan Roberts experienced that unique atmosphere created when an entire village was filled with uncontrollable excitement. People climbed on the pulpit rails, sat on the balcony steps, scrambled onto the window ledges, shouted and pushed in the entrance lobbies. Women fainted in the packed pews; strong men threw themselves down and wept loudly; amateur soloists and reciters pressed themselves forward and took over right in the middle of Evans address. Hour after hour, until five o'clock in the morning, men and women stood up to confess sins and receive the Saviour, and some of these acted strangely. Evan Roberts accepted everything, except loud shrieking and wild gestures. W. T. Stead heard him sternly rebuking one disorderly group, saying to them, "He who would walk with God must come to His house in a spirit of prayer, of humility, of awe. If we truly walk with God, there can be no disorder and no indecency."

More often, Evan Roberts himself was hand-clapping and exhorting people to go on and on. He listened in silence while a rough man prayed with his hands clenched together and his voice going higher and higher because of deep anguish and terrible grief. How quickly he would respond to need. To the rebel he would say, "Don't fight any more with Him who died for you." To the despairing one, he would recite an old gospel hymn, "The noontide is past and night draws near but the door of mercy is yet ajar." He often invited people to sing, "Throw Out the Lifeline" or that haunting gospel song, *"A welsoch i ef."* ("Say, Have You Seen Him?") which contained a great verse of assurance.

Now interceding; now interceding.
For us, still pleading is he
O my Father I entreat
By my wounded hands and feet.
Let them live—they are purchased by me.

It was probably at Pontycymer that a singer introduced *"Dyma Gariad fel y Moroedd"* ("Love Like the Oceans"), which became the anthem of this revival. Miss Annie Davies of Maesteg, with her sister, Maggie, and Miss S. Jones, came under conviction at one of the Pontycymer meetings and felt they should offer their beautiful trained voices to the Lord. Evan Roberts wisely told the emotional girls to go and pray about it for a day or two, even though he felt sure that the Lord was going to use them. All three girls were mightily used, but Annie Davies seemed so one in spirit with him that he often allowed and encouraged her to echo his message and appeal in her own choice of songs. At one stage he also used volunteer soloists, but he told the Bala students in June 1905 that he had stopped this when a spirit of envy and competition had driven the Holy Spirit from certain meetings.

Every hour at Pontycymer was filled with meetings and conversations and he managed to get only two or three hours of sleep each night. Yet his hostess, Mrs. Maddocks, said that Mr. Roberts seemed quite fit and full of vitality. One day he took some services at Pyle and Abergwynfi which converted many people. Even on the last day he got up at 4.00 a.m. to meet the night-shift colliers and hold a prayer meeting; then he took three other meetings before tea. Still not satisfied, he asked the evening meeting to pray for two colliers who were atheists. This was the result:

Where I sat, I saw the evangelist full length on the
floor of the big seat in most excruciating agony, his face

51

smeared with burdened tears. He tried to bear up as well as he could and, holding on from seat to seat, to get out. [He was] crying out with his hands upwards, "O Lord, stay Your hand, or I shall die. I am dying. This is too much for me to bear." He wept to the door and through the street. . . .

Then the evangelist came back after weeping every step to the house of these two who had been prayed for. He announced the good news that one had given himself to Jesus, but the other was hesitating.

Evan Roberts was soon showing many signs of emotional overload and overstrain, yet he reacted strongly when someone suggested that he take a rest. Instead of taking it easy before entering the Rhondda, he went off to the mountain village of Ynysybwl where he first challenged the church members to think of their friends and neighbours who were already drifting and sinking. A very emotional scene followed in which people were pleading with others to surrender, or naming them in prayer. When Roberts called on unsaved people to stand, seven young men in the gallery rose up and confessed Christ.

Evan Roberts behaved as an outspoken evangelist at times even though he was primarily the quiet, humble instrument of revival. Most of the stories from Mountain Ash show him as purely the catalyst, moving quickly from meeting to meeting and, in each case, telling how revival would begin and explaining why they should pray for the baptism of the Spirit to "invest each of you with power to work for the Lord." Yet there is also one report from his Ynysybwl mission which gives an unforgettable picture of the effects of Evan Roberts's pleading with sinners and backsliders.

I want you listeners to receive Jesus. I know you are in sympathy. Do you see Him coming from the judgment

seat with a crown of thorns on His holy head, and blood
flowing down His cheeks, and His back flayed by
whipping and His face reddened with the bleeding, and
that heavy cross on His back as He goes to Calvary—to
die for you and me? I know that not one of us would
not have wanted to have a chance to help Him carry it.
But you need to turn that sympathy into a flame of love
before you can embrace Him as Saviour. Who can forget
Him?

Awstin, the *Western Mail* journalist whose revival
supplements are still a major source of information, noted
that some people were literally shaking while others were just
shouting out. He looked at Evan Roberts's radiant face and
saw him shouting and clapping his hands and crying out, "O
blessed place!" It was abundantly clear to everyone that God
had given Wales a different kind of messenger who would
not necessarily be a Bible expositor or eloquent preacher but
a man with a burden. God had sent him to warn, exhort, invite
and plead lovingly. Underlying this was a great compassion.
On one occasion, he was heard crying out passionately, "How
can I repay Him for the privilege of going through Wales to
proclaim His love?" His next mission, to the Rhondda
Valleys, gave him a great opportunity to do just that.

6

The Rhondda Aflame for Christ

ot far from the township of Tonypandy, the long ridge that separates the two "Rhonddas" rises to a peak called Penrhys. A long, circuitous road connects the two and there is a summit spot where travellers could rest and look down at the miles of terraces. After sundown they could watch dark shadows fall on the collieries and houses. A chain of light would ripple down the valleys as the street lamps began to glow. In December of 1904, the watcher would have seen whole clusters of light coming from the windows of a hundred chapels. They were already opening their doors for the third or fourth revival service of the day.

Using our imaginations for a while, let us join the crowds who are hastening eagerly toward those lights. Let's mingle with the hundreds of newly bathed miners and their wives and children, all dressed in simple, clean clothing. The men look tired and still hungry after a hurried meal, but they are on their way to a different kind of feast. At the gate, families with children are directed to the balconies or to side vestries, but there is room inside for us close to the church officers and visiting missionaries and preachers. All around us are the foreign guests from every land who have come to catch the revival flame and take it home, like a spiritualised Olympic torch. No one is sure where the revivalist will appear because he will go only where the Spirit prompts him. Eventually he enters quietly and humbly and sits just in front of the pulpit, which is usually reserved for nursing mothers and their babies. He has made his way through a singing throng in the street and has been stopped by anxious enquirers many times on the way. Now that he is inside, he is obviously affected by the tremendous heat and airlessness, by the whimpering of children, by the arguments among those who have blocked the steps to the balcony, and by the irritable shouts of people out in the porches. They know they will not get a seat until some miner and his wife leave the chapel to get ready for the night shift.

At a quarter-past-six someone shuts the vestibule doors to prevent more people from barging in. Those left outside start their own revival meeting. A reporter is already hard at work, sitting in a side pew at the front, and writing down the names of important visitors, such as clergymen, colliery managers and the miner's agent, who are given a pew near the front. What a surprise to see the "big seat" occupied not by the deacons but by the chairmen on duty that evening and also two lady soloists. Many people are singing in rich harmony, but the vocalising fades and dies away as soon as Evan Roberts stands up.

Such scenes became familiar to the men from the national dailies and religious journals who travelled to the Rhondda to hear Evan Roberts. They were amazed to find a young preacher who had no oratory; a prophet who would not pronounce fiery judgments. A local man told one of the pressmen, "He seems to be just talking and explaining things and then giving a smiling invitation." The Rev. William Evans, a local Presbyterian minister, attended several meetings and had this to say about Evan Roberts's preaching

56

method, which some clergymen deplored:

> Since the revival began he has not taken a Bible
> verse and made comments as preachers do. (He did that
> at Trehafod but that was an exception.) He rarely
> ascends the pulpit if he has enough room in the lower
> seat. His habit is to speak gently and naturally. He
> drives the message into the hearts of many by means of
> his questioning. His sentences are short and his proverbs
> are homely, natural and even "folksy" at times.

Well-structured expository preaching, however desirable,
was just unworkable at this time when each service was
dominated by testimonies, prayers, pleadings and songs. A
sermon which the Rev. Williams Evans heard was interrupted
about thirty times by pleas and excited comments. He
marvelled that somehow the revivalist could use these to
illustrate his main theme. To the visitors, especially those
who knew no Welsh, it sounded chaotic.

Some enthusiasts, such as John McNeill of Peebles,
claimed that the setting aside of formal worship and of the
usual preaching modes was the sign that a new age had
dawned:

> What is the use of praying for years, as we have been
> doing, "Lord, send us whomsoever Thou wilt send, in
> whatever way Thou pleaseth" Then, when the Lord has
> taken us at our word, we get nervous. Be not afraid if
> the Spirit breaks up for the time being the deadly dull
> formality. . . . Avoid sending for leaders, so called, to
> take charge and make it respectable. Do not insult the
> Holy Ghost in that fashion.

Influenced by such men, Evan Roberts insisted that first
place should always be given to the Spirit's prompting which
must never be ignored or questioned. When helpers tried to

reduce the interruption, he told them: "No one has the right to check it, for that would be authority and control coming in. No one is to lead except the Holy Spirit." The Holy Spirit, he said, was not just some unseen force but a Divine Person who must be praised and adored in His own right and must also be obeyed totally:

> Who prompts us to pray to the Holy Spirit? Look at our hymnbooks. They praise the Father, they praise the Son, but very few praise the Spirit. But I will praise the Spirit as long as I live. I shall praise the whole Trinity. In praising I shall obey in everything and the Spirit shall lead me in everything.

Thoughtful Christians may have said, "Surely the Scripture says 'Worship in the Spirit,' not 'worship the Spirit.' The Lord said that the Spirit would glorify HIM." Then the idea of absolute obedience to the Spirit sometimes led to such results that five years later Evan Roberts and Mrs. Penn-Lewis wrote, "To place the Holy Ghost as the object of obedience, rather than God the Father through the Son and by the Spirit, creates a danger of leading believers to rely upon a 'spirit' rather than God on the Throne who is to be obeyed by the child of God, united to His Son; the Holy Spirit being the *media* through whom God is worshipped and obeyed."

During the revival, the twin principles of worshipping and obeying the Spirit gave dynamic force to meetings held in every village chapel and hall. Team members even went down the mineshafts to pray and testify alongside the colliers. Evan himself raced from chapel to chapel, at all hours of the day, until the swift currents sapped his emotional powers whilst the physical condition sapped his energies.

When journalists kept writing enthusiastic reports about a "revival in song," they must have been thinking about the

Rhondda Valley meetings where almost every chapel had its soloist. In Gosen Chapel, Clydach Vale, for instance, a lady sang, "O that we should be like Him," a little girl sang, and then the people sang, "Love Like an Ocean." A miners' agent named Tom James sang just one line, "Come to Jesus just now," but others freely invented four more lines such as, "He'll forgive just now." Even Mr. Roberts found it a bit overpowering when the people sang the last line of "Crown Him Lord of All" seventeen times in succession, in English and Welsh.

Sometimes when he could not stop the flow of praise, he just sat back and smiled. He still rebuked those who tried to hush the singing. Sometimes he threatened to leave a meeting if anyone tried to interfere in any shape or form. When one leader dared ask Evan Roberts to cut down the singing, he said, "Would you stop the dawn chorus of birds and allow just a few to greet the rising sun?" Only exhibitionist behaviour would cause him to stand up and say, "The Spirit cannot be with us now." He used volunteer singers if they didn't show off or take over. He loved to get the unspoiled children to sing old gospel hymns. Even greater liberty was given to his own group of gospel singers who led the meeting before he came in. Annie Davies, Miss S. Jones and Miss Rees always sought guidance from the Lord to ensure not only the right choice of solo but the right time to underpin the message.

At this stage, Evan Roberts made full use of the zealous and well-trained "Christian Worker Bands" who would walk in and out, scramble over pews, push people aside, and climb over balconies in order to kneel down and plead with some guilt-laden man or challenge an undecided person. Unfortunately, he also took no action when overzealous workers began to shout out, "Here's another one," or when an excited deacon shouted out too loudly the name, address and personal details of a new convert. Many friends felt this was forcing things and Evan gave up the practice later on. Other groups which he encouraged were the "Witnessing Bands." They went into the streets and alleyways and brought all sorts of people in, especially after the taverns closed. Often he exhorted others to join in:

> We must all be workers and sincere in prayer. It will not do for us to go to heaven by ourselves. Friends, we must be on fire for saving others. We cannot do so without being workers. . . . O that we were filled with the spirit of the Great Lover.

It was during December 1904 that Evan Roberts began to extend and develop the practice of directly questioning Christians to make them display their true colours. Awstin was at the meeting in Van Road, Caerphilly, when Evan asked, "Will everyone who will confess Christ rise?" When only forty responded, Evan professed to be astonished. "What! Is this the number?" he cried. The Rev. Tawelfryn Thomas, who was standing near him on a temporary platform, shouted out, "No. No." So the people were challenged again. They realised that they had not come to be entertained but to "show their side." In every Rhondda village, he questioned people about their Bible reading, their prayer times and their desire to witness for the One they loved. When he was challenged by a bold atheist at Tylorstown, Rhondda, Evan Roberts commanded all the believers to rise to their feet. Many were too embarrassed to stand up and were upset when they saw others pretending to confess Christian in order to escape notice. These "testings" seemed to put Evan in the driving seat whereas he had claimed he would stay out of sight. These events worried Christian friends as much as his many statements about special guidance by vision and voices.

Whatever the difficulties and misgivings, they did

not in any way affect Evan Roberts's triumphant procession through the Rhondda chapels. The glowing accounts in the main newspapers aroused great excitement and longing in places far from the Rhondda. Because the Christmas holidays were close, a number of business and professional people travelled into the valleys. Sometimes there were groups of gentry who drove in from nearby house parties. Famous preachers, authors, missionaries home on furlough, arrived by every train, and their first question was: "Where can we find the flame burning?" or "Where can we find the revivalist?" The generous people of the Rhondda welcomed them to their homes.

Evan Roberts allowed a great deal of speaking time to distinguished visitors, such as the black-robed Father McTaggart, Gipsy Smith, John McNeill and Dr. F. B. Meyer. Their words often provoked a fresh outburst of song and prayer before Evan took over again. Out of pure courtesy he gave the freedom of the platform to a converted footballer, a converted army sergeant, a trade union leader, a well-known entertainer called "Uncle Franklin," and a very eloquent American visitor who shouted: "Some people think this revival is like the fizz of a bottle of pop. No! It is the fizz of a fuse and the dynamite is at the end of it."

Perhaps the greatest sensation occurred on 22 December when Evan gave time and opportunity to a Turk and then to an Armenian whose people had suffered at the hands of Turks. He wanted to illustrate one of his personal burdens: "If you do not love the brethren there is no unity. If you have received the Saviour you should be one with each other." Evan often rebuked those who prayed for only their own chapel, denomination or country. One of his finer sermons, based on the Archdruid's call at the National Eisteddfod, advocated peace and unity at every level of life.

It seems sad, therefore, that the freedoms given to English and European visitors caused discontent. Giving them the best seats was bad enough; now they were given time to make platform speeches instead of being content to join in the prayer and praise. To ministers like Dr. Morris and William Evans, it seemed an abuse of the spiritual liberty that Evan Roberts had advocated. Another prominent Welsh preacher, Dr. Cynddylan Jones, sent a letter to the *Western Mail* (December 22nd) to warn off the eloquent professional evangelists. Even the friendly journalists, Awstin, said these outsiders' long speeches were embarrassing. Evan Roberts never really solved that problem. How could one say, "You all have full liberty in the Spirit to speak as you are prompted, but you are not to make speeches which trespass on the liberty of others."

Instead of following the revivalist through the thirty or more Rhondda meetings, some of which were described as "The Day of the King's Visit," it seems best to choose paragraphs from two fine addresses. (These Rhondda meetings are described in writings by Stead, Lewis, Holyoake, and Francis. See "Suggested Readings.") These sermons seem to refute allegations that Evan Roberts had no depth in his preaching. Dr. Morris also warned readers that notes and bare print could never reflect the true quality of any sermon preached by a man full of the Spirit.

Extract One

Blaenycwm, 1 December 1904. Sermon: "The Way of Victory." Notes and comments made by Rev. W. Evans. (Twelve hundred people were present.)

After almost three hours of continuous prayer and praise and reciting of remembered portions of Scripture, Evan Roberts entered through the vestry door just as they were singing "*Buddugoliaeth*," the hymn of victory at Calvary. He made some inspiring remarks about being on the victory road, where they need not fear anyone because they could be more than conquerors through Him that loved us. This was followed by a number of interruptions as people appealed for help or asked for songs or made comments which the revivalist took on board. Rev. Evans forewarned readers that "the petitions and verses and lines from hymns were influencing the thought as he took hold of them and spoke. That would account surely for so many different ideas being conveyed in the address."

Actually, Evan had two main themes interwoven—"God's three gifts" and "Man's four responses":

God's second gift is His beloved Son. Have you ever considered how difficult it was for Abraham to place Isaac, his son, on the altar? If you have, you can think of the feelings of the Heavenly Father when giving His own Son. It is a feeling that cannot be described. Now, if the Father has given Him, have you received Him? Do you mark this, friends? If there is anyone here who continues to refuse Christ, and refuses Him unto the end, the thief on the Cross will stand up in the Judgment as a witness against you. He received Him in his wretchedness. You enjoy health and are in God's house and have seen God saving twenty thousand in this country. Receive Him, friends. You had better go out this moment if you are going to reject Him forever. A soul is not a thing to play with. You cannot redeem a soul after losing it. If Christ is worthy of acceptation at all, He is worthy now. . . .Remember He will never come down to disobedient and stiff-necked people. If you are disobedient, ask Him to bend you, not to save you but to bend you now. Do you wish Him to bend you friends? Sooner or later you must be bent. Either grace or wrath will bend you. If you are not willing for God to bend you, friends, it is better for you not to be called church members. "Woe unto them that are at ease in Zion."

When Evan Roberts repeated his call to be cleansed of unconfessed sin, freed from doubtful things, and prepared to confess Christ openly, there was an immediate response. As usual, he urged them to be resolved to obey the Holy Spirit totally: "We do not ask you to obey a Society but this Divine Person. Not merely ask for Him, but give yourselves heart and soul to Him. Bow to Him now."

An observer counted thirty-five people committing their lives to Christ as he ended his exhortation. Some people were confessing their offences to one another. Others were weeping bitterly. And some just sat there, "looking as awful as if it were the Day of Judgment."

"This was the most wonderful meeting in my life," said Rev. Evans. "You had to be there to get any conception. After being there six hours we parted, having felt, seen and heard things that the world knows nothing of. Thanks be unto Him."

Extract 2
Sermon at Hopkinstown Pontypridd. 16 December 1904
Theme: "The Challenge to Abraham to Obey God's Call."

> Everyone must obey and go where God directs him. That is the great lesson we have to learn. . ... If God calls, we must obey. Do not ask, "What will become of me? " It does not matter what,. . . God is a God of light. He has plenty of light to shed upon your path. "I am weak," says a man. It does not matter. God is strong. He is a God of all power. If God be for us who can be against us? The path will be made light for us. We shall not lose our way. Nobody ever lost his way who followed Him. You must keep near to your Leader. If anyone loses his way, it is either by going too far behind, or going before God. If He says, "Come after Me," we are to follow. If ten thousand be against you, do not be afraid. God is with you. If you are filled with God you are not afraid of anybody except God.

Such pleadings and warnings flowed from Evan Roberts for the best part of an hour. At the last he shared his certainty about victory in the coming battles.

> God is the great power and we are brought in as fellow workers. Let us rest upon God. The Lord shall fight for us. If we believe, there is nothing that God denies us. Go back to the promises. Go to the last chapter of Matthew again, and to the last verse. "All power in heaven and earth is given unto me." Shall we believe that? ALL POWER? ALL AUTHORITY? If you believe that, the victory shall be with you. . . . Many will try to stand against us. It is better for them to stand aside. The Lord's chariot is going with mighty impetus. . . . Woe unto anyone who stands before the Lord's chariot. Many will try, but I tell you, "GET ASIDE," for the Lord is in it.

Just before the last meeting of the Rhondda revival mission, Evan Roberts was asked to send a telegram to all the churches in Wales, advising them to keep their chapels open over Christmas. He would not do this and neither would he issue a special Christmas message as some friends asked. Awstin, of the *Western Mail*, was present at the service and heard his hero giving a final word of guidance, "Never to lose sight of Jesus." Evan not only spoke these words but sang them in English and also in Welsh, "Cadwn ein golwg ar Iesu." It caught the imagination of the crowds who went home singing it.

Awstin asked him afterwards in a private lodging called Brynfedwen, "Would you agree that the Spirit has given you those words as a Christmas message?" It appeared everywhere in print and so did Evan's final challenge to the Rhondda churches: "The Church has been sleeping but she is awake and is putting on her armour now, and marching triumphantly. But do not make a mistake. God cannot do a great work *through* you without doing a great work *in* you first."

7

The Refining Fire

I f Evan Roberts had intended to have a good rest over Christmas, his hopes were soon dashed. Reporters were knocking on his door an hour after his arrival on Christmas Eve. Some turned up even on Christmas Day, and press photographers appeared in the Boxing Day service at Moriah. Those seeking interviews were ushered into the little parlour but were given one firm message: "I have nothing whatever to tell you. I know nothing except what I am told by the Holy Spirit." He agreed to take a small part in two chapel meetings but wisely withdrew when enthusiasm became too fervent.

In the first week of January, Evan Roberts came by invitation to the busy town of Swansea with its numerous and elegant chapels. Most of these had already felt the revival blaze and were expecting great things. Leading people from all denominations came along, and one senior Anglican marvelled that "Evan Roberts refuses to recognise in any way sectarian differences. He has no new gospel to proclaim, no new doctrine, no fresh sect to form." A distinguished visitor from France, Pastor Cadot, came in search of the miraculous meeting which he had read about in the national newspapers.

Bible teachers came from Russia, pastors from Germany and Scandinavia, evangelists from North America and missionaries from India, China and Africa. Some tried to join in the worship, and some fellow Celts in Cornwall and Ireland brought special messages. Others waited for the blessing to fall on their own souls. They yearned to be baptised in the same way as this soft-spoken, young Welshman who stood before them.

In the pews and in the aisles sat scores of people who had travelled from every county in North Wales to see and hear for themselves the wonderful works of God. It was not difficult for them to find lodgings with those who had long since migrated from their farms and quarries to the South Wales coal mines. These were the people who took the name of Evan Roberts on their lips when they went home to tell what wonders they had seen. (The effects of this are described in *Voices From the Revival*, chapters 7 and 8.)

Many of these visitors noted and admired Evan Roberts's extraordinary skill in keeping meetings informal and free. At Swansea he delivered more traditional sermons on the "Omnipotence of God," the "Omnipresence of God," and "The Glory of the Lord." There was also plenty of open time for prayer, testimony, singing and exhortation.

The first serious murmurings against his meetings were heard in January. Guests were giving mini-sermons instead of testimonies. Others were abusing the liberty of the Spirit by uttering long, eloquent prayers or by behaving like cheerleaders. Several ministers protested about this but the revivalist said once more, "Everyone must be allowed to do whatever he or she thinks best, for no one must control the meeting except the Spirit."

Less than a week later, Evan himself started questioning some singers and testifiers because he suspected that they were not coming forward for truly spiritual reasons. More and more frequently he pointed the finger at those who were "drawing near with their lips but having their hearts far from God." In the midst of a very free and easy session, Evan would suddenly call on everyone to bend to the Spirit or to "remember to worship the Lord in the beauty of holiness." The chief reason for his zeal for purity was that he was utterly convinced that the unsaved would not be converted until the churches were cleansed of superficiality and sham.

The meeting in Babell Chapel, Cwmbwrla, a suburb of Swansea, shows the price that Evan was paying for his tremendous intensity. D. M. Phillips pictured this heart-rending scene:

> The testimonies having ceased, he begins to speak of the nearness of the Divine Presence. In a few moments he fails, having been choked by his feelings. He breaks down entirely, and his groanings and tears overcome the vast audience. He sits in agony of soul, and the effect sways the people. A few were able to keep their mental equilibrium and it was fortunate that they did, because they succeeded in drawing the attention of others from the pitiful state of the evangelist. . . .
>
> Shortly the scene changes again. The whole audience is on its feet, swayed by intense enthusiasm and pouring out its feelings in various ways. The visitors are startled and possessed with wonder. One or two of them shout, "Hush," but what was the good of that? It would have been as well to say "Hush!" to the thunder's mighty roar or the ocean's swelling tide.

At the end of this service, Evan made a passionate appeal to them. "God has conquered us here this afternoon," he cried, "but He has done so with His love. What if He had done that with His wrath? He has touched us tenderly, friends."

In a later meeting in that chapel, Evan Roberts sat down at first and listened to many wonderful prayers followed by some choruses which were repeated over and over. He suddenly realised that this was becoming meaningless and insincere.

> The evangelist suddenly got up and cried, "STOP!" One singer persisted in singing but Mr. Roberts several times cried, "STOP, STOP, PLEASE!" When the singer did stop, Mr. Roberts declared that he had, before doing this, asked for wisdom. If they obeyed the Spirit by singing, they could also obey by stopping. In some meetings the Spirit had been quenched by certain people who got up to do things. He had been told by the Spirit to tell such people to sit down. He had at one time allowed the meetings to proceed, but now he was directed to prevent the quenching of the Spirit by anybody who might get up to show themselves. "I know," Evan said, "when anyone gets up unmoved by the Spirit, and they also know it."

In his biography of Evan Roberts, D. M. Phillips explained this stopping of prayers and praises which seemed so contrary to the spirit of the revival. He wrote:

> It is as fire to his soul to hear a deceitful man before the Throne of Grace. We have seen his eyes on many an occasion flash with holy indignation when hearing such.

This may have silenced some hypocrites but it also put off some of the ordinary believers. Equally upsetting was the use of public questioning to expose people's values and attitudes and to discern their degree of spiritual life. What people grumbled about most was having to stand up to make an affirmative reply to each of the questions. There were times when it looked as though Evan was conducting a drill session. It sounded like spiritual bullying and was sure to get a very mixed response.

In the last of the Swansea meetings, Evan Roberts seemed to overreach himself, and this may well have caused him to drop this questioning style soon afterwards. Arriving late as usual, he accused the very tired people of being cold-spirited. Then he commanded them, "Let all who have done their best for Christ, stand up." Two women cried out, "I have tried to do my best," but the rest stayed very quiet and several resentful ministers sat firmly in their places. At length, the Rev. Pennar Griffiths, who was known as a revival enthusiast, turned to Evan and told him that he could not stand up either because, "I have done my best for Him, but not all that I have done was as clean and pure as it might have been."

There was an unexpected reaction to this stern questioning in one Swansea chapel. Two young men stood up and denied that they had been mocking. "We are seeking the truth," they said, "if you have anything to give us." Then one of them issued a challenge: "You ask the Power to save us and we shall believe you." Evan Roberts had no answer to this except to call on the whole congregation to pray fervently. All the crying and groaning and agonised wrestling in prayer left them cold. They would clearly have preferred a debate but Evan was not equipped for this. He cried out, "Don't argue with them; pray for them."

Dr. F. B. Meyer stood nearby and he challenged the two men to think seriously about a verse in First John which speaks of a sin unto death. He asked them to say, "yes" to God as an act of will, if not an act of faith. At this point, Evan broke in with a reference to an Old Testament story of three rebellious young men who were swallowed up. The result was another jeering reply from the agnostics: "Don't try to frighten us. We have waited fifteen minutes without any effect. How long have we to wait?" Evan then found more verses in the Old Testament where Israel was commanded to stand and wait for the Lord to act. So he cried out: "We have to wait. We have prayed. We have cried unto the Lord and He is going to answer." Still nothing happened and the meeting was closed suddenly.

Evan Roberts looked so defeated and drained that certain friends thought it best to escort his mother away from the place. Dr. Meyer wrote to his friend that he could never forget the sight of that tearful face and the kneeling crowd pleading sadly for the two "obstructionists" who had dared to challenge the Almighty to convert them if He could. This was a sad ending to the Swansea mission but, in the mercy of God, there were a number of encouragements in the next few days.

Evan Roberts's spirits revived quickly as more visitors came to plead for the blessing to transmit to their cities. His local secretary could show him daily letters from Europe and America, begging him to come to them. Best of all, there was an atmosphere of expectancy as the winds of revival grew ever stronger and the mercy showers swept up the Neath Valley from mining village to mining village. When Evan came to Tonna he called on God's people to ask the Lord for breezes from Calvary. Instead, there arose a hurricane of intercessory prayer. Awstin wrote, "There was a Babel of voices, but a beautifully harmonious Babel, breaking forth simultaneously in prayer and song." Exactly the same thing happened in an all-day prayer meeting in a chapel which is close to the present wildlife park. Sometimes Evan Roberts seemed to be lost in silent communion with God. Yet, whenever the people's praise slacked off, he would step out of the pulpit and cry out, "Draw near to God with your hands and your hearts made clean: O pray, people, pray that we may be bent." Thus he urged them on until everyone was praying fervently for someone else.

The grand climax of the Neath Valley mission happened at the little mining town called Resolven. It had a population of only about 3,000, yet on Tuesday evening over 1,000 were crammed into each meeting. Hundreds of people from the surrounding villages had to stand at the doors unless they managed to hasten down from the mountain straight after the afternoon milking. There was plenty of joy and fervour long before Evan Roberts arrived. There was also a sprinkling of curious watchers whom Evan Roberts spotted and denounced. In the crowd that day stood David Matthews of Aberdare, the future evangelist who observed:

> The spiritual atmosphere pervading the worship of the people so thrilled him when he came that his countenance seemed to be luminous. . . . Wherever he felt the perfect liberty of the Spirit in a service, his eyes glistened, his face became almost transformed and his smile radiant. Burdens lifted, sighings fled, Christ glorified. What else mattered? With boyish joy he entered into the spirit of the service. Changing moods were apparent. Invitation hymns suddenly turned into rhapsodies of praise. A sombre *Dies Irae* issuing its dread ultimatum to sinners, warning impenitent mockers of impending doom, uttered by those inspired voices, would resound through the building, filling every soul with unspeakable awe. Sensitive to these changing moods of the Spirit, Mr. Roberts would reflect them in his face. The meetings in Resolven were unique.

The last meeting was at Glyn-Neath. The little railway halt there was suddenly flooded by visitors, many of whom were dressed in national costumes. Inside the spacious chapel, people were praying in several languages simultaneously—it sounded like another Day of Pentecost. Still Evan Roberts was not satisfied and kept calling out: "Let us pray to the Lord to send out workers. There are too many persons here and not enough workers. Have you all prayed for the salvation of sinners in this meeting?"

His spirit had discerned the greatest enemy force which

could stifle a national revival. That enemy was the complacency of churchgoers and the self-centredness of new converts who would not transmit their faith to others. Every evangelist today could testify to the dragging effect of scores of "spectators" who turn up at mission services to see what might happen, not to plead with the Lord that something will happen.

About four years after the revival faded out, Evan Roberts addressed this problem and the linked question of failure to testify. These words appeared in a tract called, "The Shame of a Silent Church":

> To believe with your heart and confess with your mouth is the first step to break the silence of God's children. Each new creature must learn to be a witness and learn to confess Christ. The silence of the church in testifying to Christ is a shameful, sinful thing. If you do want revival, then consider this, "You shall be witnesses unto me."

8

The Furnace Glare

The last fortnight of January was the turning point in the revival. It started in great excitement and mass applause, but it ended in depression, perplexity and bitter criticism. The first meetings were held at a village on the moorlands above Aberdare. A hundred years before, this township had played a great role as a pioneer of the iron industry. In 1905, it had come almost to the end of that rich Welsh-speaking culture in which religion, drama and the arts had been honoured. From this place, the great Caradog had taken the finest of choirs to a famous journey through North America. Now it was just a road and railway junction, but still a useful venue for religious assemblies.

Never had it seen such masses of visitors as in mid-January 1905, once Evan Roberts's coming was known. Hundreds of converts from the first revival meetings at Aberdare now hastened up the long hill to the chapel, to meet the man whose message had changed their lives. Over the high moor came the men from Maerdy, Ferndale and Tylorstown in the Rhondda Fach; over the steep Rhigos Pass walked whole families from Rhondda Fawr. They stopped to hold prayer meetings when they needed a breather on the uphill climb; they lifted their voices in songs of praise as they descended the last slopes towards Hirwaun. Meanwhile, the little railway station saw a strange sight as the courtyard filled with a mixture of South Africans and Russians, Indians and Irishmen, Norwegians and Dutchmen, and Canadians. There was even a party of Americans who simply wanted to say when they got back home, "I was there when miracles happened." Among these visitors were those who had been sent by their churches to beg Evan Roberts and the people to pray revival down on their communities. Inevitably, the press was there also and it was their glowing reports which brought hundreds to Hirwaun and Penydarren. Sadly, there were also far too many people of whom our Lord would have asked as always, "What went ye out to see? A reed shaken by the wind?"

There was such a massive invasion that it soon needed great courage for latecomers to get in further than the chapel gateway. An amusing account can be read in Chile Pine's book, *Revival of the Welshman's Soul*:

> One bright, frosty night I set out with a friend to see that irresistible being who had shaken the Welsh-speaking world. Swiftly the train carried us to Hirwaun. Through the lanes we made our way to Bethesda. We found a surging crowd in the gateway. We forced ourselves into the tide and were caught by two opposing currents, for as many were anxious to get out as were to get in. Several times we were washed back to shore. An old acquaintance hailed me and implored me to retreat before I lost my life. I began to give way, but my companion urged me to try again, so I grimly pressed forward. Inch by inch we advanced—sometimes lifted off our feet by our impetuous brothers and sisters. At last we passed safely through the lobby and entered an aisle.

They expected to see a fierce prophet, and were amazed to hear Evan Roberts speaking gently, pleading with people to accept the love of Christ, and sometimes breaking into floods of tears. Evan was heard saying that he wanted to enter into the sufferings of his Master, who had experienced indifference so often. It was in the chapel called Ramoth that the revivalist showed another side. He jumped up suddenly, lifted up his arms and demanded total silence. Then he began to make an all-out attack on the insincerity and hypocrisy which he said he could see like a creeping infection in their worship. He asked how people who came to church only once a year could possibly sing, "I Need Thee Every Hour." "SHAME!" The word rang out across the audience like a pistol shot. David Matthews heard it and then saw people bowed down all over the chapel and crying out as though they had been smitten by plague. There were very many conversions that day.

A few days later Roberts told his friend Sidney Evans that he was afraid to speak words that had not come from God: "I remember how in one meeting a voice said to me, 'Cry out the word Judgment! Judgment!' Praise be to the Spirit, I was prevented from doing so, else Mr. Self would have manifested himself at once." Often he searched his own heart and tested his thoughts to find hidden sins which would surely take him out of God's way. (Would to God that all evangelists today did this!)

The last days at Hirwaun were free of all strain and Chile Pine wrote: "He had the happy smile of an innocent boy, full of the joy of living. When he appealed the people were melted with a love they could not comprehend." A correspondent from the *Brecon and Radnor Express* (26 January 1905) listened with delight as Evan encouraged the aged and the children to take part. He told them, "Each soul is of equal value in the sight of One who is out seeking to save souls." The Rev. John Williams (Brynsiencyn) had come down from his Liverpool chapel to hear Evan Roberts's message. He marvelled that a Spirit-filled man of God could be so sparkling and free.

> Whatever he said was alive. Every sentence gripped you. . . . Deep soberness and yet bright smiles played across his face. . . . One minute you see bleak midwinter in his visage but the next minute you feel as if you are in the middle of May with the sun shining, birds singing and everyone delighted.

On Thursday morning, which happened to be free, a small group accompanied Evan to the snow-clad Rhigos mountain above Hirwaun. Mr. H. Roberts, his walking companion, recalled:

> We were all on pleasure bent and each one of us enjoyed the morning in a different way according to each one's temperament. It was a fine morning in January. Snow covered the mountains round about and we longed to be as pure as the white flakes that lay thickly at our feet. We did not climb in sober fashion. We climbed as young people should. True to our youthful nature we were happy and yet at the same time serious. The snow attracted the attention of the revivalist who said in Welsh: "White is the snow and white should be our lives. Now! Upward to the mark, and to God be the praise." As he looked around the mountains, magnificent in ruggedness and lovely in mantles of white, he exclaimed, "How wondrous is every part of Thy work!" We climbed upward in a merry mood, yet we were conscious that God was near. When we were within a few yards of the top, the revivalist took out his Bible and began to read a portion of the Epistle to the Ephesians.
>
> When we made our way to the top, the scene was magnificent. We bowed our heads in prayer to Him who made us all. Evan and one other person made public

supplication to the Throne of Grace. . . . I have omitted
to tell you that on the way up, Evan Roberts wrote on
the snow a word which denotes the key to this revival:
L-O-V-E .

While they were discussing this theme during the
descent, one or two members of the climbing party spotted
a group of small boys who were playing near a frozen pond.
The others all passed by, but Evan Roberts always believed
that children should be treated as real persons and precious
souls, loved by his Saviour.

He went up to them, called them to them and asked them
if they could sing. Some of them said they could but the
others sniggered. He threatened to go away if they laughed.
The little boys went on their knees in a double row, facing
each other. No one told them to do so; they did it of their
own accord.

At his request they sang "Throw Out the Lifeline" or
"Taflwch Rhaff Bywyd." It was a sight never to be forgotten.
He gave them some money and left them with an injunction
to do all they could for Jesus. They promised that they would.

From every town and village in the Swansea and Neath
Valleys there came stories of how Evan gave the boys and
girls full freedom to pray, sing and testify. The same
travelling companion has left us this memorial written in
1951:

> Two meetings remain in memory. The first one of
> these having a shining light around it. The gallery on
> one side was full of children. During the meeting, when
> some were praying simultaneously, these children broke
> into singing. Just as the Pharisees tried to suppress the
> children in the Temple, someone tried to hush these
> children. At once the revivalist got to his feet and, with
> a pleased smile, he said, "Suffer the little children to
> come unto me." So they went on singing.

Yes! This was a truly happy time when children loved him, friends surrounded him, famous people visited him and local poets asked permission to read out tributes about Evan and the revival. A favourite recitation, called "The Return of the Amen," depicted a great procession of exultant praisers marching through the whole of the land. On the final night two thousand people crammed into Bethel. No wonder Evan Roberts preached about the power of Pentecost to sweep away divisions of language, race and denomination. It was happening before their eyes. The time of blessing continued as he moved on to the mining village of Bedlinog on the Friday. It seemed doubly sad, therefore, that things were so different when he returned to nearby Dowlais.

As soon as Evan Roberts entered this town, where a score of furnaces thundered night and day, he had a strong feeling that he had entered enemy territory. In one or two chapels he behaved as if he were frozen and very uncomfortable. In nearby Heolygerrig he left most of the meeting in the hands of Miss Annie May Rees and Miss Annie Davies because he felt the people in the meeting were resisting him. When he entered the massive Hermon Chapel, he felt such a noticeable coolness that after a short while he put his coat on and said loudly, "Who can remain here?" Next day he would not even enter the huge Bethania Chapel where two thousand people had come to see wonders.

At first the revivalist was inclined to blame himself for the people's resistance to the Spirit. He became so tense that his hosts got very anxious even though he was so gracious to them. Gradually he began to hint that a few persons, or perhaps one, who was not far away, was hindering the revival by criticism. Could he possibly have known that the Rev. Peter Price was already preparing his notorious letter to the *Western Mail*, condemning the entire mission?

Meanwhile, the revival team had moved downhill to the sprawling industrial town of Merthyr. Here Evan Roberts took up an openly evangelistic approach and there is a moving account in the *Baptist Times* (2 Feb., 1905) of how he dealt with those who sought to receive Christ into their lives. This incident took place at Penydarren where he preached on "The Love of God."

One young woman seemed to be very confused and fearful. Evan Roberts said to her, "Do you believe? You must believe and then the feeling will come."

A voice cried, "She thinks she is too great a sinner."

Then Evan Roberts said, "But the chief of sinners was saved." Others rose one by one amidst prayers and exhortations in Welsh and English. The evangelist exclaimed, "Do not fight any more with Him who died for you." Then the people sang a hymn from the 1859 revival: "The noontide is past and night draws on. The door of mercy is not yet closed."

While the Merthyr mission was winning so many souls for Christ, the local press circulated stories about Evan Roberts's irreverence, hysteria, mesmerism and improper pressures upon impressionable females. Several church leaders spoke scornfully about excesses and disorders, but Dowlais was the home of an even more hostile minister. The Rev. Peter Price, a Cambridge graduate, a skilled counsellor and a dedicated young pastor, had put his faith in reasoning and discussion as an effective answer to the rising secularism and atheism of his time. He was displeased when an unqualified Welsh preacher turned up in his area and at once gained spectacular successes by his highly emotional exhortations. He sent to the *Western Mail* a letter which caused a nationwide debate. He claimed that a genuine revival movement in his area had been spoiled by the coming of Evan Roberts and his imitation revival. By some strange irony, things were happening that week in the Merthyr meetings dramatic things which were bound to make Price more antagonistic. Some people were even more convinced that there was something false and showy at the heart of the Evan Roberts revival. Others were convinced that these events were Pentecostal "signs following."

On the second day Evan Roberts stopped a meeting and said, "Someone wants to surrender now." This happened two or three times and always someone stood up. People were excited and awestruck and asked, "How is it possible that each time he makes a prediction, someone is there waiting to yield." Exactly the same thing happened at nearby Troedyrhiw on 1 February. This scene could not have been more dramatic if it had been planned by a clever producer.

> Presently Mr. Roberts stood up, not to speak much but to make the declaration that someone had "decided," and that all that was necessary was that he should be asked to stand up. Immediately a convert was announced. A man was praying that God would save that afternoon. "Oh! He is saving," rejoined the missioner. "There is another one who has yielded." At once came the announcement of another convert. "Diolch Iddo," then rang out. The evangelist, as if startled by having made some discovery, stopped the singing. "There is another one here," he exclaimed quickly. Immediately came the reply, "Here she is.""Yes! That's right. Diolch Iddo!", he gleefully rejoined, and a peal of praise followed. His countenance soon assumed a serious aspect. He buried his face in his hands and was evidently engaged in prayer. He again interrupted the singing with the declaration that another had decided.

Again at Saron, Evan predicted a dozen individual decisions to turn to Christ. Each time someone surrendered, the audience marvelled. Hundreds began praying and praising at the same time, until the voices rose in one united hymn of praise to the "Great God of countless wonders." However, some observers realised that these scenes were putting a terrible strain on Evan Roberts's mental powers. Others publicly dismissed his strange new powers. An investigator, A. T. Fryer, was told bluntly that:

> Evan Roberts's immobility is only apparent. He is transfixing everyone with his gaze. For a long time he reviews methodically the rows of faces. It is the gaze of a practised physician. By the time he gets up to speak he has made a mental census of the audience. He knows what souls are ill at ease. He predicts conversions and detects hindrances. He waits for the audience to reveal itself to him and then gets up and tells people what they know already, yet they are puzzled—amazed.

Such an explanation would not hold water unless it could be proved that everyone who decided for Christ made a visible or audible sign. Many a timid soul never showed such signs, yet Evan Roberts perceived their need. Even when his line of vision was obstructed by pillars, he still "saw." Others knew of instances where people were agonising outside the chapel, in the burial ground or the porch, when Evan Roberts suddenly came out from the building to pray with them. Finally there were converts who testified in writing that when they were on the run from the Spirit, they would sit at the back of a chapel and then hear Evan say: "There is a man here tonight who has tried to run away from the Spirit of God. He is here tonight and he is going to yield." When they did yield, their stories caused fear and amazement to their friends.

There is no doubt about the authenticity of these events, nor are we suggesting human manipulations. Nevertheless, there were dangers. English journalists made it so sensational that people flocked to meetings to see more of the same. Contemporaries such as R. B. Jones questioned whether there was need of such dramatic proofs when there was deeper and more enduring evidence that the Holy Spirit was setting the seal on the revivalist's messages. Surely the worst danger of all was that he would depend more and more upon such signs and allow himself to be guided by such evidence without taking the step of checking his words and actions with a group and not privately. A letter written by Evan to his friend Sidney Evans (Appendix C) shows a growing awareness of this problem.

Meanwhile, Evan had collapsed and was obliged to remain housebound at Dowlais. In a time of deep depression, he announced that the Spirit had now forbidden him to go on to Cardiff. Critics said this was not the voice of the Spirit, but the voice of a man full of doubts and fears. All these strange events in Dowlais and Merthyr mark a turning point in the revival, as far as it involved him. Instead of clear sunlight, Evan Roberts was now enduring the furnace glare, and he suffered.

9

Sunshine and Storm Clouds

hen Evan Roberts suddenly cancelled the mission to Cardiff, which had already been planned and announced, he caused great disappointment to his supporters, confusion to his secretary, and anger among the citizens who saw this as an insult. But the village of Nant-y-moel, near Bridgend, was overjoyed that he was coming their way, and huge crowds turned up at Dinam Chapel. By nightfall, scores of visitors had moved in from Cardiff and were looking for rooms. As usual they discovered how generous and hospitable the valley people could be. Among the visitors were many who had come to watch rather than to receive. Sometimes a meeting would "go cold" until some godly person would rise and ask the Lord to forgive them all for quenching the Spirit. On the other hand, there was a wonderful meeting at Saron after Evan Roberts had urged more and more to confess Christ. Awstin wrote:

> The night meeting in Saron Chapel (where the revival fire has for weeks been burning brightly) was from the outset unique in its spiritual temperature. The

crush was in itself an indication of the intense expectation prevailing. Notwithstanding the "strangeness" of the previous night's meeting, this was a Pentecostal gathering. The prayers and hymn-singing, which had been remarkable in the morning and afternoon, culminated in high tension from the time of the opening of the night service. Very tenderly Mr. Evan Roberts, soon after entering the building, asked those who had not received Christ to abstain from singing, for they could not possibly sing from their hearts—an appeal which silenced some, but which elicited a tremendous outburst of hymn-singing and simultaneous prayers.

Mr. Roberts remarked that the service was a powerful illustration of the fulfilment of the promises of God. The promise of the previous night, that he would give His presence at this meeting, was amply fulfilled already. Another outburst of prayer and song followed, the repeat of several of the hymns being extraordinary in frequency and fervour. The evangelist, dwelling upon the need of obeying the Spirit in all things, pointed out the need also of a pure heart in individuals who have a share in the work of winning souls.

He then invited the congregation to sing "Great God of Wonders," and the response was thrilling. The people stood and sang again and again with intense fervour, repeating the last four lines about twenty times. And with the singing came prayers in Welsh and English, singly and simultaneously, so that the service became simply indescribable.

Perhaps because of fatigue, Evan Roberts treated the congregation in one Ogmore Vale chapel so sharply that an English visitor cried out, "What is the meaning of this? We stand appalled." Even when people started confessing faults and calling upon the Lord, he said very sharply, "Where is the fire?" Suddenly the atmosphere cleared and Mr. Roberts now wanted to keep the meeting going all night. The first meeting at nearby Maesteg was disrupted by a gas lamp breaking and by someone's foolish attempt to strike matches for candles. Evan stayed perfectly calm, persuaded the crowd to sing hymns in the pitch dark and finally urged them to remember that they were under God's constant care.

Signs of overstrain were even more apparent the next day. Entering a chapel at nine o'clock, he announced that the Spirit had fled because people were too confident. In the Tuesday meeting, he launched another attack on members superficiality, disobedience and unholiness. Suddenly he began to talk about "obstacles arriving" and "obstacles departing," and many people looked around to see who was there. Afterwards people said that the only obstacle was Evan Roberts's troubled mind. They believed that he was now feeling the effects of growing criticism. Some longed to defend him and were filled with anger against the "agents of Satan" who were trying to destroy the revival. Evan himself began to describe every grumble or whispered remark and every challenging question as the work of Satan. The man who had once delighted in a bit of humour was now easily upset by a grin or a whisper. Sometimes he behaved rather like a nervous trainee-teacher who condemns the whole class because one or two pupils are mischievous.

An afternoon meeting at Caerau on 16 February shows how quickly he could react. Inspired by a gospel song and by a little boy reading from Isaiah 53, "He shall see the travail of his soul; he shall be satisfied," Evan Roberts began a passionate exhortation:

> If you say Amen to anything, you should say it after those words, "and shall be satisfied." The Son of God is to be satisfied. There will be a vast song of the redeemed. Have you done anything to bring together that vast throng? What would you think if you had a king to wait upon you and serve you? Yet here you have a greater than a King. The Son of God came not to be served but to serve. How many of you are willing to wash the feet of the disciples?

Suddenly he broke off and turned to the sorrowing Christians and asked them, "Have you any fault to find with Jesus?" Of course they all shouted, "NO!" Once more there was a burst of fervent singing.

At that peak moment, Evan stopped the meeting and announced that there was someone in the congregation who wouldn't speak to his brother. He called for that person to confess his sin, threatening him with divine judgment and ordering him to leave. Because no one admitted this fault, the people had to remain on their feet a very long time. Some were shaking as Evan warned them sternly: "God will not accept any praise from us until this is cleared up. Dead flies cause the ointment of an apothecary to send forth the stinking flavour." Some accepted this kind of rebuke from a man whom they took to be a prophet; others felt it was a mistaken act done by an overtired young man. The rest of the week went very well and many people were saved, cleansed, restored and reconsecrated. Nevertheless, this mission was a world away from the joyous, love-filled revival meetings of November and December. Storm clouds were rising before he moved into the next valley.

The Afan Valley, above Port Talbot, is a long, narrow ravine where dawn comes late and dusk comes early. A string of little villages have somehow hung themselves on narrow ledges above the collieries, each one with its family shops and its chapels. In the damp, chilly days of mid-February, most of the chapel caretakers had provided generous heat for their buildings. Unfortunately, this meant that once the chapels were filled with excited crowds who packed the aisles, blocked the windows and cut off the airflow through the lobbies, the atmosphere became intolerable. People got very restless and even the best soloists went out of tune. Once or twice Evan felt so choked that he ordered someone to smash the window panes.

If the physical environment seemed unbearable, the spiritual environment oppressed him even more. The news that Mr. Roberts had displayed a remarkable gift of detecting those souls who were secretly trying to come to Jesus, had been spread widely by the main newspapers which said that all his predictions had come true, so many people came along to check this for themselves. Aged people from that district used to tell how they had often heard people passing by on their way to a revival meeting and shouting to each other, "Let's see how many he will pick out this time," or "I wonder if he will pick so-and-so, for he is a big fish and a big sinner, we know." One of the first things Evan Roberts said was that they had no real concern for the lost and had failed to pray for them.

Such shallow-minded people enjoyed the singing of simple choruses like: "The upline to glory is clear. The upline to glory is clear. I am in the express for the kingdom, and bound to land safely up there." They enjoyed colourful testimonies given by noted ex-sinners, smiled at peculiar prayers or actions, and listened politely to visitors' speeches. Evan Roberts could feel this superficiality as he walked into a chapel and it filled him with a burning desire to put an end, once for all, to the deadly spirit of casual interest and idle curiosity. He preached about holiness and obedience, and warned that if any people persisted in their disobedient spirit, he would be obliged to point them out: "If I have to ask someone to leave, however unpalatable a duty it might be, I will have to do it."

At an evening meeting in nearby Pont-rhyd-y-fen, Evan Roberts became visibly upset and started to threaten someone with divine punishment for "making a mockery of what was so divine. . . . Mocking what has cost God his life-blood. I saw no one, for my eyes were closed, but the Spirit saw. Ask God to forgive you. Don't ask God openly, please. I don't want to know you." After carefully scanning the congregation, again he urged someone to ask for forgiveness and then declared that the meeting could not proceed until the obstacle had been removed. "If you don't ask for forgiveness, will you go out?" asked the missioner in a tone of deep concern. Let them not think, however, that he wanted to frighten them. The remonstration went on for another ten minutes, but no one owned up.

In the first meeting held on Monday at Cwmafan, Evan Roberts walked in and almost at once threatened to close the meeting because too many had smiles on their faces, not of pleasure but of mockery. He rebuked them for disobedience and failure to confess sins. Everything was working up to the triple explosion which shook South Wales between 21 and 23 February 1905.

At "Tabernacle" in Cwmafan, after four hours of prayer and praise, Evan Roberts entered and at once uttered a prayer that God would forgive them all for their disobedience, hypocrisy and hardness of heart. There had been no signs of hysteria previously but now there was loud sobbing and groaning. As he called out again, "Watch out because the Spirit is here; you cannot escape the message of the Spirit," the atmosphere seemed to grow denser, as if a thunderstorm were near. English visitors couldn't see any reason for the sudden change. They sat in silence as if stunned.

At that crucial moment, Evan Roberts announced that he had a terrible message to convey. He fell to his knees and the people waited and feared greatly. Then he began to cry out:

> "There is a soul lost because someone has been disobedient to the promptings of the Spirit. . . . Too Late! Too late!" He broke down again and cried out, "O forgive, Lord! Forgive! Oh! Dear people, it is too late! Too late! A soul gone!" That great cry of lamentation resounded through the chapel and people fell prostrate and cried out in sympathy. Some attempted to pray but he actually stopped them from praying and cried in tragic

tones, "It is too late, too late." Then he explained that he was prohibited from praying for the soul that was lost and that this was the most terrible message he had ever had to deliver.

News spread like wildfire that Evan Roberts had condemned someone's soul to irreversible ruin by forbidding anyone to pray for him, because the Spirit said so. The God who spared wicked Nineveh had apparently ordered his servant to pronounce certain judgment on one unidentified human being. Twenty-four hours later came the news that this same Spirit had banned him from entering a Briton Ferry chapel where he was awaited. People were not slow to ask, "What Spirit? . . . God's Spirit, his own, or a deceiving one?" Even while the debate was raging, they heard the amazing news that Evan Roberts had now cancelled all mission engagements. Naturally the main newspapers treated this as a nervous breakdown or worse, until a further announcement was made: "Evan Roberts will remain in the house for six days in a silence which had been commanded by the Spirit."

These three extraordinary events convinced thousands of people that the critics had been right and that Evan Roberts was unbalanced. Revival converts wondered uneasily whether he had been deceived and brought down by Satan. A few wise leaders remembered that Evan was a very inexperienced young man and could make a young man's mistakes. A social psychologist, Dr. Fursac, attributed what he called eccentric behaviour to the excessive strain of four months of serial meetings, all-night sessions, and crises. He wrote this verdict after seeing Evan:

> Our organisms cannot support such pitiless tensions and violent repeated shocks, shaking the nerves and exhausting the brain and body. From these factors is born a complex state whose dominant traits are exaltation of the ego and diminution of physical/mental energy.

91

The next two chapters will attempt to examine the changes in Evan Roberts's public image, assess the impact of weeks of visionary experiences, present his words and actions in spiritual terms, and consider the effects of the "Week of Silence." This objective assessment is not intended to be an insensitive verdict on the Lord's anointed messenger, but hopefully will help us to see our own infirmities and weaknesses more clearly and thus lead us to cry again, "Lord, lead us not into temptation; but deliver us from the evil one. Amen."

10

Personality and Pressure: An Interpretation

uring the first months of the revival, Evan Roberts was greatly admired. Tall, slim, sinewy, clean-shaven and with an ivory-hued complexion, he had wonderfully tender eyes and a radiant smile. Because of his modesty and naturalness, the church leaders and journalists often described him as "the transparent man." He was virginal in every sense of the word. Many a young lady was happy enough to work with him, sing for him and do humble tasks for him, but he treated them all with scrupulous courtesy, as if they were all his sisters. When female soloists travelled with him, he took his own sister with them. He had no desire to be some kind of "cult leader" with female devotees.

Evan Roberts was not very confident in the company of more mature people and he detested committees. He stayed well back in conferences and had no time for group sessions and consultations. He tried to avoid being recorded on phonograph and did not at first agree to being photographed. He cold-shouldered any journalist who wanted to turn the spotlight on his role. He allowed his secretaries to handle hundreds of letters and sift all requests for private interviews.

Finally he banned all announcements of the next village or chapel he would visit.

A small group of close friends who knew him well understood that Evan could loosen up in their company and sometimes join in their amusements. Young men testified that he was a pleasant travelling companion who put their comforts and needs first. But everyone also knew and accepted that sometimes Evan needed space and time on his own. Then he would withdraw from them all into an "upper chamber" to pray for them or perhaps to meditate on God's will.

As his public ministry developed, Evan Roberts became well-known and respected for the humble, gracious way he treated older people. He often encouraged them to testify or pray, however hesitant they were. Others remembered him best for the way he inspired the trust of children; others for the way he listened to and helped young men. Those students who met him at Bala College testified that he had understood their problems and had warned them against the ever-present sins of self-pride and self-confidence, which afflict most youths and which had troubled him also.

> Satan used to come to me and say, "Hast thou heard of Evan Roberts and the wonderful meeting he had at such and such a place?" This was a great temptation to rejoice and so to foster pride.

As the revival reached its peak and hundreds of people declared openly that God had anointed this youthful messenger and given him unique powers, Evan began to protest. His replies were quoted in *Smith's Weekly:*

> I am not the source of this revival. I am only one agent in what is going to be a multitude. . . . I am not the one who is moving men's hearts and changing men's lives. Not I, but God working in me.

> I know that the work which has been done through
> me is not due to any human ability that I possess. It is
> His work and it is to His glory.

He explained further: "I have nothing for them. They must rely on Him alone who can minister to their needs. When you go to a window you do not look at the glass but through it at the scenery beyond. . . . Then look through me, but see the Lord." Evan knew that his modesty needed to be enriched by a Christ-like meekness of spirit in order to prevent secret pride. He surprised many friends by quoting Newman's lines, "Pride ruled my will," when he was in prayer. A famous American evangelist named R. A. Torrey knew all about this need. He sent Evan a letter thanking God for raising up a new instrument but adding a little warning:

> I am praying that God will keep you simply trusting
> in Him and obedient to Him, going not where men shall
> call you but going where He shall lead you, and that He
> may keep you humble. It is so easy for us to become
> exalted when God uses us as the instruments of His
> power. It is so easy to think that we are something
> ourselves. When we get to thinking that, God will set
> us aside. . . . May God keep you humble, and fill you
> more and more with His mighty power. I hope that some
> day I may have the privilege of meeting you. Sincerely
> yours.

Evan amazed everyone with his liveliness and joyousness, but he was not an extrovert and he detested showy people. He would leave a meeting if the presiding minister drew attention to him, or if someone urged him to go to the front and take over. He walked out of one great meeting as soon as some admirer called out, "There was a man sent from God and his name was Evan Roberts." For much of the time he played no open part in a meeting. He told his friend Sidney Evans: "It would spoil the work and rob God of His glory. Is it not important to keep ourselves in the background? "

It is still difficult to explain, therefore, how and why Evan Roberts gradually moved into the forefront and became more and more directive in January-March 1905. There could be many reasons for his growing forcefulness and directiveness.

Firstly, there was the great problem of his own super-sensitivity. Probably he could not help feeling inferior when men with high degrees or high reputation were present. He must have been well aware that he was an unqualified preacher with only six weeks of adult pre-college education and with only a year or two's experience of public speaking. In the National Library there is a letter from some London businessmen complaining that they had come down to meet the revivalists and had gone almost all the way through a conference before they realised that he was present. The young revivalist was even more self-conscious when he went into English-speaking cities or into the cosmopolitan cities such as Liverpool. His sensitive spirit also knew that clergymen were disparaging his informal manner and his restless movements in the pulpit. It embarrassed him that the journalists kept talking about his physical features such as the pale face and magnetic eyes and the nervous voice and "signs of hysteria." When he was confronted by skillful opponents, he always countercharged with a battery of questions, and was then criticised for being too assertive. Yet the Rev. D. M. Phillips always feared that he would not cope with the most skillful hecklers and would never stand up to an atmosphere of bitter hostility.

Secondly, as an evangelist he felt more and more dismayed as people responded so coolly and casually to urgent messages. Those who live in this age when the fear of God is almost forgotten, would find it hard to grasp what it meant to men like Evan Roberts to realise how the shallow people around him were not conscious of sin and judgment. He told one friend that he was so filled with burning desire that he could not get to sleep and wanted to go straight back to the chapel to exhort the people again. The vision of thousands of lost souls filled him with anguish and when people rejected Jesus he would cry out, "Is it possible that Welshmen will be found at the Judgment?" This was accompanied by a still deeper passion resulting from his many visions about the sufferings of Jesus.

A very experienced and sympathetic minister, the Rev. Thomas Phillips of Norwich, tried to account for this:

> A type of suffering arises from sympathy with the redeeming purpose of Christ. To watch with Him and work for His Kingdom is to be hurt by everything that hurts Him. To follow Him is to take up the Cross. Our Cross is like His in so far as it is caused by sins and endured in order to help others live.

Thirdly, Evan Roberts the exhorter, never restrained his indignation when church members finally confessed their secret sins and hypocrisies. In some of the revival meetings, where he had detected this "hiddenness of sin," he felt he had to deal quickly and decisively with those who were coming under conviction. Quite a few people were surprised by his extreme behaviour when dealing with something as ordinary as two quarrelsome deacons spoiling a meeting. Suddenly his frame would quiver and tears pour out as he cried, "Oh! Bend them! Lord. Oh! Speak to them! Oh! if you don't make peace, go out at once!" He would then fall down on his knees in the pulpit and sob bitterly.

These three feelings would not have changed his attitude were it not for a fourth factor— his growing conviction that he was called to the same kind of task as the lonely Elijah; the abused and misunderstood Jeremiah who challenged his faithless nation; the quiet priest Ezekiel who obeyed all commands of the Spirit; and the stern John the Baptist who rebuked people in order to prepare them for the One who came to baptise with Spirit and fire. During the second phase of the revival, Evan also seemed to identify with St. Paul, who bore the burden of disciplining unworthy churches and removing obstacles. This seemed a vital task because he was utterly convinced that, "When the churches are aroused to their duty, men of the world will be swept into the kingdom. A whole church on its knees is irresistible."

Such a convicting work had to start somewhere. The way in which he dealt with hypocrites, deceivers, boasters, quarrellers and dishonest church members seems to be in line with St. Paul's injunction to Titus to deal strictly with moral offences and impurities. However, this advice needed to be balanced by another Pauline injunction addressed to Timothy (1 Tim. 5:1-2), where the servant of the Lord is told to be as gracious and humble as possible .

The greatest tragedy was that just when Evan needed to come to terms with his own zeal and to see more clearly the limits of his role in the revival, his sensitive soul was exposed to a terrible testing. He was called an unbalanced crowd stirrer, an exhibitionist, a hypnotist and even an occultist. The singers were called chorus girls and the team was accused of making money out of the revival until someone revealed how all fees were given to deserving causes. Every day he could read new, bitter charges; in every meeting he was challenged by agnostics and others. Even worse attacks came from within the churches, above all in a letter to the newspapers from the Rev. Peter Price of Dowlais, who described Evan Roberts as a self-deluded actor, and as a prophet of Baal calling down false fire by his incantations. This letter acted like a whirlpool, sucking in a large number of hostile comments. For weeks the correspondence columns were full of such choice words as "bearer of false fire," "crowd stealer," "profaner." One senior minister alleged that Evan Roberts had gone on an ego trip and was being turned into a cult figure.

Evan apparently accepted all this as a refining fire. Indeed, he had forewarned his mother that a time of suffering was coming, and told her that he had asked the Lord for grace to suffer patiently. D. M. Phillips paid tribute to his response:

> Not a single bitter or discourteous word will he say about them. On the contrary we hear him more than once exclaiming, "Oh! these must be prayed for." He at once petitioned the Throne of Grace on their behalf. It is not in him to take revenge on anyone. On the contrary he believes in living in the spirit of forgiveness towards his villifiers.

A number of Evan Roberts's supporters were not so forgiving. They sent letters denouncing the critics as agents of Satan. Unfortunately they also exalted Evan so much that the Rev. Ioan Williams of Llanelli said publicly that, "The thoughtless multitudes are turning him into a public idol." Surely Evan Roberts must have noticed the strange silence of some ministers who should have defended him.

In an essay entitled, "Y Dau Diwygwyr," the late Principal Geraint Jones, of Swansea, showed that his father, R. B. Jones, and his circle admired Evan Roberts but kept their distance, mainly because they disliked his informal addresses and very personal testimonies which took the place of expository sermons. Was that enough reason to stay silent? Only the Rev. John Williams from Liverpool issued a public statement praising Evan Roberts's lack of exhibitionism and calling him self-possessed: "Judgment and common-sense were evident in the midst of the most intense emotion. He was entirely natural, with no shade of self-deception and no flavour of pride ."

The crucial question is: How far did the assault affect him in the long run? Did all-out condemnation of this kind change his personality, especially in public life? Once upon a time in South West Africa, a primitive tribe invented an ingenious dart whose poisoned tip could not be dragged out of an animal's body. At first the beast would feel no pain, but it became slower and weaker and more confused until it fell. In such fashion, the arrows from Price and his fellow huntsmen could have wearied Evan's soul and confused his mind.

The first sign of strain was that he gave up his belief that there should be no direction of meetings. He told one congregation in mid-January, "In times past I allowed meetings to proceed, but now I am directed to prevent the quenching of the Spirit by those who get up in order to show themselves." He suppressed anything that looked contrived.

The second sign was that he would stop meetings as soon as he detected an unloving or proud spirit or any signs that an evil spirit was present.

Third, he began to walk out of meetings after five minutes because he claimed to have discovered obstacles there.

Fourth, he was so worried about the charge of falsity that he used his old questioning technique to force people to expose their inconsistencies. For example, he would cry, "Will all who bear no malice stand up!" Or, "Let all who have not forgiven their enemies stand up!" Or, "Let all who have done their best for Christ stand up!" Some would cry out for forgiveness or would say, "I have tried to do my best." Many others resented such treatment and just kept to their seats.

As Elvet Lewis commented in his book, *With Christ Among the Miners,* "It was the growth of these practices that led to some unhappy incidents both by way of attack and defence." The judgmental attitude seemed so out of keeping with his private image that many were perplexed. Critics picked on Evan's use of the word "rhaid" (must) when calling upon the Holy Spirit. They accused him of being "a director, not a disciple," and asked why he dared to pretend that he was, "the infallible authority on the actions of the Holy Spirit."

One man was even more satirical:

> If Mr. Roberts controlled his emotions to a greater extent than he does at present, and if he endeavoured to know their working reasons more accurately, he would not attribute so many things to the Holy Spirit. If his own emotions lose intensity at a certain period, he must not take that as proof that the Spirit has departed from the building.

Even the editors of the *Cambrian News* turned on Evan Roberts and dismissed his claims:

> Why such claims to special insights and divine orders and supernatural visitations? Isn't he subject to the same mental laws? This is overheated imagination which is a fatal blow to real, inspired religious movements.

If all these pictures of inward and outward pressures on the revivalist's soul are accurate, it becomes easier to accept the tragic events of his last revival meeting in "Tabernacle" in Cwmafan. After it was over, some observers said that Evan was in a very strange state; others suggested that Satan had somehow deceived him into denying the possibility of mercy to a particular man. It cannot be denied that in the heat of the moment, Evan Roberts was claiming powers for himself that no individual can ever have. It is perhaps significant that Evan Roberts did not appear at any other meeting and that he rarely spoke in that way again. It may well have been yet another learning experience for the young evangelist. A year or two after these events, Evan Roberts, after conferring with Mrs. Penn-Lewis, explained the tragic errors in February and March as evidence of Satan's power to exercise control even over a servant of the Lord, by entering into the heart, influencing the mind, and troubling the spirit of a transparent man.

These words can be read in the first edition of *War on the Saints:*

> The Baptism of the Spirit takes place and the Holy Spirit fills the spirit of the man. But hidden secretly in him are habits and dispositions by which an evil spirit breaks forth into activity. The result is that for a time his heart is filled with love and his spirit is full of light and joy, and his tongue is loosed to witness. Ere long, a fanatical spirit may be detected, or a subtle spirit of pride or self-importance, concurrent with the other pure fruits of the Spirit, which are undeniably of God.

How such a modest, self-effacing and sensitive man, so keen to be out of sight, could gradually, in his public ministry, turn into a very directive person, is not just a riddle for psychologists to solve. It should be accepted as a solemn warning to all those who are called to such special ministries in our day and generation.

11

The Visionary Experience

f the strange happenings at Cwmafan had upset many of those who had championed Evan Roberts as the consecrated instrument of the Holy Spirit, the other two events which took place at Neath caused the enemy to scoff and the friends to wonder. Both the cancellation of a preaching engagement and the retirement into total isolation were said to be the result of "Spirit command." This brought the question of visions and voices to the fore. Those who were sure that he was "God's anointed servant" looked for other reasons for all these events. D. M Phillips believed that, "the reason for the seven-day silence was involved in an unbounded thirst for a closer communion with God." David Matthews, a notable revival convert, saw it as a perfectly natural literal response to Bible verses:

> The special word in Ezekiel came home to his soul with such power as to compel the belief that the Lord was leading him to do the same. Many of God's children have had Scriptures impressed on them in the same way. There is no mistaking the force and power of such experience.

Surely these two unusual instances of visionary guidance must be seen against the background of all those earlier experiences which were never questioned by friends or pastors at the time. They were probably not tested until around 1908 when Evan and Mrs. Penn-Lewis examined his revelations in order to discern which were truly inspired and which were subtly misleading. It is essential that this new and detailed review of the evidence does not cast doubt on the validity of that great New Testament promise: "I will pour out my spirit on all flesh. Your sons and daughters shall prophesy. Your young men shall see visions" (Joel 2:28 and Acts 2:17).

During the time when he was being called and prepared, Evan had again and again known an intense feeling of the presence of God, which caused his body to shake and his face to shine with peace and joy. Then, after the bending experiences, he was given special visions showing how God would send him to the young people in Loughor and exactly how many would respond. One other vision in this period predicted a great conflict between Satan and the Archangel of God. After the revival got underway, Evan Roberts told congregations about three or four visions which all seemed to point towards a great time of triumph. A vision of a white horse and of a key which opened the Gate of Life can be traced to the Book of Revelation. The most striking vision was of a candle's feeble rays being eclipsed by the rays of the rising sun. This signified that present forms of spreading the gospel light would be eclipsed by the radiance of revival.

Some friends felt that he should have kept many of the visions to himself, for his own encouragement. Evan Roberts should have remembered the warning Jesus gave about not sharing pearls with the earthly, sensual people who mocked what they couldn't understand (Matt. 7:6). He could have done with far more reticence, especially when he revealed

things to reporters. He confessed this temptation to his
friends: "The Evil One often tempts me to speak my own
words but, praise Him, the Holy Spirit through His wisdom
overcomes me, the world and the devil in all his wiles."

Once his mind and body became tired and overstrained,
he began to find it hard to distinguish Satanic suggestions
from the Spirit's promptings, and even harder to discern
which "voices" were only echoes of desires within his own
mind. Evan could not always see when his visions and voices
were psychical and not spiritual. A year later he told the
students that he was not even sure whether the Spirit
suggested things or actually spoke.

During December and January, Evan Roberts
experienced a new series of visions, each of which was
centred upon biblical scenes, such as Jacob wrestling with
the angel, Elijah being helped by ministering angels, Jesus
in the wilderness and Jesus in the garden of the agony. A
book which was given him at this time seems to have caught
his imagination. It was called *The Gospel in Art,* and
contained many pictures of the Passion which bore a striking
resemblance to his visions. In a Rhondda Valley meeting, as
some woman cried to God for an unsaved son, Evan broke
into loud crying and said that he had a clear vision of Mary,
Jesus' mother, and her tears at Calvary.

One night when he had to be given a drink, he had a
sudden pang as he saw that sop of vinegar being offered up
to the Man on the Cross. In a Hirwaun chapel in January,
the thought of Christ's sufferings came to him so forcibly
as to make him feel helpless. He wept, sighed and cried out
in the most heart-rending manner. He emerged "transfigured"
and overwhelmed.

David Matthews wrote about this costly experience in a
guarded way:

When this incident was far in the past, he told us that he had asked God to give him a taste of the agonies of Gethsemane. Probably, in his later experience, such a request would have been unthinkable. He and others, who were prominent at this time of visitation, were but minors or novices in the things of God. The fact remains, and I am a living witness of the incident, that the prayer was answered in a terrifying manner. Falling on the floor of the pulpit, he moaned like one mortally wounded, while his tears flowed incessantly. His fine physical frame shook under crushing soul-anguish. No one was allowed to touch him and those seated close to him frustrated any attempt at the assistance which many willing hands would have gladly rendered. The majority of us were petrified with fear in the presence of such uncontrollable grief.

Matthews said he wondered what value or meaning there was in such an experience. Yet there is some evidence that it gave him a deeper empathy with the soul-anguish of others, and that it inspired an even stronger desire to convince the rejecters of Christ. He could not bear any longer to see indifference when he spoke about Calvary.

His friends were relieved when the more dramatic visions stopped, probably because they feared that if Evan Roberts relied on visions he would not rely on the normal ways in which the Spirit of God gives guidance, that is through the Scriptures and through insights shared with a fellowship. On the other hand, there were admirers who considered the visions to be the highest proof that he was a unique prophet of God. How easy it would have been for Evan to convince himself that such unique experiences made him a very special person. There were times when the promptings of a "voice" caused his friends more concern than the visions which now faded into the background.

One day he was in a chapel where ninety percent were English speaking, yet he refused to speak in English, not because he was unused to this but because "the Spirit has forbidden me." When a group came over from Swansea and asked him for a New Year's message for that town, Evan closed his eyes in prayer and at once said, "No! the Spirit says no!" He gave no reason for this. Another group came with Mr. Tudor Rees and made a plea that Evan would soon come to their district. Without even a pause to pray this time, Evan Roberts said, "I am not unwilling to come but the Holy Spirit tells me not to go there yet." It is little wonder that a sympathetic minister from Llanelli told his audience in February, "Mr. Roberts's language in regard to the Holy Spirit's operation is confusing and his visions and predictions are very mysterious."

Peter Price dismissed it as manipulating the Holy Spirit. Even more damaging was the letter from a spiritual man from Llandovery alleging that all the visions and voices were profane because Evan Roberts never had apostolic gifts and never healed the sick, prophesied or spoke in tongues. A stern letter from Omega of Llanelli charged Evan Roberts with: "trifling with the Name of the Holy Spirit. . . . He is prostituting the people's idea of the Third Person and is speedily assuming the role of a Delphic oracle." Omega went on to ridicule Evan Roberts's "pretence" that the Spirit had stopped him from visiting cities when the truth was that he was afraid of cities. He said the revivalist should stop making a scapegoat of the Spirit.

This debate became open conflict when Evan Roberts suddenly announced that the Spirit had commanded him not to go to Cardiff despite previous agreement. He was interrogated by a minister:

"Are you sure that you are not mistaking bodily weakness or some reluctance, as an answer from the Spirit?"

Roberts: "I am as certain that the Spirit has spoken to me as I am of my own existence."

Minister: "Will you come in the future? "

Roberts: "Yes! as soon as I get permission and not before."

Minister: "What about the girls? Shall they come?"

Roberts: "No, they shall not. I have asked the Spirit about that, too. The voice said to me, *'If you go I shall not go with you.'*"

Minister: "Do you care nothing about the great disappointment of the crowd?"

Roberts: "I can't help it. I am not going with this voice ringing in my ears. . . . I will go anywhere He leads, but I will not go anywhere without Him."

At the time he was hearing this actualised voice, Evan Roberts was heading for a bout of nervous prostration and depression and perplexity, which kept him abed for a few days. He needed to know how and where his relationship with the Spirit had gone wrong. Just then a tutor from Trevecca College, John Young Evans, came to see him and to offer his counsel. The *Western Mail* devoted three columns to the talks. First of all, Evan told him that ever since he had been filled with the Spirit he had been physically conscious of the Spirit's prohibitions and commands. Sometimes, he said, these were so contrary to his own desires that he had to accept them as trials of the flesh from which his spirit might emerge stronger and purer. He said he had learned by experience that if ever he spoke or did anything before seeking the mind of the Spirit, he was at fault and his prayers were hindered. Yet, in this matter of avoiding Cardiff and going elsewhere, he doubted whether he had received genuine Holy Spirit guidance.

He was very relieved when the learned tutor produced examples of positive and negative guidance from the Book of Acts and from the lives of monks and missionaries and Welsh heroes. It seemed to make sense of his own decisions and actions. Was he not also a chosen messenger? Thus his spirit was uplifted and his heart was at peace. His face began to shine and brighten and he said exultantly, "The burden has passed away; I will trust God to put all things right." From that time until the middle of the year, he had full confidence in the voice of the Spirit which called him to obey in all things.

Because of the flood of requests for visits, the Rev. Mardy Davies, his secretary, agreed to draw up a planned itinerary and then got the newspapers to publish a list of Evan Roberts's future engagements. Almost immediately a hostile critic wrote, "If all his movements are prompted by the Holy Spirit, why is someone drawing up pre-planned engagements?" If this objection had come to the ears of Evan Roberts, he would have reminded everyone of his first resolve never to forecast the next meeting in case the Spirit decided to send him elsewhere. Surely a new crisis would arise over this somewhere. The blow did fall at Briton Ferry not very long afterwards.

On the appointed day, the great crowds had gathered at a Briton Ferry chapel. A team of gospel singers had begun the time of praise which usually preceded the arrival of Evan Roberts. Into the chapel came a flustered Mardy Davies who went straight to the pulpit and read out this strange little note: "Tell the people that I shall not come to the service. The Spirit prohibits my coming. I must pray here for the salvation of souls. The Spirit prevents my coming and I cannot speak."

There were cries of disappointment, perplexity and even anger in the chapel. From all accounts, the Briton Ferry meeting was still a great blessing, but scores of visitors were very upset and many local people were asking pointed questions about Roberts's absence. Some rushed to his lodging in Neath to find out what had gone wrong this time. Among them was the French psychologist, Dr. Emil Fursac, who wrote down Evan's explanation: "I had prepared to go to the service and had put on my overcoat and gloves and had a hat on my head when a voice said to me, *'Don't go, Evan!'* Whilst I was washing myself, a voice had spoken to me in Welsh, *'Do not go to Briton Ferry!'* Now the voice repeated, *'Do not go!'* I went back to my room. I sat on a chair, and I was compelled to pray for the salvation of souls. Then came a second explosion greater than the first and I was forced to sink to my knees in great agony of soul. The voice went on saying, *'Do not go this evening!'*"

Of course the growing band of Evan Roberts's critics ridiculed the whole thing. They challenged him to admit that this was only a cover for his own need to retreat and rethink after the disgraceful way he had behaved recently. Even friends and admirers of Evan Roberts could not convince themselves that the mighty Holy Spirit would give a last-minute order which countermanded earlier guidance. It seems highly unlikely that such an abrupt change of orders could be given, not through reading the Bible or praying or listening to friends, but through an inner voice speaking to God's messenger while he stood in the bathroom and then in the hall waiting to fulfill his mission.

The best thing his supporters could have said was that Mr. Roberts was very inexperienced and that he had been under great strain. Perhaps some of them remembered the closing remarks of the Rev. Iona Williams at Llanelli: "I cannot shake off the thought that it might be a good thing for the stability of this revival if Mr. Roberts now retired into seclusion for two or three months."

As this strangely prophetic suggestion appeared in the *County Express,* it could have been brought to Evan Roberts's notice. It was while that debate was still raging that the last of the supernatural commands was announced. People heard the news that he was under orders to shut himself up within a room, and close the door to all visitors except for Annie Davies to bring in meals. The crowds of visitors melted away and the pressmen were also excluded. Awstin alone had access to the *Journal of the Week,* and Awstin was permitted to publish the special letter of explanation. Rather unusual letters were given to his hosts, Mr. and Mrs. Rhys Jones of Godrecoed, and another message was sent to a nearby church.

1. To his hosts:

> I don't know what to tell you for this is very remarkable. Because, first of all, I am your guest, and yet the Lord does not permit me to see either of you. I hope you will not think hard of this. He will surely bless you for this hospitality.
>
> . . . The Lord has cautioned me several times not to attempt to say a word. Now, father and mother, if the Lord says I am to stay in this room for any length of time without seeing any person, are you willing? But why should I ask you. Of course you are, for the sake of your son. There is no need to ask you to pray for me—you could not help praying for your son.

2. To Bethlehem Green Church: per Mr. Jones.

> It is a difficult task to say, "Thy will be done," but we must so say. Otherwise His will cannot prosper to the extent He wishes it. This week I am obliged to humble myself under the mighty hand of God. It is easier to say, "Let Thy will be done," than to do His will. The condition of prosperity is "In His hand." Not our plans but His Divine scheme. . . .
>
> Lord, accept my will to do Thine own Divine will.
> Yours in the bonds of love.
>
> Evan Roberts

3. To the Press per "Awstin."

> In reply to your first questions. 1. I must remain silent for seven days. 2. I must remain at Neath for this period. 3. As for the reasons, I am not led to state them. 4. One issue of this silence is—if I am to prosper at Liverpool I must leave Wales without money—not even a penny in my purse. (Luke 10:4) . . . 5. We read of Ezekiel the prophet (Eze. 3:24-25), that his tongue was made to cleave to the roof of his mouth, and that the command was, "GO! shut thyself within thy house." My case is different. I can speak. I have the power, but I am forbidden to use it. It is not for me to question why, but to give obedience.

> P.S. I am sorry to cancel my engagements. It is the divine command. I am quite happy. A divine peace fills my soul.

There are crucial questions that need to be answered. Was this retirement only an act of a merciful God that was intended, as Eifion Evans says, to save him from spiralling excess, ruin and eclipse? Or was it, as James Stewart claimed, an essential experience in which "one's whole life and personality lies naked before Holy God for the transforming work of the Spirit"? What new freedom did Evan Roberts obtain; what mistakes were corrected; what new truths were unfolded; what new commission was given in these last visionary experiences?

In the fifth *Western Mail Revival Supplement,* Awstin used Evan's notes to compile a record of his experiences during those six days. He said that on the first morning a voice spoke to him in English and in Welsh, commanding him to read Isaiah 54:10—"My kindness shall not depart from thee, neither shall the covenant of my peace be removed." He wrote in his notebook, "It was not an impression but a voice." On the second day he spent some time meditating on the words, "Let there be light." On the third morning he meditated on the names of Jesus. On the fourth morning his theme was, "Praising the Blood of Jesus."

Other visions of the Cross were not so pleasant. Even the afternoon pot of tea reminds him of the terrible thirst of the Crucified One—not only for water, but for the lost souls of men. The note ends: "I thirst for Wales, England, Scotland, Ireland. I thirst for the world." A highly imaginative paragraph imagines the brooks and the rain clouds being forbidden to satisfy the thirst of Jesus on the Cross. Another morning he heard a voice within his soul telling him to be ready to be forsaken and rejected for Jesus' sake. He was beginning that two-year journey which ended in a full acceptance of the doctrine of identification with the Crucified One which he preached a year later.

As before, there were Satanic voices tempting him to think of going off to the Holy Land before he had completed his work. In hours of discouragement and depression he explored ways to defeat Satan.

He wrote: "Satan came to me but he was driven to flight. The father of lies and the accuser. I told him, 'You may as well go for I am determined to win.' He was not long before hurrying off." This kind of experience was not new but there was a significant sentence in his notes, "Speak, Lord, in such a way that I may differentiate Thy voice from the cunning of the Evil One." It looked as though the old problem was settled once and for all that week. On the sixth day, in the early evening, Evan Roberts heard the unmistakable voice of the Holy Spirit once more. The first message was similar to some contemporary messages in that it used words and phrases from the Old Testament prophets when it wished to denounce old leaders and pronounce blessing on new ones. The second message was really giving a new commission.

This solemn day had begun with Evan praying and

fasting, and making a new vow to obey only that which God himself would command and, secondly, to take every least thing to God in prayer. He wrote out a vow to give obedience to the Spirit but, also, to give ALL the praise and glory to God. He then drew three heavy lines under the word ALL, but a voice was heard saying, *"Draw a fourth line!"* He did so without asking the reason. Finally he wrote down a plea, "Here am I! An empty vessel. Take me!" He then committed himself to the task of reaching the millions for whom Jesus had died. After the vows and the covenant came the divine promises:

> *Take thy pen and write. Lo! I am the Lord who hath lifted thee up from the depths. I have sustained thee thus far. Lift up thine eyes and look on the fields. Behold! They are white. Shall I suffer thee to spread a table before my enemies? As I live, saith the Lord, the windows of heaven shall be opened and the rain shall come down upon the parched earth. . . . Open thy hand, and I will fill it with power. Open thy mouth, and I will fill it with wisdom. Open thy heart, and I will fill it with love.*

It is hardly surprising that many of his friends discovered soon afterwards that Evan Roberts was expecting greater and more notable manifestations of the Holy Spirit's power working through him. But the words also heralded the coming of a new and wider ministry. He ceased to be a passive instrument or catalyst of revival movements in which the Holy Spirit was in entire control. Instead he chose to set up revival missions to Liverpool, North Wales, and perhaps further afield. The old dream of winning one hundred thousand souls for Christ was calling him onwards once more.

There was still one important work to be done in Evan Roberts's spirit during that week of silence. He needed to have the last traces of self-examination and ultra self-consciousness wiped out, and all tendencies to be too masterful. Under the guidance of the Holy Spirit, he wrote down the words of a new prayer. By his command, it was printed and circulated for use by hundreds of the converts. It became a kind of manifesto of Christian humility and service:

> Holy Spirit, purify and make all Thine own, to Thy glory and keep me to the end in Thy service. Teach me to serve and let me be not weary in serving. Give me the joy of the servant. Teach me to be as humble as I wish to be and as humble as Thou, the Holy and Just One, wilt have me to be. Fill my heart, which Thou cleansest, with work. Direct my steps towards work— not my work but Thine. Make clean my hands so as not to soil Thy work—work hallowed by sweat and tears—work which has all the riches of God in it, upon it and behind it.
>
> My God, draw me to Thy work. Keep me in Thy work. Let Thy work hold me fast, and make me a power to draw others to Thy work. Own Thy work at this time; own it for the Atonement's sake. Think Thee of the intercession of Thy Holy Son, Jesus, and of Thy sons, Thy servants. Give me a baptism of work.

One of the first expressions of this new yielding to God was a little poem which seems to sum up the change in his soul.

> *This was the prayer of the flower at the end of the day.*
> *Bend me down low, lest my faith should decay.*
> *And when the dawn broke, on its knees it still lingered.*
> *Thanking the Lord, for the prayer had been answered.*

God bended the flower with the weight of the blessing,
And washed it all white in the dew of the morning.
Then the blessing was shared and the heart of the giver
Expanded with love, and the mind became clearer.

On the last day of the week of silence, Evan Roberts received a command: *"Rise from your bed! Open your lips! Pray!"* He renewed fellowship with his hosts, his team and his friends. He explained to them that he would now follow First Corinthians 1:17 in preaching. They noticed with gladness that he had lost the weakness and the strain, and was quietly waiting for further guidance. Awstin kept copies of the brief notes he sent to his hosts, apologising for his strange order not to approach him, and assuring them that their obedience and goodwill would bear eternal fruit. One day he shared his experiences with Maggie and Mary Davies and other close friends. However, he avoided even the most serious visitors and gave only one message to a press representative: "Tell the people, my faith in God is stronger than ever."

Certainly his friend and biographer, D. M. Phillips, believed that this had been a creative experience and a health-giving one, in the spiritual sense. He wrote, "I have not the least doubt that he had a clearer conception of God's counsels, love and grace."

12

Return to the Place of Blessing

fter the week of silence, Evan Roberts relaxed with friends and family until visitors began to swarm in once more. A troublesome cough kept him indoors for a few days, but he kept a promise to attend a chapel anniversary service at Penuel, Loughor. Scores of people rushed into the chapel and were surprised when they found their hero sitting quietly in a pew. Then they heard the minister announce that Mr. Roberts would not be speaking, but wished to lead the congregation in saying the Lord's Prayer. That was all.

As if he were remembering the first years of preparation, Evan took long walks along the river paths where he had sat and prayed with his band of youths. He went past the yard of that colliery where he had once witnessed to fellow colliers. He decided to visit his uncle's forge at FForest, Pontardulais, where he had written his first poems and prepared his first sermons. Once more a crowd came and besieged the workshop and urged him to hold meetings in the village. He retreated to Loughor for a day or two. Arriving by train a few days later, a horde of sightseers and autograph-hunters found that Evan and the singers had gone

117

on to hold special meetings at Newcastle Emlyn. The members were delighted to see him in that "Bethel" where he had received his great commission. He stayed with the Phillips family while the two lady evangelists were put up in the Cawdor Hotel. At first, Evan avoided interviews with the local people, but on the Monday evening he entered the "big seat" at Bethel. He issued a warning message to all who were there purely out of curiosity, but the rebuke had no effect.

As soon as it became known that he was going back to Blaenannerch, in obedience to the Spirit's command, people rushed to make arrangements to follow him. People from dozens of little farms finished work early and put on their Sunday best. The larger families got wagons ready for the journey across the hills towards the coast. Joined by quarrymen from the Presceli Hills and fishermen from Newquay, they had filled Blaenannerch chapel by three in the afternoon. The place was packed with excited people.

Evan Roberts came in with his helpers and a few students. He began at once to rebuke those who had come only to satisfy curiosity and therefore were not ready to receive gifts from the Lord. Miss Maggie Davies began to sing, "If I've Jesus, Jesus only" in an off-key voice that made certain men on the gallery laugh. At once, Evan Roberts's face went bleak and he shouted out: "God will not be mocked. This place is terrible. It is ill-fitted for a display of indifference." He could not bear to think that anyone would behave so carelessly in that almost-sacred place where the Lord had bended and broken him. As others prayed, he thought he could still hear scoffing, and his face changed. The local *Cambrian News* reporter, a hostile witness, said that he seemed to convulse and groan as if in agony:

> All eyes were turned on him. He lay a limp, inert
> mass on the reading desk, with outstretched arms as if

pleading. Suddenly he straightened up and, with a look of decision, he dramatically pointed to the gallery and declared that some person there possessed a heart full of scorn, scepticism and sarcasm. That was an obstacle to the path of the Spirit, and the cause must be removed. He tearfully appealed to him to repent or quit the building. . . . Half a dozen people prayed simultaneously for the person denounced, while the missioner gasped for breath and trembled like a leaf. He implored people to pray and the response was general. Meanwhile he continued to sob, with his face buried in his hands. "Lord, bend him before it is too late," he prayed as he sobbed convulsively. No response was made from the gallery and Mr. Roberts again looked dejected and again failed to read the verse he had selected because tears were blinding his eyes. "Ah!" said he, "Bending is inevitable sooner or later. The patience of God has limits. He will not punish His servant for the transgression of others for long. What if the Spirit tells me to ask that he may be struck down for his contumacy?"

Under this pressure a little boy shouted that he was the scoffer, and two men stood up asking for forgiveness, but Evan insisted that the Spirit was still guiding him to someone who was "older than the three who had confessed."

Such claims seemed to confirm an earlier *Cambrian News* editorial which said: "When he thinks he hears voices and fancies he is receiving divine messages, and that he is being enabled to look into the intentions of those who attend revival services, he is probably on the borderline of a nervous breakdown and should be under medical care."

In the next meeting Evan announced that God had taken pity upon the scoffer because: "Heaven has answered my request. Sometimes it has occurred that the answer was not given so directly and I am distinctly bidden to cease praying for someone." What kind of authority was he claiming here?

Even his admirers questioned whether his prayers could move heaven to delay or accelerate judgment.

Evan Roberts acted just as sternly when he reached Newquay where the first sparks of revival had once glowed for a while before resistance began. His anguished cries and strange actions in that chapel were like those of a father whose sweet little children have turned into difficult adolescents. Such was the force of his passion that men and women confessed their sins and made restitution as soon as Evan called to them.

In one such meeting he called to a man to confess his sin and actually claimed that, "The Spirit has given me that man's name and age." Many doubted whether any man could be given such knowledge from above about any person's name, personal details and destiny. When Evan was made aware of all these feelings, he challenged the people to believe: "Some of you are sceptical of the reality of this manifestation, but let there be no doubt about it. Put the matter to the proof and leave it to God's decision." When he was asked to explain the shocking things he had said, he replied, "I have to be severe at times."

Only in later years would he question whether it was the Holy Spirit who commanded these things, and whether he had used power aright. If the main services were rather stern, the cottage meetings were quite different. He held meetings at a gentleman's house in Henllan and a Captain's house not far from Capel y Drindod, where he had first sensed that great things were about to happen. When he was told by someone that an aged, bedridden saint longed to meet him, Evan and a friend named Williams borrowed bicycles and rode out along muddy tracks to the man's cottage. He spoke briefly but movingly about the love of God to the family and addressed a crowd of villagers who appeared out of nowhere. All through that meeting the aged man held his hand within his own.

Another story was circulated about how a farmer's son borrowed someone's bicycle and rode to Newcastle Emlyn because, as he told his family: "Something impels me. I have been restless all the morning in chapel and I cannot form any idea, no, not one." When he got home he told everyone how the revivalist had been so kind and encouraging and that "he seemed to know all about me and seemed to expect me." This young man told Evan, "I desire greatly to do all I can for the Master," and received this gentle reply, "Just obey the call and your efforts will be truly blessed."

The last days of this journey into the West were very relaxing. Evan took his sister and Maggie Davies and a few students to Ty Llwyd cottage where he sat in his favourite chair. A little crowd gathered outside and listened to them singing revival hymns in the parlour. Mr. Joshua Eynon, who was a local photographer, obtained a good picture of Evan Roberts, Sidney Evans, John Phillips the tutor, a student group and the four lady missionaries. After he left, the local correspondent went out of his way to show that Evan had aroused no resentment, whatever he had said. He cited a prayer spoken by one of the revival people in a chapel meeting:

> Thanks be for what Thou, O Lord, hast done through Mr. Roberts. Give him strength as he has nearly worn himself out in Thy service. Bring forward more men of his kind so that Wales may be on fire. Amen.

One rather strange incident has to be recorded as it concerned future developments. Some Newcastle Emlyn folk had asked for one more meeting before his departure. Instead, he sent his former tutor, John Phillips, with a prophetic message for them:

> *I AM what I AM, the Creator of Heaven and Earth and the Sustainer of every creature. Blessed are they that obey my commandments, for in them and around them I shall be as a flame of consuming fire. . . .*

This fits in with a statement he made to Mr. Young Evans and others after he had returned to Loughor. Instead of apologising for his severe words spoken in the West Wales chapels, or answering those who claimed that his behaviour had stifled the revival, Evan began to hint that they were all going to see greater manifestations very soon.

13

The First Revival Mission
(Liverpool, April 1905)

here is little doubt that Evan Roberts was nervous and uneasy about this mission from the start. The first thing he did was to make a public announcement that he had given away all his personal savings to Moriah Chapel, to the family and to certain good causes. He was determined to travel to Liverpool in apostolic poverty, but a Christian friend paid his rail ticket and another escorted him and lodged him in that northern city.

He was not sure exactly when to go and took his time in deciding whether to take singers and other helpers. He knew a programme had been arranged, although he had insisted on his freedom to change plans if the Spirit commanded him. Evan felt uneasy that the organising committee had publicised the mission. He told them: "Please do not announce in what meeting I will preach. The people must come for the Lord and Him alone; otherwise the Holy Spirit will withdraw Himself." He must also have sensed that many city ministers were very uneasy because they had heard about his words and actions in West Wales.

During the Liverpool mission, Evan Roberts was

destined to face the wealthy leaders of the Liverpool Welsh business community along with a galaxy of scholarly preachers and theologians. He was expected to meet with distinguished journalists such as Sir Edward Russell of the *Liverpool Daily Post* and Mr. Hodgson of the *Daily News,* who had once described him as a, "man with the heart of a child." Hodgson thought that Evan was too terrified to speak to him at a meal because he "seemed to think of us as vivisectors."

Some journalists never understood that Evan always avoided interviews until he had clear proof, as D. M. Phillips said, "that a correspondent will adhere strictly to facts without magnifying them." In all fairness, the senior Liverpool journalists gave a very balanced view of the mission. An interesting magazine called *Porcupine* explained why their scepticism had changed into admiration in one week. Then Sir Edward praised him for sticking to his true work of evangelising and converting instead of getting involved in political, social and theological issues which were best left to others.

Long before the mission began, excited people were planning to come from all over North East Wales. Evan Roberts was the topic of the day in chapel societies, luncheon clubs, hairdressers salons and the chambers of commerce. Already there were many prayer groups who spent hours in passionate intercession. Meanwhile, the committee, under the chairmanship of the Rev. John Williams, had worked out rotas of chapels to be used, stewards on duty, and singers on call. They had a list of distinguished guests and they had special tickets to ensure that outsiders could get seats. They even had the city police force to help with crowd control. Yet all these arrangements collapsed under the sheer weight of numbers. Humphreys of the *Caernarfon and Denbigh Herald* described one of these chaotic scenes:

Two policemen stood by the door but, in spite of their efforts, things were getting very disorderly. Older women were climbing over the railings to reach the door quicker, and they were falling on other people. They were snatched up by the police and thrown inside the chapel like sacks of wool. Some shouted that they were suffocating. Others fought with the policemen as if they were to blame. . . . When one reached the gallery, things were at their worst. The air in the chapel was just as if a man had opened a furnace door. You can imagine the noise, with some outside pleading to get entrance, and others shouting at us to hold the doors tightly lest anyone come in. We were well-nigh suffocating as we were. Across all this tumult I could hear the voice of someone reading the scriptures. . . .

Before long, the well-organised mission services looked like the revival—all over again: solos, prayers, cries of confession, children's songs, congregational hymns, more prayers; all came in quick and bewildering succession. If anyone tried to restrain this, Evan Roberts would say, "Scores of people are quenching the Spirit and disobeying His promptings." Such behaviour attracted more and more people who came to observe but not to have their lives changed. To such people he cried, "Have I come here to divert and amuse you, and not make things clean?" Often there was a very slow response to his "burden" message. Humphreys commented: "I believe the churches had a shock when Evan Roberts came. His emphasis was on the spiritual state of the hearers, whoever they were. Were they obedient to the Spirit's call or were they stiff-necked and unwilling to bend? Did they believe there was no need to be convicted of sin because they were members?"

Despite his own dissatisfaction, many of Evan's meetings proved to be a great blessing, such as the Seacombe Presbyterian service where his preaching on "Who Shall Dwell in Thy Tabernacle?" caused scores to cry to the Lord for greater purity of life. At the Bootle chapel, the theme was, "Christ is the Physician of the Dying." Here he pleaded again for simultaneous prayer for the salvation of souls. Almost immediately converts began to appear, and he asked members to help them, saying, "Don't let the stewards take your crowns."

It was at the height of one such meeting that Evan stated that a person who was in the farthest part of the topmost gallery was ready to give himself to the Lord. No steward had found the man; yet, even as the people watched, someone stood up and confessed. Doubters said this was either a case of occult powers or of very sharp sight. They were utterly confounded when in the midst of another mass meeting in the 6,000-seat Sun Hall, Evan detected that a hypnotist had entered the meeting and was trying secretly to control him. When the man confessed to a theatre audience that this was the truth, hundreds of Christians endorsed the verdict of Dr. Hugh Jones of Bangor, in the journal *Yr Eurgrawn:* "Inasmuch as he lives so near to his God and is so fully consecrated to Him, it is not surprising that he should have revelations concerning men, such as are not permitted nor will be permitted to any others."

Tragically, the use of such powers caused such confusion and conflict that in later years Evan confessed to a fear that he had been tricked by Satan into using them too drastically. The first clash took place in a meeting intended for backsliders and others. Evan noticed that the place was full of complacent churchgoers. Then he said that five people were hindering the work and that they needed "bending." After a great deal of whispering and groaning, Evan began to rock back and forth and then pronounced judgment: "Don't ask God to save. He is not listening now. Three of these five preach the Gospel. There will be an awful bending one of these days."

The chairman, a Rev. W. C. Evans, asked, "May we not

Portrait of A Revivalist

Evan Roberts and the Welsh Revival

Brynmor Jones

Photographs are exerpts from *The British Monthly* February, 1905 "The Revival in Wales."

Mr. Evan Roberts

Miss Maggie Davies, Miss Annie Davies
Miss S. A. Jones

Rev. Rhys B. Jones

REV. EVAN PHILLIPS, OF NEWCASTLE EMLYN

Evan Roberts Revival Visits – South Wales Valleys

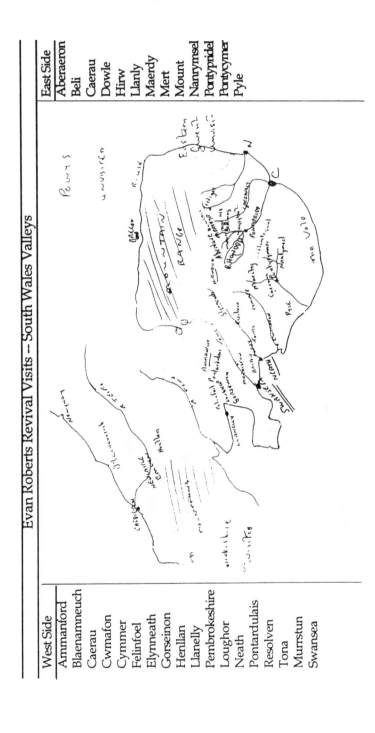

West Side	East Side
Ammanford	Aberaeron
Blaenannneuch	Beli
Caerau	Caerau
Cwmafon	Dowle
Cymmer	Hirw
Felinfoel	Llanly
Elynneath	Maerdy
Gorseinon	Mert
Henllan	Mount
Llanelly	Nanrymsel
Pembrokeshire	Pontypridel
Loughor	Pontycymer
Neath	Pyle
Pontardulais	
Resolven	
Tona	
Murrstun	
Swansea	

Evan Roberts in North-West Wales

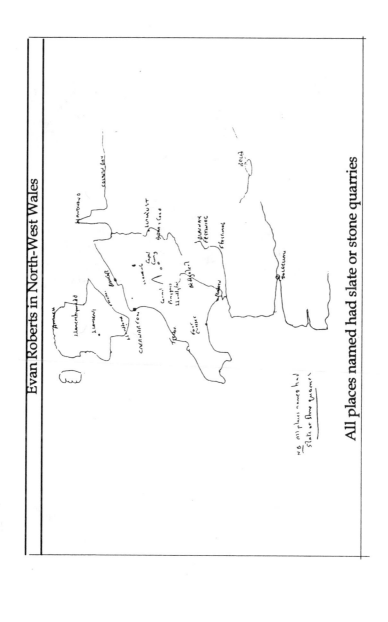

All places named had slate or stone quarries

Mrs ROBERTS.

EVAN ROBERTS HOME LOUGHOR

MR ROBERTS.

Mr EVAN ROBERTS

MISS ROBERTS

Mr DAN ROBERTS

O! Ysbryd Sanctaidd, tyr'd i lawr
I ogoneddu Iesu mawr:
Plyg yr eglwysi wrth Ei draed,
A golch y byd mewn dwyfol waed.

PISGAH SCHOOL.

MORIAH CHAPEL.

give thanks for those who have been saved?"

"No!" was the sternly authoritative reply, "He will not receive any thanks. He will receive nothing. He has locked heaven."

Afterwards people murmured that such statements were presumptuous. The next time that there was conflict was on an evening which should have been the high spot of the mission. The Lord Mayor and his Welsh wife had decided to hold a reception in the civic centre. This was to be attended by many leaders of Welsh churches and by the Welsh business community. Evan Roberts was driven in the official coach to the City Hall and ushered into the reception chamber where he behaved with perfect courtesy as the Lady Mayoress made the introductions. The Rev. John Williams made it known that the revivalist did not feel led to make any formal address, but the reception remained friendly and lively. The president of the Free Church Council and a representative of the Anglican Church took part in the welcome speeches. The official party then entered the coach and were driven to the vast Sun Hall where six thousand people filled every tier.

Suddenly Evan Roberts broke away from the party on the dais and said he wished to speak from the front of the platform. After bowing his head in prayer, he projected his voice to the farthest, highest corner of the hall. Now he challenged everyone to make sure that they had come for cleansing and for confessing Christ by a simple raising of hands. Trouble flared up as a minister sitting behind him on the platform grumbled about this testing. He told the minister to ask God's pardon and make public confession. He said to him: "Do not be surprised if your arm hangs by you so that you will not be able to raise it forever. Do as you please, but you will be carrying this sign of disobedience as long as you live". While the people were still wondering, Evan Roberts called on someone to rise and confess, and he virtually identified him: "Not an Englishman and not a woman; not a deacon or a preacher; but a minister. Pray God to bend him." Two Liverpool ministers then challenged him to take the offender to a private room and thus clear the names of the others. At once he left the meeting.

The crisis did not seem to affect the revival mission although some ministers were wondering whether their missioner had the right to treat murmuring as an unforgivable sin and decree such judgments. The Rev. David Adams wrote: "We sometimes fear lest Christ and Calvary be hidden from our view by Moses and Sinai. . . . We believe that Evan Roberts does not get the amen of the people when he ascends Ebal to pronounce curses." However, the people reacted in a different way to the message of judgment. In each meeting that week scores took part in the joyous singing and testimony centred upon Calvary and Christ's love. Two hundred people decided to come to Christ the next evening and then two hundred more soon afterwards.

By this time there was an equally vocal, "Evan Roberts" faction, whose members prayed in the public services that "the ministers of Liverpool be made to bend," or that "your servant shall be protected from all attacks of the devil, from hatred in the press and on the platform."

Even a dangerous accident during a pony and trap ride to Hilbre Island, when he was thrown out almost under the wheels of a coal cart, was viewed as sinister. Evan refused to cancel meetings, though in a state of shock, because, as he told a friend, "This is another of Satan's tricks, but he has failed again."

The next blow fell on Tuesday, 11 April, in the Welsh Wesleyan Chapel. As soon as he arrived he said, "This place is not clear. What is it friends? There is something extraordinary the matter here." After moaning and struggling he declared that God was making him give out a message for the new "Free Church" (a recent breakaway church). The message was, "The foundations of this church are not on the rock."

"I was willing to go there, he said, "but I was not allowed. I would rather not have delivered it but somebody must say it."

As an invited missioner, did Evan have the right to enter inter-church affairs? The Rev. John Williams said he had nothing to do with the message and wanted no feuds. Other church leaders also disowned it and denied that it was divinely given. These controversies seemed to unleash the full wrath of all who had been lukewarm about the revival mission from the beginning. Some resigned from the planning committee, some let it be known that only 760 decisions had been recorded, and some took refuge in silence.

The final storm broke at a men's meeting on the Friday night when the Rev. John Williams was away preaching. Faced with hundreds of disturbed men, Evan sat for two hours without opening his lips. On behalf of the offended pastor of that denounced Free Church, a certain minister asked, "Were you reconciled to your brother minister before you came here? Why dost thou trifle with sacred things?" Several prayed that Satan should be silenced and enmity cease, but it was too late. Evan made no answer, and the Rev. John Williams was not back yet. As the acting chairman tried to close the meeting, the Rev. H. H. Roberts stood on a chair and began to state his views, but he was shouted down. During the shameful wrangle that followed, the revivalist left the chapel. What a dishonour to the Lord and what an opportunity for the enemies of revival.

When the Rev. John Williams came home from a Wrexham preaching festival, he took prompt action to stop the strife. He contacted four Liverpool specialists who examined Evan on the Sunday morning and signed a joint bulletin: "Mr. Roberts is physically and mentally sound, but suffering from the effects of overwork, too many meetings and far too many visitors." On Sunday evening, Mr. Williams announced this, asked for good order and warned people that "preparations have been made for dealing with any breach of the peace."

When Evan Roberts came in at seven o'clock, he began to weep and pray on his knees in the pulpit. After two hours of this he began to smile and then exhorted them lovingly to consider the True Shepherd as depicted in Ezekiel 34. Meanwhile, some of the ministers had offered to be reconciled and Evan Roberts was able to smile and sing again. The last meeting closed in peace and sunshine. Evan Roberts was in his most winsome mood, his face radiant and his mind resourceful and alert. Someone noted that he never once attempted to give a word of prophecy.

As the congregation sang, "Till we meet," Evan still smiled, but he must have realised that he would never set foot in a Liverpool chapel again. Others were invited to that battlefield where Satan fought against the Holy Spirit, but Evan had to go into the hills of Wales for the healing of his wounds.

14

Walks and Talks in North Wales

n 18 April 1905, Evan Roberts was once more on a train which was taking him into new experiences, but it was for a sad reason. Once he had travelled in obedience from the college to Loughor; once he had travelled in great joy from Loughor to Aberdare; this time he was in wounded retreat. He was entering unknown territory.

Many friends and admirers came to Lime Street Station to wish him Godspeed. Businessmen had paid for a reserved compartment for Mr. Roberts, the Rev. John Williams and the two lady evangelists. He completed his journey with only one companion and was driven up to Capel Curig, close to Snowdon, where a room had been booked for him at the Royal Hotel. A friend, Edward Williams, sent him a book and he felt well enough to write a few letters. One of these was a cheerful and forgiving letter sent to a Liverpool minister who was grieving over the rift between them.

It was a healing time and he told one friend, "I desire to receive something of the heat and light of a fire on the hearth." He told another friend, "I wish to be more happy and useful." Early in the mornings, Evan would be out cycling or walking along the lanes close by the lakes. In the twilight hours, he would take out a boat and row across shallow Lake Ogwen under tall Tryfan, or explore the shining waters of the twin lakes between Glyder and Moel Siabod. In that beauty and majesty, he could rest his oars and pray.

Sometimes he loved to sit in his room and gaze at Moel Siabod, "shrouded in grey, tinted cloth." As his strength returned, Evan arranged to climb Snowdon's peaks with some friends on a May morning. Afterwards he wrote a little poem to send to friends.

> *The mountains are high—my hope is higher.*
> *The mountains are strong—my hope is stronger.*
> *The mountains will depart—my God never.*

Only a few visitors were allowed, including Dr. McAfee and Dr. Williams from Liverpool. A few days earlier, he had written to his friend D. M. Phillips to tell him that the cure was working and he was ready for service.

> My soul has been possessed by the peace of heaven. My bodily strength is much improved. Each sinew is stronger the nervous system more peaceful and normal; the circulation meeting no obstacles, flowing in full harmony. My mind is clearer, the memory revived and the imagination ready to wing its flight.

One day some friends called and took him down to lunch in the Llewellyn Hotel at Beddgelert. He was asked to put his name in the visitor's book. Instead, he wrote a few lines of verse composed in honour of the 1826 revival in that town. As he glanced through the lounge window, he saw children at play in the school field. At once he asked the vicar to permit him to go and call the children together. At the end of his talk he asked them to make a solemn promise and they all shouted, "Mi a wnaf fy ngorau." ("I will do my best.")

This was by no means the only time he stopped to talk with children. One reporter saw Evan talking to some little lads about the harm that their smoking would do to their bodies and pockets. When he begged them to put away the habit, the lads handed over cigarettes to their teacher. Evan next asked the children about memorising the Bible and told them, "This is the best time in your lives to store God's words in your minds, so that it will be a blessing in later days." Then some children began to recite verses, but a carriage came along to take him away and he shook hands with each child. True to form, Evan thanked *THEM* for the spiritual feast they had given him. Always he honoured children.

As usual he was completely at ease with young people and interested in their well-being. One weekend he travelled all the way back to Liverpool to attend the wedding of John Thomas Jones and Ann Daniel. The pastor, the Rev. John Williams, invited him to read a Scripture portion, but Evan also sang some snatches of a Welsh hymn. At the reception he was in top form, making puns and riddles.

During one of his visits, Evan Roberts was introduced to the famous Welsh politician, David Lloyd George. They encountered each other in the Rev. John Williams's company. Apparently their first dialogue turned into a polite duel of words.

> D. L. G.: "I am very sorry I have not been able to attend any of your meetings as yet. I would certainly like to see you."
>
> E. R.: "Yes, and I would like to hear you some day but I am busy, as you see, with all these wonderful meetings."
>
> D. L. G.: "Perhaps I can come and visit you some time when I am free."
>
> E. R.: "Yes, and I should like to visit you if the Spirit permits."
>
> D. L. G.: "This thing I know. My work is to wield the sword but your work is to build the Temple [Nehemiah 3]."

In fact, they met twice more, the first time at Lloyd George's home near Criccieth, and the second time in the parlour of the Mayor of Caernarfon, where a press photographer was present. There is a postcard depicting the "Great Welsh Parliamentarian" and the "Great Welsh Revivalist," clasping hands at the fireside.

By the second week of May, Evan Roberts was taking far more interest in chapel meetings. One weekend he cycled down past the Swallow Falls into Betws-y-Coed and then over the old bridge and along the lovely River Conwy to Llanrwst, where he dined with the Chairman of the Borough Council. That day he was asked to send a special telegraphed message to the Welsh missionaries on the Khassia Hills in India, where another revival had broken out. Then, on the Sunday, he gave an address in Griffith Ellis's chapel on, "The Christian's Work and Witness." It ended with a simple and straightforward appeal:

> I fear that many hearts are ready to beat fast here, but are yet too weak to reveal Christ, for they are not brave enough. If you are feeling weak, ask for the Spirit's strength. . . . The simple Gospel was, and is, "Believe on the Lord Jesus Christ." Can we ever pay our debt before we die? With what? With our time and talents? But these were given to us. No. Be baptised with the Spirit and then go out to work with zeal and fire.

He was still not strong enough to take the communion service that night, but he began to say a few words about drawing near in full assurance. Then he simply collapsed in the "big seat" and cried as if he were heartbroken. The people were amazed at this emotional scene.

The journalist Morgan Humphreys, who went with him to several chapel festivals, said that Evan was sometimes heartbroken and sometimes shining with pleasure. "He would be content to be out of sight the whole meeting as long as this would help."

It was inevitable that as soon as he arrived at a singing festival in Bethesda, he was surrounded by excited converts. When he came to the Preaching Festival in another "awakened" village called Ffestiniog, crowds surged into the chapel and surged out again as soon as they were told that Evan had slipped into the chapel house. He was persuaded to speak at Peniel and Tabernacle chapels, which had known the full revival flame. At once he began to accuse them of disobedience and fear of others' judgments. After the appeal was made, most people raised their hands but Evan knew that few were really under conviction and announced that he would like to deal with the deceivers. The church officers refused to send a report to the local press, yet the people did not mind such rebukes.

The revivalist was given enough VIP treatment to have turned his head. The High Sheriff of Meirionethshire, Mr. G. H. Ellis of Penmount, escorted him from the railway station at one end of Blaenau Ffestiniog and took him through the narrow crowded main street to the west end of the town. Later on, he took him for a carriage ride to Minffordd near Porthmadog. There was another huge crowd waiting to greet the man, "who is high in God's counsels." At the end of that visit, he was driven again to the station where scores had come to say farewell.

When Evan Roberts returned to Betws-y-Coed, a letter from Jerusalem was handed to him. It was an invitation from a former resident of Betws-y-Coed to come and stay at his guest house if and when he was able to fulfil his desire to go to the Holy Land. Evan at once wrote a grateful reply saying, "I'm afraid I cannot stretch out my hand to it at the present moment. If the Lord intends me to visit that land which flows with milk and honey, it will be a happiness for me to stay." By then he knew that plans had been made for him to do a mission in Anglesey.

At every halt along the railway from Betws-y-Coed through Llanrwst, Conwy, Bangor and Gaerwen, Evan Roberts was met by a crowd of people pleading to see him. The bookstall clerk at Bangor Station asked him if he had a message for the people, to which Evan Roberts replied, "Tell them to read their Bibles." He had to change trains at Gaerwen Junction in Anglesey and was told that the county's M.P. was there waiting to shake hands with him. At the tiny Rhosgoch Halt, a group of farm workers and estate workers were there to greet Evan and his companions. For three weeks the whole of Anglesey was to be in a ferment. Several newspapers commented that normal work had come to a standstill even before the Whitsun Festival.

The Whitsun weekend was Evan Roberts's last opportunity to go exploring. He spent Friday in Criccieth, Trevor and Caernarfon; Saturday in Llandudno and Conwy; Sunday in Pwllheli and nearby Abererch. He was told that he was not far from the birthplace of John Elias, the preacher. When he eventually got there, he scribbled a proverb in the visitors' book, "If you wish for a fragrance when dead, you need to be a fragrance when alive."

As they crossed the Eifl passes to the tiny village of Trevor, a little incident showed his impish humour. Morgan Humphreys remembers:

> Four of us were walking up the long hill from Trevor's quarrying village on the seacoast of Gwynedd. In order to lessen the burden on the horses, we walked. Then Evan saw a steamroller out in a safe place on the side of the road. The boy in him was aroused. He asked each of us, "Now, which one of us will dare to drive this in order to save us walking up this hill?" Well! No one was man enough. So then he contented himself with composing a poetic rhyme addressed to that machine. He did this with the help, or hindrance, of other members of the company .

Little wonder that the Rev. John Williams told readers of *Yr Ymofynydd* (*Enquirer*) that "the revivalist is as natural in company as a boy. He throws himself into every innocent merriment, but he never loses an atom of his dignity, nor an atom of respect."

On Whit Saturday he went on a trip to Llandudno. He spoke cheerfully to many of his fellow passengers and to crew members before going ashore at Llandudno to lunch. Suddenly his peace of mind was shattered because, just outside the Cambridge Restaurant, a boy was shouting out headlines: "Forthcoming wedding of Evan Roberts to Miss Annie Davies the singer." He rushed out, bought a paper and found to his horror that this story had been copied from an English newspaper called *The Christian Worker.* This meant that many friends and admirers would read this pointed note, "He is going to marry Miss Annie Davies who travels with him frequently." Evan was really upset by this false news and it took all John William's wisdom to calm him down. Evan had already endured a *Daily Chronicle* story about his emotionalism and an untrue story that a Bangor gentleman had been persuaded to bequeath money to the revivalist. This was his "baptism of fire" on the eve of the revival mission.

In the afternoon, Evan entered a soldiers' prayer meeting in the military camp somewhere near Conwy. Some of the recruits in this camp were revival converts who longed to set the camp aflame. Their leader, ap Harri, used a large tent in the middle of the camp to conduct meetings in which soldiers prayed and testified. Now they felt that they should also meet in the town on Saturday evenings and even try to hold an open-air meeting. Evan Roberts spoke in Welsh and English and challenged them to become soldiers serving the Spirit and the Lord. Twenty-two responded and he told their leaders, "This is like the dawn of the revival."

On Saturday evening, he went over to Pwllheli, to D. M. Phillips's revival meetings. Once the local people heard that he was there, the crowds poured in and it was decided to hold the Sunday service in the farmyard, like an old time "Camp Meeting." That night, after a good meal in the Rev. H. Roberts's house, he slept a little but then he had a vision of Jesus who, he said, was looking smiling and pleasant. Now he was sure that the mission would succeed and he came down and shared this with his hosts at the breakfast table. A friendly minister who sat nearby was puzzled to see that Evan Roberts was weeping even while he was rejoicing about the vision. Tears of joy were a rare event among the reserved North Walians. Evan Roberts had been warned that they would not accept any novelties in their services, revival or no revival.

There was one more informal visit which Evan Roberts made during his North Wales tour and it should be included here although it took place a month or so later. He had received an invitation to speak to the students at Bala Theological College and he turned the meeting into a counselling session. Sitting in the midst of the students, he listened to their spiritual problems and tried to give clear-cut advice.

> First Student: "You said that it is essential to love Christ above everyone and everything. At times I feel that I do, but at other times this feeling is not present with me. Do you consider such a one a fit and proper person to preach the Gospel?"
>
> Evan Roberts: "Yes I do. We must not place too much emphasis on feelings. We cannot be in a passion of feeling all the time. If so, there would not be a place for faith."
>
> Second Student: "I feel that my life is not pure enough. Can I pray that I may be filled with the Spirit? There are some things that I am conscious should be sacrificed, but I cannot do so."

Evan Roberts: "Had I a personal conversation with you I would know what those things would be. But remember that we cannot in this world be without sin. Self will come to the fore."

Third Student: "Should I pray in public while I feel that I am doing so out of egotism?"

Evan Roberts: "No, you should not. But you should pray in secret until that egotism is consumed.

After many more such questions the revivalist gave a final word that these students never forgot: "Pray for the Spirit and for wisdom. We must take care to be wise. Produce an ounce of ridicule and you lose a ton of power. If the Spirit of God is leading you in prayer even for half an hour, heed not any man. We receive the power from God, and the wisdom is to regulate the use of it."

The time has now come to turn to the actual preaching that took place during the revival mission in Gwynedd, but it is an undeniable fact that people involved in that students' meeting and in some of the incidents recorded in this chapter received a great and lasting blessing, not in a crowded chapel but in the freedom of a personal encounter with God's servant.

15

The Second Revival Mission
(North Wales, Summer 1905)

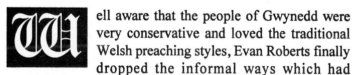ell aware that the people of Gwynedd were very conservative and loved the traditional Welsh preaching styles, Evan Roberts finally dropped the informal ways which had surprised people in the first days of revival. If R. B. Jones, the author of *Rent Heavens,* had been able to attend or to hear first-hand reports of the North Wales Missions, he could never have written, "Mr. Roberts gradually ceased to speak at his own meetings. He could but sit silently in the pulpit and take no part—a spectacle rather than a prophet." R. B. Jones was thinking of those hectic revival meetings in South Wales. Unfortunately, his remarks have been parroted in many forms ever since.

In the summer of 1905, Evan Roberts was not just a voice raised during a prayer service, or a teacher speaking to a fellowship where no one spoke until the Spirit moved. This time he was principal guest preacher who took two arranged services per day, instead of dashing wherever the Spirit sent him. This time he was not disrupted by people's cries and demands. The sober, attentive listeners rarely broke into groanings, or joyful shouts or impromptu songs. The president of each service was a local minister who kept close control.

That is why the reporters noted a strange incident in Gwalchmai when the presiding minister, the Rev. Thomas Williams, suddenly jumped to his feet and began to work up crowd excitement. Even more unexpectedly, this minister invited people to yield to Christ with him, saying, "Oh, I am trying to do it again, though I have been preaching for years, unworthily enough. I feel a strong desire to give myself again." His words triggered an explosion of confessions and anxious crying unto the Lord.

This was certainly not the norm. Evan Roberts seemed ill at ease in any meeting where a disorderly element crept in. He agreed to hold some meetings out in a field or yard because of the extreme heat, but he would often fall silent if he felt that only a crowd of curious visitors were there. Mr. Hughes of Llanrwst travelled all the way to Brynsiencyn in Anglesey and stood waiting for more than an hour before Evan Roberts came:

> He spoke for about five minutes while the wind was blowing and each little breeze shook the leaves of the trees. He said, "I do not believe that the Holy Spirit is at work here. If he were, he would be troubling every being just as those leaves are shaken on the trees. It is the breeze that causes every leaf to move; so should it be here also, if indeed the Holy Spirit were at work in our midst." He sat down suddenly and that was the lot we had from Evan Roberts on that occasion.

There were no quick results or mass surrenders this time but, as Mr. Humphreys declared: "Evan Roberts was not cast down by his lack of success. Sometimes he was shining with pleasure because the Holy Spirit was evidently working."

Indeed, there were other, more memorable days. There was a village called Llanddona in South Anglesey where

Evan Roberts was invited to speak in a parish church for the first time. The vicar's address was full of peace and goodwill and so were Evan Roberts's opening remarks:

> Why should Christians who are brethren in the family of God maintain so great a distance the one from the other? We shall shortly part from each other here, but let us each and all strive to be found in that company where there is no parting.

It was the same message that he had brought for the attention of this Anglican - Nonconformist gathering—the urgent and vital matter of confessing Christ openly, and the problem of obstacles:

> It is the devil who is trying to hold you back. He has a rope of three strands binding you. The first strand is to tell you that you are not ready, the second that your feeling is not ripe, and the third is that you cannot hope to live up to your profession if you submit now. That is how the devil keeps you prisoner until death comes and makes you for ever his own. . . . Thank God, Christ also has a rope of three strands. First ask Him to take you as you are. Then ask Him to forgive your sins. Then ask Him for strength for the future. This three-stranded rope of salvation is enough for the present, the past and the future of every sinner.

Many people showed signs that they longed to have this assurance, and the vicar's prayers were more than answered. It was a typical Evan Roberts sermon in that instead of expounding a text, he gave them a picture drawn from their own experience and used this to illustrate the doctrines of salvation. He could take it for granted in both church and chapel that the people were so familiar with the Scriptures and with their creeds and confessions that all he needed to do was to apply them directly to their own minds and hearts.

In North Anglesey, in the village of Cemaes, another journalist saw Evan Roberts standing on a hay cart outlined against the glow of an evening sun, which lit up the cornfields and bathed the distant peaks with sunset glory. About two thousand people stood in the open air on Whit Monday, and an even larger crowd assembled at Llanfachraeth, where:

> All the windows of the farmhouses are open and occupied with spectators. Dozens of others are perched on dizzy heights overlooking the square. At the far end of the cobbled square stands a lorry fitted up as a platform, roofed over with sailcloth, with the John Elias pulpit in front. At the other end are large iron gates. Through the wicket-gate, people have been admitted all the afternoon in single file, careful note being taken of the number. There is nothing here to distract attention. In the shade of the surrounding buildings, the congregation is protected from the hot rays of the sun. A few drops of rain fall and at once hundreds of umbrellas shoot open. A second later they are just as instantly closed as the Reverend John Williams compares them with those who "put up umbrellas to shut out the kingdom of Heaven."

As news of the bold and authoritative preaching spread far and wide, six thousand people made their way to Llangefni, nine thousand to Holyhead and uncounted hundreds to the open services during the association assembly. The castle precincts were the only space large enough in Beaumaris where hundreds crossed the famous bridge to meet him. Even these gatherings were eclipsed by the huge July meeting in the Eisteddfod Pavilion at Caernarfon where ten thousand people stretched its space beyond the limit. Countless numbers followed him to Bala where he was invited to preach on the "Maes" (Town Square) where some of Wales' greatest preachers had stood. Evan Roberts could not thunder like them, but his voice echoed exhortations towards the hills and the lakeshore.

It was in the huge mass meetings that Evan Roberts spoke most severely because he saw that he was surrounded by church leaders and staid chapelgoers who needed to be given the vision to pray for the lost and the courage to witness to them. The "Four Points" he proclaimed long ago at Gorseinon were applied to this urgent task. *To confess Christ* was not only an initial act of faith but a willingness to speak to others about Him. *To put away doubtful things* meant to search out and destroy all that would ruin their witness. *To obey the Spirit* meant willingness to reach the lost. He saw himself as the Lord's special messenger who would rouse the churches for their task of saving the nation. In Anglesey, Caernarfon and Bala, he repeated the challenge *to witness in every possible form:*

> It will not do for us to go to heaven by ourselves. We must be on fire, friends, for saving others. To be workers will draw heaven down and will draw others to heaven. Without readiness to work, the spirit of prayer will not come.

His most forthright charges to professing Christians were prompted by the fact that even the recent converts seemed to care little for the plight of other sinners. Again and again, Evan found himself speaking to audiences which were stiff and uncomfortable, even to the point of leaving the chapel while he was making an appeal to the unsaved. In desperate concern, he pulled out all the stops as he called for "tears":

> Tears will be shed here today that perhaps no man
> will ever see; but God will see them all and will preserve
> every one of them. God anoints the name of His Son
> with the tears shed out of love for Him. "What a foolish
> weakness," say some, "Shedding tears for such a thing
> as that." Weakness to shed tears! What? Remember the
> Son of God, for our salvation cost Him many a tear. It
> was not weakness that caused the Infinite One to shed
> tears. What is said about Him? He offered up prayers
> and supplications with loud crying and tears unto Him
> that was able to save Him from death. He was heard in
> that He feared. . . . If you have not wept under the
> influence of the Gospel, there is reason to fear that you
> have not commenced to live it rightly. When we see and
> love the Son of God, we cannot restrain our tears. True
> love for Him presses out our tears. . . . To shed tears is
> a sign of the power of love.

"If all Wales were to resolve to obey the Spirit, in a short
time the country would be transfigured," he cried to the
departing church members. Somehow he seemed unable to
move those who had seemed to repent and find peace with
God during the revival. Evan had to accept at last that flame
hardens where it does not melt.

Some allege that Evan Roberts's failure to provide a
foundation of exposition and instruction was the cause. Yet
there is little evidence that the annual conventions of W. S.
Jones and R. B. Jones in Gwynedd and Clwyd had any
deeper or more lasting effect, even though they expounded
from God's Word the great biblical doctrines and then called
the people to holiness. The more likely reason for the
coldness was that from Christmas Week to Easter week these
people had sat through dozens of meetings and endured hour
after hour of emotional pressure. Some wanted more
excitement, but most of them were too weary in their minds
and spirits to take systematic teaching in formalised services.

Since this was a revival mission, Evan Roberts also had messages for the unconverted and the backsliders. He preached with passion and breath-taking sternness because he saw that they had been touched emotionally but not truly convicted and converted during the winter revival meetings. The following three extracts show how he sounded the alarm to the unconverted, acting as God's faithful watchman.

1. At Amlwch, probably during an "Association" sponsored public service:

"Are you so close to the table of the Lord and still refusing to partake? There is a grave for the body, but eternity for the soul. Yet, despite this, people neglect the soul more than the body. You who still refuse, go into the secret place tonight and there, face to face with God, you tell Him, 'I am rejecting your Son.' TELL HIM, IF YOU DARE! . . . God struck His only Son, my friends, but woe to anyone else who strikes Him. Go with Jesus to the Upper Room, but take heed you do not have the same intention as that traitor. Go to the courtyard and take the scourge from the soldier's hands and strike the Saviour. DO YOU DARE? . . . Would you refuse to help carry His cross tonight? Go to the hilltop yourself. Send the soldiers away from there. Take the hammer yourself and drive the nails through His hands and feet. IF YOU DARE. Then ask Him, 'Jesus of Nazareth, why are You hanging on the Cross?' Then listen to the answer spilling out slowly in agony: 'IT - WAS - FOR - YOU.' O friends, the Spirit will not reason with you forever. Perhaps it will be the end for some tonight."

2. At Caernarfon Pavilion, 4 July 1905:

"Thanks for the Name—the Name of Jesus. There is sufficient room for all in this Name. There is eternal freshness in it. Do not stand on the Name. Determine to be IN the Name. Does your life glorify the Name? Trample not the Name, nor disrespect it.

147

"Remember that God is going to care for this Name. God will have glory to this Name from all, one way or other. If there are some here who are trampling on the Name, move on, if you please, AT ONCE! Remember what Name you are endeavouring to trample. Have you felt how near GOD is? He is fearfully near; so near that He sees all things."

3. On the High Street (Maes) at Bala, 7 July 1905—"The Coming Wrath of God":

"Is there anyone here refusing salvation? There is a great meeting to come—not on this side but on the other side. It will be the prayer meeting of the refusers. Whatever is the intensity and the earnestness here tonight, all will be put in the shade by that strange, unique meeting. It will be a meeting of praying and shouting. The rejecters of Christ will be shouting for the rocks to hide them. If you are determined to refuse Christ, then go close to the rocks to practise shouting. Call on those rocks to fall on you, and for the mountains to hide you. Go close to the rocks to see if you will be possessed with terror. And if you will be terrified, come to the Rock of Ages. Pray for the Rock of Ages to hide you. This is the safe place for your life—the shadow of the eternal Rock. You will hear the music of the storm, but no fear will possess you.

". . . All who reject Christ will be in the prayer meeting of the day of judgments. All classes and grades. If they refuse to bend here, they will have to bend there. Are you Welsh people who are here? Do you see? Or are you blind? How is it with you—the rejecters? Where will you be spending your eternity? Do you know what is eternal woe? How is it to be with reference to eternity? That is the great question. One of two things it must be. Oh my dear countrymen, do not be so foolish as to reject, and do not wait till tomorrow. Trust in the arms of the eternal love.

"If you are determined to reject the Gospel, never come

to a meeting again. Why? Hell will be more awful to you if you do come. Enjoy this world as much as you can, because no happiness will await you after crossing. Oh! be in Jesus, friends, before going to the judgment. If you are lost you shall see Jesus in the judgement—but infinity will be between you and Him there."

16

The Last Revival Missions
(1906)

van Roberts was in high spirits when he came home from the summer mission in Gwynedd. He wrote to friends predicting another time of blessing, and he sent out a bilingual "Message for God's Churches" which attracted some notice. In it he reminded people that revival was God's achievement alone and that men are only the instruments. The secret of revival was not a new technique or a new doctrine, but awakened people and renewed churches prepared to obey the Holy Spirit fully.

When he came to the Llandrindod Convention in August, he felt he ought to appeal to God's people to remove all hindrances such as the unloving spirit. He challenged them to "give your all to Jesus; give your best to Jesus. These are the claims of Heaven. Don't talk of YOUR claims. . . . We have not the presence or the power of God because we are not honest and we rob Him of His glory. We must all get out of sight."

During the autumn months he struggled against discouragement because he had no clear leading. He told his friend D. M. Phillips, "It is a mistake for me to try to arrange

151

and carry out my future. People cannot understand why I do not move, and I fail to understand why I am staying." Then one morning he received a letter from church leaders in North Wales asking him to come again and conduct a seven-week mission. The Free Church Council in Gwynedd had appointed a Central Mission Committee which set up a chain of meetings reaching out into the more remote districts. It didn't occur to anyone that it might be dangerous in midwinter for Evan Roberts to move every day from some overheated chapel into the chilly streets and the frozen roads. It was so cold that one reporter almost collapsed and Evan forced him to take over his glass of hot milk before they went out again into the wild weather.

Allan Raine, the novelist, has left us a vivid picture of what happened in fishing villages like those on the Cambrian Coast, when it was known that Evan Roberts was coming. The men did a special spring cleaning of the public lanes through which he would come and the women decorated and whitewashed all their cottages. When the revivalist entered their chapels, the villagers responded not to his simple theology nor to his plain speaking but to "his message of love to the sad, the struggling, the sinning denizens of this lower world. . . . He preached not, but spoke to his hearers—one human soul conversing with his fellow travellers on the road of life. His sympathetic voice reached every part of the chapel and spoke to everyone's heart as if it spoke to it alone."

One night, Evan Roberts and Mr. Humphreys were returning in a carriage and pair when they saw a light on in "Rhydbach Chapel"and decided to go inside for a rest before driving on to Pwllheli through a silent and lonely countryside. According to Humphreys:

> The chapel was quiet too. When we opened the door
> we saw that there was an officers' meeting. Only the
> minister and elders were there in the chapel. Evan

Roberts was at the height of his fame and the little company marvelled to see him come in so unexpectedly. Yet he was given a great welcome. He went into the pulpit and gave out a hymn. The woman from the chapel house put her head inside the doorway at the side of the pulpit. Then she vanished after taking one look at the man in the pulpit. In a moment or two she was back with her husband and children. Evan Roberts was praying and the people were coming in from somewhere. It was obvious that a buzz had gone abroad. By this time there was a congregation of about thirty. Now Evan Roberts fell silent and someone else began to pray, and he was followed by other hushed brief prayers. Then, in the quietness, Evan Roberts brought to an end his own prayers, greeted everyone warmly and went onwards to Pwllheli along the dark, silent roads.

After preaching at Criccieth and Porthmadog, Evan was due at Caernarfon. When they reached the village of Penygroes, they turned aside into the quarry-scarred Nantlle Valley and paid a brief visit to Capel Mawr near the main quarry entrance. For years afterwards, the local people told visitors how Evan Roberts had refused to give any message because he had heard people cursing and blaspheming on the steps up to the chapel. Things were much happier back at Penygroes where scores of children joined readily in his catechising. He made it a lively occasion and in the end called them all "scholars."

The visit to the royal borough of Caernarfon was rather a test for him because the council members and church leaders came out to meet him. Also he was expected to meet up again with its brilliant MP, David Lloyd George. On 12 December, 1905, Evan had written to him, "Permit me to congratulate you on your present success which is a great honour to you. Through this the land of Wales has been honoured too. May the Wisdom from on high keep you and uphold you in the future. Just a brief note with best wishes and my thanks." This time he sent thank you verses because Lloyd George had told his agents to postpone a Liberal Party conference in order not to interfere with the revival mission in his borough.

On the first night of the mission, Evan Roberts was driven down to the town in a carriage and pair, and was shown off to the admiring people. Going inside the great pavilion he gazed from the platform at the crowds of talkative visitors and then stayed absolutely silent for two hours. Some took that as a rebuke and they were certainly more reverent at the second meeting. Let us hasten to the final meeting where Evan sat with his head lowered once more, murmuring prayers until he felt the hour had come to speak. His first words astounded them:

> All who have watchfully listened will have noticed that Jesus came into this meeting at its commencement, but He went away and then came again. We must testify about Jesus.

In the deep silence that followed he began to give encouragement to those who were afraid or ashamed of their own sins. Evan said, "Do not go on carrying the burdens of the past forever." He had put his finger on a major problem for many revival converts.

When Evan Roberts moved on to Port Dinorwic, he had already decided to speak mainly about discipleship and obedience to the rows of young people who had been purified in the fires of revival. Their need was to know how to move forwards from, "Christ living in all of my heart" to, "Christ ruling over all of my life." However, he had a message of love and forgiveness for the undecided and another message for souls in conflict.

If there is a storm within you, He can still it.
If there is night within you, He can call up the dawn.

Somehow Evan Roberts felt compelled to talk repeatedly about ways to practise the presence of God before beginning prayers of intercession:

> There are those who desire to pray but who pray silently. Throw yourself upon the Holy Spirit for it is not easy, but neither is it impossible. We take hold of ourself, but the Spirit says, "Let go!" We offer prayer, but while we are praying the mind is looking for words to express thoughts. Then there is not the smoothness of expression that attests the power of the Spirit. The head is working but the heart is frozen. Let the heart be full of warmth and then the mind will work it out. We stay too little in the presence of God. Suppose we would remain for half an hour in silence and the Holy Spirit would search us. Could we stand this? O Lord, crucify this indifference.

As the first week came to an end, Evan Roberts requested a meeting with the Central Mission Committee and showed them how terribly weary he had become. They agreed that the planned itinerary could be postponed until after the general election. But Evan told them frankly that he would like to visit fewer centres and stay longer. As he said to a Swansea friend, "I need more time to plumb the depths where the fish lie."

The next place to be visited was Llanberis which stands under the western flank of Snowdon. The Rev. Ferrier Hulme and Rev. Samuel Chadwick needed a guide to take them along stony tracks, but they finally caught up with Evan in a hillside manse and spent the morning in prayer and testimony. They told readers of the *Methodist Times* that he was in fine form, his face glowing, his eyes sparkling and

155

his mouth filled with laughter. He was surrounded by praying saints who had heard the divine promise and believed that the Lord had given him a holy authority to bring revival to their district.

Together they went to the slated chapel in the village of Dinorwic whose cottages and chapels overlooked vast quarries on one side and the bright Peris Lake on the other. The blind pastor, the Rev. Puleston Jones, brought the English guests into the big pew and sat them next to a bilingual reporter. After the prayers and hymns, Ferrier Hulme felt led to testify. Meanwhile, Mr. Roberts and three or four ministers came in from the Manse and began to utter loud petitions. A reporter noted: "One after the other broke down and the meeting just gave itself up to the all-conquering Spirit. Many were blessedly baptised. After the tumult came a great calm of quiet joy."

The next day they moved to Rhostryfan from whose slate cottages they could see across a tapestry of fields and woods to the Caernarfon Bay, Anglesey and Ireland. The whole meeting was given over to pray that Christ would be crowned in every country of the world. A short walk took them to Carmel, the gray village of slate. Slate walls, gateposts, stiles, signposts, doorsteps, shop fronts, tombstones. The quarrymen of Carmel and their families had tough, enduring bodies but they also had slate-hard souls until the revival broke them. A hillside chapel called Brynrodyn had been chosen for this meeting which was filled half an hour before time with eager people who sang rapturously. We can share with Chadwick and Hulme two of the thrilling scenes:

> One hour later the Spirit sent a perfect hurricane, a hot wind which speedily resulted in boiling hearts and scalding tears. I always find it easy to pray in this atmosphere even though there is no other English speaker present. Immediately afterwards Evan Roberts

prayed with amazing unction and in a few moments the place was shaken. Oh, how mightily he prevailed! God filled him so full that he shed tears of unutterable delight. The fountains in all hearts broke loose and the people gave themselves up to adoring the Lamb—O, the bleeding Lamb! . . . In half an hour, what a change has come over that quiet throng. Their tears are wiped away and all faces have caught the glow of gladsome peace. They are calmer now but their intellects are wonderfully alert. The writer has reported seventy meetings and has never known Evan Roberts keener.

As the revivalist travelled homewards his soul was rejoicing but his body was exhausted and his face was thin and drawn. Avoiding Loughor, he went with Dan Roberts to stay with the Lloyd brothers at 6, The Promenade, Swansea. He held one "seiat" class and took one gospel service, but most of the time was spent in "retreat" in an upper room. One visitor reported, "The sound of his prayer rang through the house all night."

Looking down from the window over Swansea town, he suddenly wanted to pray for the ungodly people. He did enter into the conversation but he left it again to pray, and everything became very quiet. He may have lost his train of thought, but then he said, "The thing is to lay hold of the promises and then enter into the sufferings of Calvary."

The North Walians were expecting him to come back, but Evan told his host that he would have to go slowly and surely in the future. In fact, that mission was never completed. Instead he accompanied D. M. Phillips to a Preaching Festival near Llandeilo. He felt privileged that they even allowed him to speak in his condition, yet that address was so dynamic that a Llandeilo printer was authorised to put extracts on a postcard and a poster. Among those quotes were:

You can be on the right track but at the wrong elevation.

Some say, "give me this feeling or that feeling," but on whom are your eyes fixed? On yourself instead of on God.

We are not receiving a message, but taking in light.

Back home at Loughor, Evan Roberts grew more and more discouraged as he saw some groups of converts following after cults in which they barked at the devil, danced and swooned, or followed healers and prophetesses. On the other hand, there were also times of blessing wherever he had fellowship with people who had yielded to the Holy Spirit. He wrote to a missionary in India: "Last Saturday was the most wonderful night I have had for over a year. The Spirit came down with such power that we were compelled to shout with our whole might. We shouted praise to Him until we felt quite weak. . . . We were only about three dozen in that old chapel at Casllwchwr. The service was a very cold one at the beginning but we repeated the Lord's Prayer three times, and then the clouds broke. Oh, that you could have been present. I had been longing for a year to see Jesus truly marching forward in His great power. . . . Last Saturday I was perfectly satisfied."

When Evan Roberts eventually returned to North Wales, it was not to an evangelistic mission but to a Keswick-type Easter convention for ministers and church leaders. He was not an assigned speaker, but an aged minister begged him to speak and he gave in after a struggle. His first duty was to explain his new burden—to present the full teaching about identification with Christ in His sufferings and death. This was his opening prayer:

Reveal the Cross through the Name of Jesus. Oh! Open the heavens. Descend upon us now. Tear open our hearts. Give us such a sight of Calvary that our hearts

may be broken. O Lord—descend now—NOW! Open
our hearts to receive the heart that bled for us. Speak,
speak, speak, Lord Jesus. Reign in every heart. Reveal
the Cross in its glory and power, for the sake of Jesus.

In his address he told them that he had been deceived
by the father of lies who had told him not to preach about
the Cross. But we must all face the Cross which delivers from
sin and works death to the self-life. "Face the Cross," he
shouted, "and you will trample on Sin, Self and all the powers
of darkness. But before we realise conquest, we must yield
all and give up the will to God."

This message reflected the main themes in Mrs.
Penn-Lewis's booklets, such as: *The Way of the Cross, Life
Streams From Calvary, It is Finished, The Father's
Love-Gift at Calvary.* The new teaching seemed to deliver
him from all his stresses. It was so simple to believe that
because of his redemptive work "Christ has given authority
over all the power of the enemy to all who will lay hold of
it." It was available for everyone who would "die to the
world" and "mortify the flesh."

Another convention, in Porth, Rhondda, was told to go
to the Cross for the slaying of all self-centredness, pride,
covetousness and temper. He said: "We must be tired of those
things before we take them to the Cross. It will not do to take
them there and to love them at the same time. Oh, to be tired
of them all and ask God to take them to the Cross and apply
the death of our Lord Jesus to them. That will give us the
full conquest of self." The same message was preached at
Llandrindod Convention in the ten minutes he was given
during the Welsh language prayer meeting where he told the
converts:

We all want the glorious liberty of the child of God
and to be delivered from the power of sin, self, and

> Satan. I want to bear witness to the power of Calvary
> to break every bond. It is for you to claim the full victory
> of the Cross. It is yours this moment if you will but claim
> it. Will you honour the cleansing Blood, by taking it?
> The Blood does cleanse and blot out the past.

At a Wednesday morning breakfast for ministers and church leaders, Evan announced, "If I am spared it will be my only aim to preach Christ and Him crucified, not theoretically but as living truth." It soon became clear that although many believers found new comfort and healing through this word of the Cross, very few churches or fellowships in Wales would go along with his new teaching. They preferred other Bible teachers who gave a different view of the victory at Calvary.

Evan Roberts's last revival mission took place at Llandrindod Wells in August 1906. The Free Church Council booked the great tent, which collapsed after vandals cut the ropes. Crowds of holiday visitors and sightseers paid scant attention as Evan testified and pleaded: "I am a sinner saved by grace. I can do nothing apart from Christ. All the glory must be His. We are nothing but He can use us. He is waiting for instruments. Shall we place ourselves in His hands?"

The prayer partners said afterwards that they felt a "terrific conflict with the forces of darkness. For three days it seemed like passing through the hour of darkness which surrounded the Cross. It seemed as if hell was raging." Soon the revivalist was so overstrained that he broke down.

The involvement of Mrs. Jessie Penn-Lewis in Evan Roberts life and work has always been a bit of a mystery. Recently discovered correspondence between her and the Rev. R. B. Jones has at last thrown light on the path which led from Llandrindod to Leicester. They were just in time to save Evan from a total abandonment of his service to the Lord.

When she stayed on to help Evan with the Tent Mission she had serious differences with the Free Church Council and visiting church leaders. Some of them rejected her special teachings about the "Cross Experience" and "The Throne Experience" which Evan shared. Others were strongly opposed to her "interference" and disliked the idea of a woman giving ministry of the Word.

Mrs. Penn-Lewis was so hurt that she told friends that she would in the future stay away from Wales. Evan, she said, felt quite shattered by these quarrels and would need some kind of getaway. Less than a month later the revivalist experienced his fourth and most serious nervous breakdown. With the full knowledge of certain Christian leaders he was conveyed to the Penn-Lewis country house, called "Woodlands", Great Glen.

The author has walked around this still peaceful district and found that the lane past "Woodlands" gave access to a former railway halt from which Evan could have been conveyed in some kind of chaise to the house where he was to spend several weeks in bed. In the next chapter it will be seen how Evan descended into a "vale" from which the Lord brought him out at last into a wider place.

17

Through the Vale of Tears
(1906-1908)

espite the flashes of inspired preaching during the summer of 1906, close friends of Evan Roberts could see the signs of another collapse coming. Invitations to preach slowed down and Evan was left wondering what to expect next. Some friends took him on visits to various towns in Gloucestershire before he went on his first extended visit to the home of the Penn-Lewises. He listened respectfully as this unusual woman, Jesse Penn-Lewis, showed him how and why he had made wrong judgments during the last stages of the revival.

During May 1906, Evan wrote a number of personal letters to the Phillips and Lloyd families. The style, the diction and the grammar all point to a man who is still trying to be a prophet. Like Elijah he can no longer see any role except to go to his own Mount Horeb and ask God to send a new commission. Neither could he see clearly the future of the faithful ones.

After brief appearances at local conventions, Evan was taken to the main Keswick in July. He soon discovered that every effort was being made to control those revival forces, which had swept through the 1905 Convention like a tide race. J. P. Clarke told people they should not have come to look for special sensations. Another leader was far from pleased when, in a tent meeting, there were many interruptions by people who confessed sins and then shouted with joy over their pardon. After the convention, a writer commented, "There have been few torrential outpourings from the Welsh hills." Then he argued that "If it is on the still nights that the dew falls, this convention must have a time of refreshing."

Evan Roberts spoke twice but broke the rules. One officer announced a new recommendation that "Visitors to the convention should not attempt to interfere with the trustees control of the meetings. They should seek a private personal interview beforehand." Someone also complained that speakers were indulging their pride by giving too much personal autobiography, which was Evan's usual habits. He never came again and the rift grew between his friends and the Keswick leaders—but the English Chairman, Albert Head, was also chairman of the Llandrindod Convention where Evan Roberts was expected to come. Though welcomed and lionised by the crowds, he was not invited to speak and had only two opportunities to influence the convention.

If relationships with Welsh leaders were strained at the Conventions they were utterly broken during the two-week mission which was organised by the local Free Church Council. Newly discovered letters written by Mrs. Jessie Penn-Lewis to the Welsh preacher R. B. Jones, show that she had fallen foul of the local clergy and that Evan Roberts had been dragged into the disputes. Some of the conflict was caused by her special teachings about the "Cross experience" and the "Throne Experience" in the lives of truly spiritual people. There was also strong opposition to her "interferences" and to the very idea of a woman giving ministry and teaching.

Mrs. Penn-Lewis was so hurt that she told R. B. Jones it was best that she stayed away from Wales and that Evan Roberts was also too shattered to do anything. He was taken quickly and quietly by train from Llandrindod to Great Glen near Leicester and carried, probably in a private gig, to Mr. Penn-Lewis's country house, called "Woodlands."

He stayed there until the Penn-Lewis's new house in Toller Road, Leicester, had been built and fitted out. "Cartref" was both a home and a counselling room and an office cum bookroom. The first floor had family rooms and bedrooms. The upper floor had two "dormers," one of which became Evan Roberts's prayer room. The plan shows that there were separate closed-in stairs from the dormer to the first landing and directly to the counselling room from which a door led to the kitchen and into a glassed-in porch which the semi-invalid could use.

Faced with this repeated criticism and murmuring Mrs. Penn-Lewis wondered where she could find support. After much prayer she wrote twice to the Rev. R. B. Jones, Porth, who was universally respected as a revival teacher. She told him how badly Evan needed to be safeguarded. "My impression is that he keeps in retirement until every trace of past strain has disappeared." She assured him that Evan was maturing spiritually at a great rate, and could now see how he had been misled over certain happenings during the revival. For a while R. B. was clearly reluctant to come to Leicester and he received a fiery letter of rebuke. But there was a private meeting in 1907, not in the sick bedroom at Great Glen but in the special suite at Toller Road, Leicester.

Mr. Penn-Lewis had purchased this plot late in 1906 and had an architect's plan (still extant) for a three-storeyed house. The plans show that there were to be two public access rooms on the ground floor (Mr. Penn-Lewis was City Treasurer) and that the first floor would have family rooms and bedrooms. At the top there would be two smaller rooms, like servants' bedrooms, which were furnished like a studio flat. These rooms had a separate closed-in stairs down to the first landing and another flight not down to the entrance hall but to the room nearest the kitchens. This gave access to a tradesman's entrance, beyond which was a sheltered glassed-in porch, where one could study and pray close to the lawns.

Those plans had been altered and it is fair deduction that this was done to provide Mrs. Penn-Lewis with a bookroom and Evan Roberts with a sanctuary. R. B. Jones was able to meet him there in private and the talks proved a blessing. A final letter sent by Mrs. Penn-Lewis from Davos in Switzerland, where the family had taken Evan for convalescence, shows that the conference had been of vital importance.

> From that day you visited Leicester, he has steadily gained and now he is able to think freely. God is pouring light in such a way that I can see the church of Christ is going to benefit greatly. After all he has been through and the way God is giving him now to be able to dissect and define the entanglements of Satan in the supernatural sphere, I see that God is training him as an expert. And I too, have been through such depths of the Cross as I never dreamed about.
>
> I see in the peaceful interval we are having that we are being specially trained for special work. I do not wonder that the adversary has raged. I knew that God was going to equip Evan here, so no wonder the enemy sought to hinder. God bless you that you should have been sent to join me in talking of Life and Liberty. No one else helped and all have failed to see clearly. You are the first that God used when I was alone.

Evan did not write at the time but he never forgot how the older man had helped restore him. He sent affectionate letters and offered prayer support during his tour of

Pennsylvanian chapels and during his rural missions and his local convention. He even dedicated a new poem to the traveller

The healing of Evan's mind and body took a little longer and it seems he was unable to stand or walk for almost a twelvemonth. Fellow Welshman, J. C. Williams, who sometimes went to pray with Evan, pictured the young evangelist as:

> Enervated by the poisonous vapours of packed meetings in ill-ventilated buildings, and by the strain of overwork. From the tempestuous multitudes he was led by the Spirit into the stillness of suffering, lying in the house of a friend week by week, month by month . . .
>
> In those weeks Evan Roberts's spirit rose in ever-ascending power and communion with God. The care of friends, the skill of the physicians, the rest and the quiet, began to play their part in the renovation of his shattered life.

Even when his recovery began, Evan Roberts had to be told by medical advisors that never again should he undertake pulpit and platform engagements. The only thing he could do was to provide informal counselling. He was hurt when revival converts, not knowing how ill he was, talked about him as a "deserter to England." Because he was listed in the *Methodist Diary* (1907) as a candidate minister, people expected him back. The editors of the *Llanelli Mercury,* ignorant of Evan Roberts's state, published the following:

> We hope that he will continue as a kind of roving commissioner for a little while. He has led us to expect great things in the future, and this would be the first fruit of what was done before. In order to keep this fire alive, it would be an advantage for him to be free of institutional ministry. . . . Wales expects more than this of Evan Roberts if there is credibility in his recent statements and promises of more spiritual stirrings.

A year or two later, there was a fuss over Vyrnwy Morgan's charge that Mrs. Penn-Lewis and Dr. F. B. Meyer had made misleading statements and had been far too secretive. Evan had to write letters denying that he had ever been held under duress. Again in 1910 he had to make another declaration that "I have not relinquished either intention or desire to return to Wales for mission work, although it is certainly beyond my power to inaugurate a fresh revival. Revival can only be given by the Holy Spirit when the conditions are fulfilled." Finally he had to answer a *South Wales Daily News* correspondent (16-17 July) who claimed that Evan had been approached by the National Free Church Council and others, with a view to becoming an official evangelist. He denied this.

Several years later, in December 1913, Evan Roberts published in *The Overcomer* a letter that was headed, "An explanation of my position at Leicester":

> Nearly eight years ago I was invited to Leicester by Mrs. Penn-Lewis in conjunction with Mr. Penn-Lewis.
>
> The Church of God acknowledges this servant of God, Mrs. Penn-Lewis, as "one sent of God." Her name sends forth no ill savour: her work can only be understood by the "faithful ones of God," whose eyes are opened of God.
>
> Now during the revival in Wales, I, in my ignorance, did not escape the wiles of the enemy, who does not leave even the elect to escape him. According to Rev. 13: 7, it is said that "it was given unto the beast to overcome the saints." This is only for a period, then even all the united power of hell cannot prevail against God's elect.
>
> Then, seeing what I saw not, understanding what had as yet not broken on my spiritual vision, Mrs. Penn-Lewis wrote me very reasonable and spiritual letters, asking me to come to stay at her home in Glen, Leicestershire.

I followed God's path; came for a short period, and have stayed here nearly eight years. But this mode of procedure is not new to me.

In November, 1904, I went to Aberdare for one day, and did not return for *six* weeks! God opened the way before me. He gave me public work, and honoured it. It was His ordination in the main. The path slowly opened as I advanced.

These last seven years of seclusion are exactly of the same pattern. But then my work was public and people could *see* the results. Now it is chiefly hidden, with its results in the *unseen* and waiting God's own time for their revelation.

I make no apology whatsoever for my conduct in these seven years. There is *nothing* to apologise for; there is *none* to apologise to. God is my Master. What He bids, I do. Where He commands, there I shall stay. Should I deviate or abandon my course of life and work because *man* fails to understand me? I will not do so.

I am responsible to God. He is my Director. It is His work I am doing; and knowing that my work is in line with His expressed will I follow it gladly, and will do so.

Those who proclaim unbelief in my work only the louder proclaim their own blindness. Have they seen my messages in "The Overcomer"? Then why could they not see the signs of God in them? Have they read "War on the Saints"—my unnamed biography? Do they not hear depths of experiences in this book calling great mysteries by their right name? Are these truths in it an unveiling of the "deep things of Satan"? And who could reveal them without knowing them?

My co-work with Mrs. Penn-Lewis in "War on the Saints" was of God. For spiritually I was too burdened to write it myself; and apart from me, neither could she write it, and it would have been useless to search elsewhere for a pen to do so. I know of none equal to her in understanding of spiritual things; she is a veteran in heavenly things. And why must she be persecuted for doing God's will? Why should these stewards of God have perpetual annoyances for opening their door and giving of their good things to a servant of God? I am called "a man of God," and surely I am so. For He has taken me at my word, made me a prisoner of the Spirit—a much greater bondage than one in two hundred thousand could conceive of. In fact, he could not conceive of it unless he had already some experiences of God's mighty works through a human spirit.

The last unpleasantness during Evan Roberts's isolation period was over was his refusal to meet or correspond with his closest relatives. A neighbour of the family said that when his mother went seriously ill, the news was not passed on to Evan because of his nervous condition. When his father went up to see him, it was not Mrs. Penn-Lewis but Evan himself who would not talk. One explanation given was that he had been set apart for a highly spiritual task and had thus been obliged to forget ties of blood. David Matthews commented: "Had he become so spiritual in his outlook that he would not permit himself to be governed by human suggestions of any kind?"

Evan Roberts came out of the dark valley late in 1908 when he was strong enough to act as a peacemaker at the Leicester Convention and to give some excellent advice to evangelists. About this time Evan was invited to go to Guernsey and spend his convalescence in reading and discussion and writing poems, such as these beautiful lines which a Christian took down:

Will the will of God, and thou
Shalt find true peace in life.
Live in the will of God, and thou
Shalt find true protection in life.
Rest in the will of God, and thou

Shalt find strength for life's duties.
Die in the will of God, and thou
Shalt find life's work is done.

In the Spring of 1909 he helped publish pamphlets, plan a new magazine and research an important book. He had all his strength and confidence back. He was visited by Professor Pike of Emmanuel College. When he entered the private chamber he saw all the signs of study and activity. Soon he found that all stories about the broken man were now out of date:

> A tall upstanding young fellow stepped briskly into the room and greeted me with a happy smile, a hearty handgrip and an utter absence of all self-consciousness. Not yet ready, I should say, for a severe nerve-strain, but there is no trace of the neurotic about him. No word of repining or recrimination, such as we often hear from those who have broken down, passed his lips. He knows himself.

Surely it could be said that the Lord had lifted him out of the miry clay, set his feet on a rock and established his way. During these weeks of restoration, Evan wrote a poem which showed how much he had learned to depend on God's keeping power in a time of trial. Its message is a blessing to all who stumble or faint:

Too weak to rise?
Then let thy hand rest on Jehovah's arm.
He holds creation by His mighty word.
Too weak? Then ask,
And take the resurrection power of Christ
For God is able, yea, the dead to raise.
Thou art too weak, 'tis true, but GOD!

Is HE? Nay, Nay! The Almighty One;
The great Almighty. Yes, His power is seen
In nature, in the heavens and all the earth.
Glance at the stars and hear them whispering thus:
We rest upon the power of His Word.
Rest thou, for thou art weary and too weak.
Rest on His Word, and let thy light go forth.

There was one aspect of this journey through the vale of tears that Evan Roberts found it impossible to forget, and that was the sense of being deserted. Discussing the problem of "trials of faith" with some Christian workers, he told them:

> The real test of the "Theo" in theology is when there is no voice from the Unseen and only the voices of people mocking. In such a hell you cannot praise the Lord, but you can keep the faith. The test is not to curse, not to turn upon and not to doubt God. Then even to care for relatives and those who need salvation. At a point when you are on the edge of giving way, you draw yourself together and gather up all the forces of your being in order to give them the right words in the right spirit. My faith has been tested and shaken by a tornado, but I knew what was required of me—TO HOLD MY FAITH IN GOD. Even in one's spiritual agonies, one's spiritual duties must be done.

Evan Roberts and his counsellors explained this time of intense suffering as a form of chastening which would fit him to deal with confused and weakened Christian workers in future. Some suggested that he had been allowed to identify with Christ's own experiences of being forsaken. Evan told the readers of *Yr Efengylydd:* "If we wish to know the fellowship of His sufferings, we must experience the anguish of loneliness. 'I am alone and needy' is the cry of many a heart today. Alone! Alone! Alone! So often we hear, in the midst of spiritual conflict, this sorrowful cry, 'MY GOD, why have you left me?'"

Mrs. Penn-Lewis desired the young Welshman to see the whole period as a process of cleansing and renewal. Sitting by the bedside of the sick man, she encouraged him to talk about all the visions and voices he had known and all the examples of his strange power to look into people's thoughts and feelings. Then she made him look frankly at the mistaken actions and the misjudgments and to ask himself how he could have been deceived. Believing he was a transparent soul and thus open to the attacks of deceiving spirits, she both instructed and comforted him with this explanation:

> The more spiritual he is, the more open he is to spirits, evil or good. If any believer will seek an experience without the Cross, Satan will give him the desired thing. Then the evidence of a false leading shows up, namely doubts and agitations, and a kind of self-exaltation because they have this feeling that God is going to do great things through them because they have been summoned. This is deception.

Evan Roberts would thus see that his recent depressions and struggles, together with the bold claims he had made in the past, were enough proof that he too had been deceived. From now on he would distrust mystical experiences, and would claim that things such as tongues and prophesyings and visions were not safe until believers had far greater wisdom and experience.

What was the antidote to deception? Mrs. Penn-Lewis convinced Evan that only those who placed themselves entirely under the power of the Cross could be sure of victory. The last remnants of self would have to be destroyed in those who were crucified with Christ. Evan told the ministers and church leaders at Llandrindod Convention:

During the last three months, the Cross of Christ has been revealed to me in such a way as it never has been revealed before. Now Christ and His Cross fill my whole vision. I have felt its power breaking asunder the self that has clung to me so long. If I am spared, it will be my only aim to preach Christ and Him crucified, not theoretically but a living truth.

In *War on the Saints,* chapter twelve, Evan and Mrs. Penn-Lewis warned others about the way in which the power of darkness tried to "drive or push to extremes what is true." Yet they themselves pushed their view of spiritual warfare to extreme lengths, at times by wresting the Scriptures to their purpose. At this stage of development, Mrs. Penn-Lewis and others interpreted Evan Roberts's sufferings as a divine plan to equip him to do battle against Satanic powers and to train others for battle. The phases in his sufferings were like the way the Israelites were trained for the conquest of Canaan. In the school of suffering and self-searching, one learned how dark powers could make war on the soul of a believer and how a man broken at the Cross and baptised with the Spirit can have the authority to bind Satan. A company of such suffering and purified ones could even co-work with God in the last defeat of Satan and all his hosts. No doubt this made sense out of Evan's dark months, and it was positive therapy for a man who needed a mission.

If Evan Roberts had been able to become a missioner and evangelist again after his recovery, he would surely have kept the vow made at Llandrindod to preach the blood and the Cross as long as he had breath. But by 1908, he was sure that the Lord was opening another great door and an effectual one. For the next seven years he was to have not **one** ministry confined to Wales but five ministries to the world, **or** at least to all Christian workers. The next chapters describe briefly what took up all his mental powers and spiritual energies until the outbreak of the First Great War.

18

The Ministry of "The Overcomer"

very church leader, pastor and evangelist must have hoped fervently that the fires of the Welsh Revival would burn onwards through Britain, Europe and the world. When it became sadly evident that somehow the Spirit of God had been quenched and the work of revival put within bounds, godly people began to look for reasons. Some blamed the "demon drink" which recaptured shallower converts; some blamed modernist theology and preaching for confusing the newborn babes; some accused revival leaders and workers of assuming that remorse and confession were the same as true regeneration; some accused the churches of failure to counsel, nurture, entertain, or make use of the converts.

Ministers such as F. B. Meyer, R. B. Jones, Cynog Williams and Nantlais Williams, made serious efforts to safeguard the fruits of the revival. (These measures are described in *The Kings Champions*, pub. 1986; and *Spiritual History of Keswick in Wales*, pub. 1990.) They wondered why so many ministers and churches had lost the vision and gone back to sleep. Was it due to carelessness, disobedience, compromise, failure to witness boldly, failure to seek cleansing and consecration, or failure to obey the divine command, "Be filled with the Spirit"? Or could it be that Satan was making war on the Church and overturning the revival? Such questions were discussed at a special conference held in St. Andrews Church, Swansea, in 1908. R. B. Jones argued that this was a new round of the spiritual battle for which the Lord would need fully equipped soldiers. Dr. F. B. Meyer believed that only united and urgent prayer would once again bring power from the throne of God.

Meanwhile, Mrs. Penn-Lewis was setting out her teaching in booklets such as: *Warfare With Satan and the Way of Victory, The Conquest of Canaan,* and *Glimpses Into Heavenly Warfare.* For the magazine called *The Christian,* she did a series on "The Hour of Peril" and set out to show "how to discern points of danger" and "how to try the spirits." She warned the churches and individual readers that until they were fully crucified with Christ to the world, they would always be deceived, divided, discouraged and defeated by the prince of this world. Only those who were hidden in Christ crucified could be overcomers, and thus be equipped to fight for a wider victory.

Evan Roberts's first task was to compose, or translate, booklets in English and Welsh. One of these compared the Church to a great rock in which a stream of living water was still trapped and thus unable to run down and make land and sea alive and fruitful (as in Ezekiel 47). Another tract called *Gwasanaeth a Milwriaeth Ysbrydol (Spiritual Service and Warfare),* called on all Christians to learn to use both the tools for serving and the weapons for fighting. A third booklet, *Croes Beunyddiol (The Daily Cross),* predicted that true churches would now pass through a time of rejection and would need to take up the Cross and go outside the city to Calvary. Finally, in the booklet *Cerddwch Rhagoch (Go Forward),* Evan said that churches had done enough crying about world wide revival; now they must "Do! Walk! Act!"

The concluding exhortation shows Evan's vision of the coming battle:

> If Satan and sin do hinder the revival, let us learn to use the cross of Christ against him. This is the weapon of our warfare for it is written, "Through death He destroys him who hath the power of death, that is, the devil." Let our prayers be that these two be destroyed. Perhaps someone will say that God cannot destroy at once. That is true, for gradual is His work of destruction. Therefore, wherever you perceive sin and Satan at work, say without delaying, "Lord destroy them." While we cling to that which is sinful or doubtful, it is impossible for us to go forward. Let's walk onward and save the world. Let's walk forward with God, in unity of spirit and mind, and in the power of the Holy Spirit.

Later that year, Mrs. Penn-Lewis and Evan Roberts met together for many days of prayer and discussion. The fruit of this was a plan to publish a magazine for Christian workers, followed by a manual for Christian warriors. The underlying purpose was to gather together all who desired to be pure and consecrated enough to take part in a cosmic spiritual battle. The lines of battle were set out in a tract called, *Four Planes of Spiritual Warfare.* Their own earnest desire was expressed in a kind of prayer:

> Oh, for a pure spirit to give only that which is pure to others. A spirit able to stand against all the devices of the Enemy. Not only against flesh and blood, but against principalities and powers, world rulers and spiritual evil in heavenly places. What can stand against such things—our body, mind and soul? Oh, no! Spirit against spirit.

One of the first joint efforts was an essay by Evan Roberts, entitled "Believe Not Every Spirit," in which he set out the best way to identify deceptive teachings. It alienated many of the newborn Pentecostalist groups by listing practices similar to theirs as misleading and liable to Satan's attack. A far more positive result of their solemn discussions was the creation of four important spiritual aids:

1. *The Overcomer* Magazine.
2. *The Manual of Spiritual Warfare*
3. The Workers' Conferences
4. The Prayer Watch.

The Overcomer Magazine

This was registered at Stationers' Hall in London, with Evan Roberts and Mrs. Penn-Lewis named as co-sponsors. Mrs. Penn-Lewis announced that the magazine would be a channel for messages from the Lord and would include answers to workers' perplexing questions. The chief aim, she said, would be, "To reintegrate all who had known deception and had found that only at Calvary could they be made whole again and find victory." Through the good offices of her husband, who was the City Treasurer of Leicester, they opened a bookroom in Cartref, Toller Road. They were so overwhelmed with work that Mrs. Penn-Lewis ended her connection with other Christian magazines.

This unique periodical had no topical news, society reports, devotional meditations, sermons or serial stories. It consisted of a question-and-answer page, a prayer news column, some guidelines on prayer, a few spiritual poems and one editorial feature presenting an essential part of "overcomer" teaching. The two founders, plus Mr. J. C. Williams, contributed eighty percent of each issue and it was financed by many trusted friends who wanted it sent to about five thousand workers in Britain, Europe, North America, South Africa, Korea, and China. Soon there were also French and Italian editions.

Evan Roberts's old dream had come true because he was at last exercising a world-wide ministry. His messages of reassurance and victory found their way into the remotest parts. In J. O. Fraser's, *Behind the Ranges* (Page 91), he tells how the devil's attacks had brought him close to defeat, but someone had sent him a copy of *The Overcomer* which met his need. "What it showed me was that deliverance from the power of the Evil One comes through definite resistance on the grounds of the Cross. The passive side of leaving everything to the Lord Jesus, while blessedly true, was not all that was needed then. Definite resistance on the ground of the Cross was what brought me light, for I found that it worked. . . . The cloud of depression dispersed. I found that I could have the victory in the spiritual realm whenever I wanted it. One had to learn, gradually, how to use the new-found weapon of resistance."

During 1913 and 1914, Mrs. Penn-Lewis was feeling very poorly and Evan Roberts contributed even more essays and poems. A few months after her return, she announced that God had told her to close down the magazine. Whole pages were devoted to the various spiritual reasons for taking this step, but the chief reason seems to have been an intuition that a different kind of challenge was awaiting her and that perhaps different "warriors" would be called to the battle. Mrs. Penn-Lewis paid a generous tribute to the vital contribution Evan had made. When *The Overcomer* was restarted after the Great War, a few of his more striking and significant pre-war articles were republished, such as, "The Soldiers Prayer," "Advice to Evangelists," "A Prayer of Confession" and a poem dedicated to all the "overcomers":

> *Stand STILL! Stand FIRM! Stand ever sound.*
> *Stand Armour-Clad—'Tis fighting ground.*
> *Then stand with victor's grip*
> *The Foe to overthrow.*

With Holy Hands unloose the bands.
'Tis Christ that brought Him low.

The Story of the Manual

The major work called *War on the Saints,* was intended to be the complete answer to the problems of a host of Christian workers and warriors. Mrs. Penn-Lewis had already sketched the general theme of spiritual conflict in her earlier booklets, but these ideas can be seen in ancient books such as: *Daniel, Revelations, The War of the Sons of Light Against the Sons of Darkness,* Bunyan's works, and Gurnall's *Christian in Complete Armour.* The cosmic warfare theme fascinated many movements and sects, but irritated anti-supernaturalist theologians of all kinds. The manual compiled by Mrs. Penn-Lewis and Evan Roberts was different in that it concentrated on deception. Its subtitle was, "A textbook for believers on the work of deceiving spirits among the children of God."

Anticipating sharp reaction to their manual, the authors affirmed that it was the product of six years of enquiry, prayer and testing of the truth. They had included evidence, supplied from contacts all over Europe, of counterfeit signs, visions, voices, and spiritual exercises. They had received authentic accounts from overseas missionaries, and had also used the testimonies of Christian workers who had come to their "Spiritual Clinic" to tell them about various ways they had been deceived or daunted. Lastly, the book used Evan Roberts's own mixed experiences which had by now been examined and sifted.

In their first announcement of the book, they warned that it was written only for "believers who know the Baptism of the Holy Spirit in such a measure that they have personal experience of the existence of the supernatural facts referred to in its pages." Someone must have changed the plan because the book was later offered to Marshall Brothers for publication. Before the edition appeared on the open market, the authors wrote to all their correspondents and their *Overcomer* subscribers, asking them to pray against all satanic devices that would hinder understanding. They were advised to pray before they tried to transmit its teaching to small circles of believers and, lastly, to "use prevailing prayer and use your authority. When the resistance is unbearable, call upon God to rebuke."

The champions of the book had a swift and sure way of dealing with criticism in magazines or in the pulpit. They said: "The measure of hostility shown to this book by readers will be the measure of the deception by evil spirits into which he or she has fallen. The book is often called singular and remarkable by those who are ignorant of its vital contents."

As further support for their manual, Evan Roberts and Mrs. Penn-Lewis devised a special column in *The Overcomer,* in which Evan Roberts asked the questions and she gave replies. The answers stated that a soul can surrender to an evil spirit in good faith; that the Christian's soul can be possessed but that Christians can resist this and can escape bondage and can even be given "authority over the enemy." The book and the articles were of great value in identifying those contemporary theories which tended to undermine the faith. Its warnings about the dangers of passivity in worship and meditation are very relevant today, whilst its promises of deliverance and victory were a great impetus to those who believed that Christ crucified and risen had all the answers.

What wounded Mrs. Penn-Lewis and distressed Evan Roberts was the degree of opposition they encountered. Welsh revival teachers were cool, denominational journals were critical, the Calvinists thought it unbalanced, and the Pentecostalists felt they were being "downed." Even the Christian Workers' Conferences felt that the Bible had been used in a selective way in order to support some theories.

Those who had studied Christian psychology could see that too many kinds of wrong behaviour had been attributed to evil spirits rather than original sin. The sections most objected to were those which seemed to say that the souls of believers could become devil-possessed. The authors had used the word "possessed" to describe what would now be called harassment, not control. On the other hand, some groups deplored what seemed to be a sweeping rejection of everything abnormal in the experiences of churches and individuals.

One source of debate was the claim that the intercessory prayers of the saints could have such force that they could accelerate the return of Christ and victory over Satan. It is certainly true that the authors gave praying people an undue importance as the co-operators with God through whom He was enabled to carry out His purposes, as we see in the following: "By prayer God is enabled, according to His laws, to carry into effect what that prayer to God asks for." Enabled! Does God need a band of prayer warriors to enable Him to work? The whole paragraph would encourage that age-old tendency to think of prayer as a way to manipulate and cause change. Such ideas have long since been corrected in later "Leagues of Prayer" and similar associations.

Only a year after the manual appeared, Evan Roberts told some friends that it had been a failed weapon which had confused and divided the Lord's people. It was too negative, he said, and there needed to be another book on life in the Spirit.

The magazine and the manual were not the only things to be produced and distributed from the bookroom. Indeed, the publications continued for eight years, with an inevitable break during the war years. Parts of the manual were distributed in the form of pamphlets and some of Evan Roberts's more striking messages were sent out separately in Welsh and English. Sadly, there was no more talk of the follow-up book which Evan Roberts had suggested. The bookroom ministry continued to fulfill a valuable function for another generation and indeed continues in new forms to this day.

The Christian Workers' Conferences

These conferences gave Evan Roberts a wonderful opportunity to use his gifts as a counsellor. He had already begun to do such work while convalescing in Guernsey in 1907. He had held several sessions with Christian workers, one of whom wrote, "What strikes me most is Evan Roberts's accuracy of insight, for he is rarely at fault in his diagnosis and his spiritual discernment."

Another group who benefited from his counselling was a party of Salvation Army officers who came over from Paris. Soon after returning to Leicester he was approached by a group of seven South Walians who wanted him to pray with them and to give them guidelines before they commenced missions. He drew a clear distinction between revival and evangelism, set out the probable difficulties and hindrances, and gave them a set of ten basic principles:

1. Together, seek from God a fresh anointing for discernment.
2. Together, before the meeting, commit it to the Holy Spirit, for Him to give each the knowledge of His will.
3. Trust God for the power of the Blood of Christ.
4. Have absolute oneness between the missioners and perfect openness to one another in speech and thought.
5. Be on guard not to be pushed into dealing with any difficulties in any way but prayer.
6. In each meeting keep your hands off souls. Let God deal with them.

7. Keep control. Let no meeting get out of hand, but avoid power.

8. Repeatedly explain the conditions on which God will work, such as putting away every known sin.

9. Do not close until the Holy Spirit's objective is reached.

10. In all missions it is best that there should be two (See Matthew 10).

Once he was fully recovered, Evan Roberts was able to take part in these workers' conferences which were held first at Leicester, then Keswick, then Matlock, and finally in London. The first time that he attended, there was a storm of praise and prayer which swept away every tension. Most often he would remain in a prayer room because he had been told by medical advisers never to speak again from pulpit or platform.

These early conferences were very open-ended, with Mrs. Penn-Lewis giving the keynote address and then workers from home or abroad raising questions to be debated. There was also a three-hour student class during which the workers were closely examined about their personal temptations, stresses, self-deceptions, slackness and mistakes. The overseas workers were invited to raise problems they had met with on their field stations. A final report was drawn up and reached about six thousand church workers, missioners and overseas leaders.

There was usually one session when Evan Roberts came into the circle or came to the tea table where he would answer questions, share his experiences and offer prayer. Instead of drawing upon commentaries or other sources, he would give a very personal view of some subjects. His talks about stewardship, meditation, burden prayers, disciplining the tongue and on healing through suffering contained many memorable things:

"Don't come to a meeting and have a mask over yourself."

"God does not promise you happiness but holiness."

"Never speak rebukingly from a fatigued mind, or from an aggravated spirit, since then we shall be harsh of voice."

A Prayer: "Keep them from overwork and from all work out of Thy will, and may they know how to roll things off mind and spirit onto Thee."

A missionary who was far away from the Workers' Conference (in Lushai, India) was given his counsel in the form of a poem entitled, "Living Before His Face."

> *All of us cannot immortal be, with pen or lip or sword.*
> *Yet each with his "Little" can build great things,*
> *Sufficient to draw from the King of Kings*
> *That praise which causes the face to shine,*
> *"Well done, faithful servant of mine."*

The Workers' Conferences were suspended during the war, and Evan played a very minor role in them afterwards. Christian workers missed his presence and many asked for copies of the talks he had given. When he walked into the 1923 and 1924 conferences, he was greeted with love and joy. The report said that some workers had been transformed into living stones. After a new secretary took over in 1925, Evan retired altogether.

The Prayer Force

Men of the revival, such as R. B. Jones, David Evans, Nantlais Williams, and Dr. F. B. Meyer, believed firmly that prayer power was the remedy for decline and the spring of renewal. At a Swansea Conference in December, 1908, this challenge was issued:

> Intercessors are needed for encircling God's messengers with persistent prayer, making way for their messages through the unseen forces, and making the spoken word effectual.

Mrs. Penn-Lewis, already linked closely with a world-wide circle of prayer, and hearing of a Prayer Watch in Pennsylvania, wrote: "How blessed it would be if a similar watch could be brought about in Great Britain, where prayer is known as a definite transaction with God, and hours every day are spent in presenting the needs of others to the Lord, and in taking Him at His word. We are to be sleepless unto prayer and watchful in our dealing with the Lord."

In various essays, even before *The War on the Saints* was published, she taught that there had to be a systematic warfare of prayer against the kingdom of darkness. It is a matter of regret that some of the teachings were very debatable. One idea was that prayerless and unrevived churches could actually delay such events as a revival or even the Second Coming. There is an "if" in Joel 2 and in Malachi, of course, but men such as Edwin Orr have realised that the desire to return unto the Lord or the longing for the Coming of the Lord is the first manifestation of God's purpose, not a cause of it.

The practical result of all the writing and speaking was that Mr. J. C. Williams set up the "Lord's Watch," which consisted of two operations: "The School of Prayer" and "The Prayer Force." Notes of guidance, prayer requests and major essays were published in *The Overcomer*. Its stated aim was that: "All missioners may realise they are wrestling with spiritual wickedness, and may know experientially how to stand and overcome." In 1911, the "Lord's Watch" sent a special warning to all church leaders. In 1912, it sent out a call for a world-wide "Aggressive Week" in which to attack Satan.

Evan Roberts played some role in the "School of Prayer." He produced a model of how to intercede for families, ministers and churches; he wrote an essay on the main distractions from praying; and he dealt with the problem of "burden prayers" which worried many.

He wrote, "The prayer warrior must not expect a conscious burden for every prayer, nor wait until he feels moved to pray. He knows that to see a need for prayer is sufficient call, and that if he waits for, 'feeling that he can pray' when he has the, 'vision to pray,' is sin."

There seems to be a direct link with the "School of Prayer" and Evan Roberts's prayer ministry. J. C. Williams and Mr. W. Scottorn and others who said they owed all they knew about the prayer life to Evan Roberts's faithful training, requested permission to publish one of his prayers for the benefit of the "Lord's Watch." This was the prayer—"That all the Children of God may have their spirits open Godward, and be filled with God-given desire for the Coming of the Lord." The expectation of the Second Advent was not shared by all members of the Prayer Watch but, in any case, Evan Roberts became detached from the Prayer Watch and became immersed in private communion with the Lord. It is time now to focus on that wonderful personal ministry of prayer which eventually shut him in with God.

19

The Prayer Ministry of Evan Roberts

Whoever ventures to examine the anointed call to prayer granted by the Lord to a faithful servant has to confess at once that he is standing on holy ground. There was something awesome about Evan Roberts's prayer life, even to those who were able to join with him on some occasions. Mrs. Penn-Lewis said that in the first few years Evan still had a small group who met in the prayer room. "Each prayed over and over until everything could be gathered into one petition. But after a while, Evan began to retire to a more solitary place where he could commune with God alone." The same writer commented, "In deep spiritual isolation the work was done, with a crucifixion in the personal life that few would endure or understand."

When and where did this prayer work begin? D. M. Phillips said that the potentiality was there long before the revival. "When most intense in prayer he becomes unconscious of everything else. Time for him does not exist. Hours glide away in a moment. He is insensible of all that happens."

Those who were constantly with him during the revival

missions testified that in the midst of all the turbulence and noise, Evan Roberts would enter a private place of prayer in which he sensed and reached those souls who were crying for help. J. C. Williams knew about the prevailing power of Evan Roberts's prayers. "As many will remember, his prayers were petitions to the Throne of Grace, so insistent, so melting, with such spirit abandonment, that men were moved and swayed as by an Unseen Hand, while the suppliant poured out his soul for the unsaved."

In February 1905, when he was laid aside for a few days, Evan Roberts told a close friend: "I would like to reach a state of prayer when my life would be nought but one prayer from morn to night. I will not be content until I experience that. At times now I fail to go on my knees by my bedside at night and morning, because I am in an attitude of prayer constantly and I am continually praying inaudibly." Such a desire could not be satisfied in the hurly-burly of the revival, nor in the worst days of his breakdown. It was in the spring of 1907 that the first sign was given.

The sign was ordinary enough. After the group prayers were ended, he felt a strong impulse to continue in prayer. Evan then said to himself, "If I obey this, I shall always be praying." Mrs. Penn-Lewis described the moment: "He dropped the matter in hand and followed that draw to prayer. He discovered a spring opened, as it were, in his spirit, out of which came a prayer-stream full of unction."

Many had expected such a special vocation to be given to Evan Roberts, because they believed that a man who had experienced so much deception and spiritual temptation and who had passed through such trials in soul and body, was being prepared by God to become "the man who would stand in the gap before me for the LORD" (Ezek. 22:30). Another godly man outside this group had also written prophetically about an "intercessor" in the Christian journal, *Life of Faith* (1906, p. 506):

> Surely it were best today, if possible, for one to give himself wholly, during the period specified, to this most responsible saving work. He can only do this as one appointed to this officially by the Lord. He must be one who is yielded completely to the divine guidance.

Mr. John Clarke was only thinking of a fourteen-day vigil; Evan Roberts had nine years of intercession, though it took different forms.

Evan Roberts never forgot the thrill he felt when he was given this new ministry. In a Welsh pamphlet sent out about 1909 and published later in *The Overcomer,* he wrote:

> Since I have been fully given to prayer, it is marvellous how the world, the whole world, has become a sphere of vision to me. It was very sweet to me to discover new spheres in the realm of prayer. But the moment I took into my sphere of prayer the whole church, the whole world, and all the powers of darkness, there came from my spirit with great joy the word "cageless." . . . Oh how sweet it was to gather the whole world under the wings of my prayers.

This did not mean, of course, that Evan Roberts's intercessory work became too comprehensive to be focused on some part of the kingdom work. As Mr. Norman Grubb said, in the splendid twelfth chapter of his biography of Rees Howells, those who have been chosen for this very special work because they have identified with souls in need and have entered into the sufferings of the Saviour/High Priest, will then be appointed to a specific, "gained position of intercession." Some will have authority to pray for healing the sick; some will have authority to pray for orphans—as Mueller did; or for mission resources—as Rees Howells did. Evan Roberts knew that he was being called to a "position" from which he could intercede continually for Christ's servants and witnesses who were exposed to deception. Such prayer was a kind of warfare which demanded qualities of perseverance, valour, self-sacrifice and, above all, vigilance.

During a day of conversations with a party of French Salvation Army officers, they spoke about the need for aggressive warfare against Satan in order to defeat and bind him. Evan Roberts continually stressed the need to persevere: "In Luke it does not say, 'preach and faint not' but, 'pray and faint not.' It is not difficult to preach. But while you pray, you are alone in some solitary place, fighting in a prayer-battle against the powers of darkness. And you will know the secret of victory." The idea is echoed in one of his poems:

> And never faint! Oh pray, full on and fast.
> Rough though the untrod way. Straight on! and last.
> And never faint, though those may rave for rest.
> The goal, not thee, is first. Pray on! thou blest.
>
> And never faint! Though strain may sigh thee down.
> Pray on! if thou wouldst fain have on the crown.
> And never faint! The end thou mayest not view.
> When bound, let nought thee bend. Press on anew.
>
> And never faint! Thy charge to God given o'er.
> Pray on! Thy tent enlarge. Enrich thy store.
> And never faint! Pray on each day with care.
> Strive for, till thou hast won, the answered prayer.

Evan was so taken up with the idea of vigilant watching that he prayed night and day and was known to fall asleep on his feet, then awaken a few hours later fresh and alert once more. He told Welsh friends in a special letter that he was like a bondservant who could not stop his work even on a Sabbath Day: "The warfare must go on every hour against unseen enemy hosts who are set to weaken the church forces." Like Moses who lifted up his arms all day long over the battle, Evan had to serve the Lord who had "taken hold of my spirit." When he was invited in 1910 to go to India he replied earnestly:

> I could not give my time to India without neglecting . my prayer work and feeling I am behind in my prayer service, and that possibly some victory is lost through my negligence. When the [crisis] of the church is through I shall be free for public work. All public work must be subservient to my prayer work.

In the same way, he shut part of his mind to Wales by stopping all correspondence and avoiding visits and visitors. Even his family were shown the door and Mrs. Jessie Penn-Lewis had to give out some explanation for all this behaviour.

> By this daily and momentary giving of himself to co-work with the Holy Spirit in every movement to pray, and in every thought given to the mind as, "knowledge for prayer," gradually his whole being was shut up to the prayer service. He could only have his spirit and mind free for outer things when God released him from this service.

Evan himself spoke at times about the necessary loneliness of the prayer warrior. He did send one very encouraging message to the "Plant Y Diwygiad" (a Welsh term for revival converts): "I see that the prayers of a special group in the church, who know God and His ways, are busily engaged in the warfare. . . . Keep at it, praying ones."

As time went on, there was a slight shift of emphasis from the militant to the pastoral and even the teaching aspects. A 1911 issue of *The Overcomer* had as its cover a studio portrait of Evan seated in prayer, with a Bible in front of him. Under this was written the verse which he had chosen, "Always labouring fervently for you in my prayers, that ye might stand perfect and complete in all the will of God." Even his pamphlet had a double title—"spiritual warfare *AND* spiritual service." In this he wrote:

> Of course it is essential for the man of God to lay down his life for the church in order that he might lead it to a higher level of spirituality.

This apostolic vision can be seen also in a poem which implies that the minister of prayer must also endure pain:

> *How hard it is to find that able mind,*
> *That careth, yes, and prays.*
> *Cares countless more than for his own;*
> *Reaps not to gild his crown.*
> *Thy spirit, groaning, inward fights*
> *With heavy burdens day and night;*
> *Thy unseen wounds not always slight,*
> *Yet heavenly faith so full of light.*
> *Thou often pressed in weary plight;*
> *The Eternal God thy only might;*
> *The burden of the churches lays*
> *Upon thy spirit all the days.*
> (The Apostle, 1912)

These are breath-taking claims, but no one who sat with Evan Roberts in the prayer room had any doubts about his authority. J. C. Williams told *The Overcomer* readership that:

> At the present moment, ministers and laymen, such as God sends, who are brought into touch with him, take away with them what they feel to be a new vision of

their ministry; a deeper insight into the spirit realities of life; the real hindrances in their life and ministry.

Many were amazed at his authority, but some were opposed to it. Others saw that the strain of the work was taking effect. Evan believed that greater prayer power required more suffering on his part. In one conversation about intercessory prayer, he told of his dream:

> The more the prayer power the vaster is the ministry.
> The world becomes his parish, the church his pasture,
> but all the powers of darkness become his foe.

The strain became so intense by late 1913 that he wrote again to some Welsh friends: "God had to take hold of some human spirit. He has taken hold of mine in spite of tiredness and weakness." Then he said cryptically, "It appears to me that God is in haste, hurrying along some tremendous, momentous, dispensational works."

This was partly inspired by a premonition that he was on the eve of a new revelation and partly inspired by a recent address by Mrs. Penn-Lewis during which she interpreted Revelation 12:4 as Satan's all-out attack on the "Man-Child Church," which would occur just before Christ's coming to rapture His people away from this last warfare.

For several weeks, Evan was plagued by discontent and told a friend: "There seems to be no place where I can find rest for my spirit. It seems there are impending changes at hand. Amen to God's will." After he returned from a brief visit to France, he seemed to want to stay in bed a great deal, or just go out for lonely walks, or sit and compose little songs.

According to Mrs. Penn-Lewis, others felt that the atmospheric pressures were about to be lifted and that the burdens were about to be rolled away. The crisis came on 19 October, 1913. On that extraordinary day, a new vision shone into Evan's soul. His old companion in revival days, Awstin Davies, went into the private chamber and found Evan and two other men radiant with light and joy in the presence of God. Evan asked Awstin why he had never spoken to him about Christ's coming and why the thought of the "translation" did not fill his mind and spirit. The reply was, "We waited for you." Now he felt a great urge to study every prophetic Scripture, share his vision with others and urge them to be "prepared to depart." Friends and workers heard him singing some new melodies.

He composed several songs of the Second Coming and put most of these in *The Overcomer*. This is one of them:

> *I'm watching for his coming, with ever present eye.*
> *I'm waiting for his presence, to fill the waiting sky*
> *No other thing shall face me: No other thing than this.*
> *His coming at this moment and my going into bliss.*
>
> *My eye is on the Saviour. My heart is in the heaven.*
> *My voice will lisp no message, but what thyself has given.*
> *"I'm coming very quickly, I am coming now for you.*
> *My word doth stand forever and is divinely true."*

Suddenly he felt impelled to announce in *The Overcomer* that he had been given a "burden on my spirit" which was to be delivered to all who understood that, like Enoch, the messenger walked daily with God. This was the word that was sent across Europe, was translated into Chinese and reached the United States in the form of *The Midnight Cry:*

> The burden on my spirit, day and night, is the imminent appearance of our Lord Jesus Christ from heaven to translate his saints. I pray God to make you

ready and to keep you ready. Although we know nothing
of how or in which hour the Lord shall appear it is
possible for us to have a revelation of the Holy Spirit
of His coming in our lifetime. It appears that the special
message of the Spirit to the prepared believer is, "Thou
shalt not die but thou shalt be caught up to meet the Lord
in the air."

Come! Is the unquenchable cry of my spirit. Only
to think that such an hour is at the door. Oh, to be ready
and to finish the work He gave us to do, and to prepare
others! Oh sinless life! Forever after this we shall be
completely spiritual and our joy shall be a hundred times
higher than we have proved in the most divine hours of
our life. Will this not cause us to cry aloud, "Oh come,
heavenly appointed hour." The times have been
measured by God. It appears today that God, through
the Spirit, is saying, "The second coming of My Son is
at hand. Be ye ready in the hope. Watch for His
coming."

The message was not well received in Britain, and some
were bound to ask whether Evan Roberts had been deceived
when he gave out a prophetic word which events quickly
disproved. By 1914 he was telling people that if the Lord was
coming soon there would have to be far greater unity among
true believers. This would not come through compromise or
pretence, but through discarding all criticism and wrong
thoughts.

Stubbornness of spirit has divided us. Should we not
seek humility from God? Prayer, repentance and a
confession of sin. Alas, that we should be divided when
the Lord comes. The devil came into the camp ten years
and split it up ten years ago by putting each man's sword
against a brother. May each one go to God for cleansing
of the spirit and for victory over Satan. The Enemy has
succeeded in making the people of God into UNITS

instead of advancing in one consolidated band. . . . We must hold to the Oneness of the Body of Christ and put our will against all divisions. We cannot go to Heaven divided. May each one sacrifice in order to be one. God can give you a spirit of toleration and peace.

Again there was very little response, and Evan began to speculate that the lack of unity would delay the longed-for "translation" or "rapture." A Californian sent a warm letter of thanks and an offer to pay the costs of distributing the message. Another American wrote:

I perceive Evan Roberts as a man raised up to lead God's people out of the bondage of demon slavery into the glorious liberty of truth and spiritual freedom. But suddenly the call of God came to him in the Translation message. Now the ringing call is heralded to all God's people everywhere, to put away all pettiness and carnality and narrowness, and to come together in one spirit in prayer for the removal of all obstacles.

Alas, this message made no difference to the debate and the divisions. Evan Roberts became even more isolated. Mrs. Penn-Lewis wrote these sympathetic words about his separation from those who did not accept his exhortation, and this included many Christian workers:

He cannot open the things of God to those who are severed from him in spirit by doubt or unbelief. Those who are around him cannot get into conversation with him, even if present in the same house, if these laws of the spirit are ignored. Thus he is a ceaseless touchstone to all who are in contact with him, as to whether they too walk after the Spirit in close fellowship with God.

Whatever else took place in that inner chamber will not be revealed until eternity. Somehow it gave added authority to his counselling and greater clarity to his *Overcomer* essays and poems. There was a break in this holy work some time during and after the brutal war years. But soon he resumed that constant communion with God which he was still practising at the time he was called back to Wales. What else can account for the unique impact he made when he was at last reunited with the faithful "saints" in the very places where God had first sent the revival blessing?

20

Farewell to "The Overcomers"

(1913-1921)

ven as the whole of Europe passed into the darkness of savage warfare, Evan Roberts's life and work passed into a strange twilight zone. After the seven fruitful and active years came seven years of isolation and apparent barrenness. In 1914, he was still an editor and contributor, a trusted counsellor, a revered prophet and teacher. By 1921, he had no links with *The Overcomer* magazine, the conferences, or the network of workers in Europe and the world. Instead, he was described as "a man of God living in another world and occupied with service in another realm."

Just before the war began, Mrs. Penn-Lewis was entering a very difficult phase of her life and was often absent from the work. She was taken away for a long holiday in the Channel Islands where the sea air would help her weakened lungs. In her absence, Evan Roberts managed *The Overcomer,* J. C. Williams directed the Prayer Watch and other helpers administered the Workers' Conferences. Not long after she returned, Mrs. Penn-Lewis announced that the spiritual warfare was entering a new phase because the End-Age of the Son of Man was dawning. She detached the Prayer

Watch, cut down the conferences, and then closed down *The Overcomer*. In the pages of explanation of these steps, one paragraph warned of a significant change:

> Our obedience to the Spirit of God will surely lead Spirit-guided workers to examine their positions and discover whether they are in their courses. It may lead some to find that they have been misled by the voices of men, or by the exterior propensity of their service, to continue in work in which they have not perceived the indications of the Spirit for their withdrawal. It will lead others to understand that God has been working towards the finish of some specific service by the withdrawal of unction upon it. It will show some that there is work they are clinging to as "given of God" long after they should have been content to let it pass into other hands, even though they may, from the human side, have special claims to it.

One is bound to ask, "Who else had a more special claim than the young Welshman who was the registered co-founder?" On the other hand, Evan Roberts also wrote a lengthy farewell to *The Overcomer,* showing from biblical examples that God had many different ways of ending the special missions and tasks of His chosen ones. No one should complain or try to keep going by his own resources once God said, "Finished." There could be a special joy in saying "I've finished the course," just as there is sorrow over failure. Now he announced that the ministration of "war in the unseen world" was over, partly because all God's servants had been instructed and equipped with new weapons, and partly because a new age was dawning when Satan would fall and Christ would reign.

Evan's article mentioned several times how God's messengers had been abused and the message resisted because deceivers hated the truth. However, he did not identify these people.

What happened to Evan Roberts during the four years of war is still unknown. As a man in his late thirties he could have been called up to the reserves or taken into some auxiliary work. That would account for a signed photograph from him to a niece in 1919 which shows him with a military-looking moustache. Yet it is also known that he was sickened by all forms of violence and that he took on his own heart the pain, grief and perplexity of many other Christians.

At a time when scores of revival converts were living and dying in the Flanders "hell on earth," and when many were rapidly losing their faith, Evan Roberts wrote: "I seem to be emerging gradually from the Valley of the Shadow of Death, along whose paths I have walked these last few years. I climb with unwavering steps."

At some point during the war years, when the Suffragette movement was strong and when many women handled posts of responsibility in business, Mrs. Penn-Lewis had passed through a remarkable change of view, which has been faithfully recorded by her biographer and friend, Mary Garrard.

She wrote and published two radical and prophetic books which sparked off a debate. They were entitled *The Ministry of Women* and *The Magna Carta of Women.* Their main argument was that the Cross had destroyed the male/female barrier as well as the Jew/Gentile and bond/free barriers. Dying with Christ into newness of life meant, she said, that women could also receive the "Word of Power." One of her most striking statements seemed to dispense with Evan Roberts and others:

> I cried unto the Lord that He would raise up a man
> to whom He would entrust the commission He had given
> me. At last I saw that there was no man. I laboured in
> delivery of my message, watching with eyes and ears

to see whether there was some hidden and chosen instructor to whom I could transmit the burden. A man who would rise up in God's time to proclaim it to the world and let me stop.

Mrs. Penn-Lewis came to believe that in this new age a woman could be entrusted with prophetic and teaching ministries.

In 1920, when people realised that Evan Roberts was no longer contributing to the revived *Overcomer,* nor expected to be present as counsellor at Workers' Conferences, they naturally asked Mrs. Penn-Lewis about it. She would only say, "It is remarkable that Mr. Roberts has never been able to take part in the work again; but his work has been carried on by others."

Of Evan Roberts's group, we know that J. C. Williams went off to Warsaw in 1921-1922, Mr. Scottorn to Riga, Mr. Johnson back to the Paris Office of *Le Vainquer,* and the Rev. Arthur Harris to the Russian Missionary Society. Evan sent Mr. Harris a very encouraging letter and expressed his hope that "some of the wealth of the Revival should be sown in Russian souls. Rivers are not supposed to be dammed. If they are, the water eventually finds a way out and over."

There was little left for Evan to do. It was announced that Mr. Proctor of Liverpool was taking charge of *The Overcomer Testimony,* Mr. Austin Sparkes was to run the conferences, and Mr. Gordon Watts was to help with policy. Mrs. Penn-Lewis spent months at Moor Cottage, Matlock, and recovered from a serious lung hemorrhage just in time to nurse her ailing husband. In July 1924, she removed the work from Toller Road, Leicester, to 4 Eccleston Place, Victoria, London, and she moved down into the Surrey hills. For three years prior to her death, she struggled heroically to attend conferences and conduct meetings.

Meanwhile, Evan Roberts had a few quiet years. During

1919-1921, various Christian leaders were taking part in correspondence-column debates in the Christian press about such issues as prophecy, signs, end times, tribulation, national awakening, and the return of Christ. But there was not a single letter from Evan Roberts except one sent to the editor of *The Christian* about the best answer to the rise of atheistic socialism. Evan's view was that all labour problems could be solved if only the workers, managers and owners were prepared to take part in earnest prayer.

What is really surprising is that Evan Roberts made no reply when a Miss Kate Drew of Coombe Down rejected his teaching on possession and secret assault by the devil. Mr. Gordon Watts issued a call for concerted prayer against the invading Satan, but Miss Drew and Dr. Schofield both refuted the theory of possession (*Life of Faith,* May 1920). Once again, Evan Roberts made no attempt to join in.

Meanwhile, he had moved to 156 Freshfield Road, Brighton, in Sussex. He bought a good Remington typewriter and began a new work of writing booklets on topics he felt to be important. The first of these, published by the Drummond Tract Depot, was *Give God the Gold.* This essay on good stewardship was not well organised and suffered from a loose use of the Scriptures. Yet it also had a number of memorable sentences about mission support:

"We need a daily ration and not a casual feast."

"How shall the heathen warm himself by the eternal fires of God's love, if we give not the money for the fuel?"

Another booklet, which has unfortunately survived only in the form of a translated essay in *Yr Efengylydd* (xvi. 163), is a solemn charge to the churches to see to their true mission, once clear of sin's mastery. It reads, in part:

Our two greatest enemies are Sin and Satan. By the Cross you get victories over them, both for yourself and for others. If you are in the clutch of the Evil One, stand upon that truth, "Dead to sin," and sooner or later you will find yourself completely free from him. And thus it is also with Sin. Stand against everything which is tugging you off from this truth. If you stand on this truth, rest assured that you will be delivered from the power of sin. Twice the apostle says in the sixth chapter, "Having been made free from Sin." That does not mean there is no sin in us but that by the dying to Sin and by the cooperation of the Lord, we have been set free from Sin's mastery. Reckon yourselves dead to sin and then I know the Lord will keep us all in unity with one another and to some extent with others who have been baptised with the Holy Spirit. . . .

Many think they have been baptised with the Holy Spirit, but in reality they have only had some special blessing. There is a baptism to be had, dear reader. If you have asked and not received, perhaps there is something for you in Acts 5:37—Obedience.

You must not stand between God and the Kingdom. Even less so your relationships. Choose. You must choose between good and evil and then you must choose between good and good—the lesser for the greater good. Choose ye. . . . The Kingdom needs are greater than the natural ones. Oh! that Jesus might have a free people—free to do His commands. Let the body of death, that is SIN, be underfoot.

A key paragraph called upon churches to see that they must take on the task of witnessing, no matter what the cost might be:

The world cries out for Life and Love and the fields are white unto harvest. Why then is it not gathered? This is SIN again—worldliness and carnality. This one is immersed in learning, this one in his field, and this one in his business. No time for the prayer meeting; no time for CHRIST.

Everyone needed to die to a whole range of sins, such as fear, covetousness and pride, he said. Evan Roberts clearly intended this message and others to be heard in every church in the land. He hoped that when entire churches got free from worldliness and learned at last to pray for the needs of the world, they would then be "all of one spirit and one mind."

He was deeply troubled by the growing disagreements between various movements and felt at times that he himself was guilty of certain sins which were making him a divider of the brethren. At some moment of self-examination he wrote down this prayer, perhaps when he knew he was leaving Leicester:

> Remove my carnal wisdom (James 3:15) and cast down the vain imaginations of my heart (2 Cor. 10). Let the peaceable wisdom from on high (James 3) dominate my actions. Let not my thoughts disturb the peace of Thy church in causing schisms, quarrels and divisions, unbearable to Thee and detrimental to the sanctity of Thy living church. . . .
>
> Let Thy church not only walk in the Light but make it Light in Thee. Let all its members walk in sweet fellowship with Thee and with one another. Let Deception be no more (Rev 12:9), and the whole world be in Thy great Light. O light of the world, shine!—so that no darkness may abide. . . . I crave this for myself and for Thy church. . . . Amen.

Evan Roberts left Brighton for Cardiff in 1927 and was given help and shelter by anonymous businessmen.

21

Welcome Home to Wales
(1919-1927)

ver since 1908, when he sent a letter to Welsh friends to assure them that he had not given up the idea of more revival missions, Evan Roberts had kept up some kind of contact. From time to time he asked a member of his group to go into Wales and bring back news of the revived churches and fellowships. When news came that the Rev. R. B. Jones and others had created a series of local conventions to teach the converts, he sent a warm letter full of encouragement. The late R. B. Jones's son kept a note sent at this time:

> Once I was greatest in their eyes and hearts, but they must die to me and be wedded to thee. Be brave and strong and take the leadership, for they must have this.

The revivalist assured Mr. Jones that he was quite pleased at this change and incredibly happy. He also made it clear to the leaders of his denomination that at that time he desired no new appointment nor ordination.

There was some grumbling about this, but no open criticism until the Rev. D. Wynne Evans's essay appeared in the *Life of Faith* in 1909. He pictured Evan Roberts as completely restored in vision and energy. Naturally enough the children of the revival were perplexed when he still didn't come home. A year later they opened their copies of *War on the Saints* and saw what seemed to be serious criticisms of their cherished revival. Among some of the authors' allegations were: "The mistake was to become occupied with the effects of the revival and not watch and pray in protecting the cause of revival. . . . Spirit-baptised souls are now locked up in spirit." They also stated that the power of God which broke out in revival in Wales had been checked and repelled by an influx of evil spirits, which God's people had failed to recognise and deal with.

Not until 1913 did Evan Roberts decide to publish in *The Overcomer* a new "Message to Wales" in which he confessed that he had been tricked by the wiles of the enemy "who does not allow even the elect to escape him" (Rev. 13:7). He asked them to pray for his world-wide ministry of intercession and to "ask the Lord that he might be sustained in spirit and strengthened in body."

Many new groups had already been formed in Wales and had continued to meet even during the war. There still exists a letter, written by Evan Roberts to Mr. King of Penyrheol Mission (1919), thanking them for support and assuring them that he would pray for their new venture. Some prayer circles met every year on a mountain where they would give thanks for the blessings of the revival. In 1919, Evan sent these faithful few a telegram which contained a heavily allegorical prophecy: "May the blessing of God be on your thirteenth meeting, like the thirteenth round of the children of Israel encompassing Jericho. My love be with you all in Jesus Christ. Amen. I Corinthians 16:4."

Evan had recently attended Advent Conventions in Cardiff and Swansea and seemed to know a great deal about the new prophetic and Adventist movements. But Evan also came to believe once more that a final time of blessing would come before the End-Days. When Mr. D. Evans met him again he found a great change in him and wrote this exciting report for *Life of Faith* in January 1918:

> Should he again be used to lead another revival, these quiet years of enforced inactivity and silence, during which great psychological and spiritual knowledge and deep experience have been gained, would be seen to have qualified him for invaluable guidance. Those who know the revivalist best know that, if he has been apparently quiescent all these years, the fires are not gone out. The glow of real revival has ever been burning steadily deep down in his mystic, spiritual nature, setting on fire the foundations of his being. Whether he will ever be publicly active again, and in eruption, is difficult to tell, but he is far from being an empty, cooled down crater, or a spent force.

A few months later, all Wales was discussing the call made by ex-Premier David Lloyd George for another awakening. He said: "The chief need of the land is not material but spiritual. The wounds of the world are bleeding and material things will not heal them. The one need of Britain is the healing of the Cross."

About this time Evan Roberts decided to renew contact with his denomination and wrote a complimentary letter to the Rev. Thomas Charles Williams who had just been made Moderator of the Anglesey Association. He slipped in a reference to "your kindness to me in the past years of revival flame, and of your intense interest in my utterances." Mr. Williams at once sent greetings and asked permission to let people know that he had heard from him after a ten-year silence. This was given and an item appeared in the *South Wales Daily News* in February 1919.

Evans's second letter contained a sermonette on the sad

state of a world where "head has taken the place of heart." He went on, "My love for Wales is in no way diminished, although abundance of love is necessary to rightly and efficiently perform the work of the church, yet how fettered is he whose health forbids the full expression of such love." Was he signalling his intention to return to Wales when he offered prayers that God would make the denomination into a "living force in these days"? He clearly believed that all was not lost, yet he had written and said nothing when revival flames appeared in East Anglia and certain Scottish towns in 1922-1924.

Every Christian newspaper had essays on revival during those years, but Evan Roberts took no part until some editor remembered it was the twenty-first birthday of the revival in Wales. Then he asked Roberts, Peter Price and Tywi Jones to reply to a key question, "What were the lasting lessons of the revival of 1904?" Price stuck to his original opinion, but Evan Roberts's thoughtful essay, printed in the *Seren Cymru* (26 May 1926), showed that he had fully analysed the revival experience and had gained a new perspective. He now affirmed that the Great Revival had not sprung out of the sands of time but had been built upon the sure foundations of godly life, abundant biblical knowledge, and the prayer meetings where particular saints had prayed for an outpouring.

Erected upon this were the four principles he had taught from the beginning. He said that the revival had restored to individuals and churches a "sense of the Living Presence as a reality," but every new experience was intended to bear practical fruits and create many new, zealous workers. He was confident that revival would come again when God first burdened saints to pray and then chose special instruments. But God's people must not just plead for the outpouring of the Spirit but must also strive to raise their lives to the highest possible level. "Make sure that your faith is equal to your prayer," he exhorted. This call was repeated in several forms in later years.

Despite all the excitement and expectation among the religious leaders of the day, no new awakening happened and many people went back to the usual denominational interests. Evan renewed his friendship with the Revs. Nantlais Williams and R. H. Roberts and was officially welcomed at an Association meeting in Llandrindod Wells. At this time, the denomination was in bitter debate over a plan to replace the very detailed doctrinal basis of the denomination by a shorter confession. Evan Roberts had friends on both sides of the debate. He had an excellent relationship with the Rev. Nantlais Williams, who led the resistance to the proposed changes and whose main essay "Torrir Rhaff" (Rope-Breaking) made him a focal point of the debate. But Evan Roberts was also respected by the assembly president, the Rev. Abel Evans, and was a lifelong friend of the Rev. R. M. Richards, the President of the East Glamorgan Presbytery. The latter asked him for some comment on the debate but the reply, published later by Nantlais Williams in *Yr Efengylydd* contained a "prophecy" about a new dispensation which would replace the Pentecost Age:

> What then is the substitute for the baptism of the Holy Spirit? Where shall the church turn for forces to deal with the problems pressing on her spiritual life? To CHRIST! The prophecy and promise of Revelation 12:10 is the pivot of the new power for service—the power of the age to come which should be taken by the believer. If the spirit of prophecy dwells in you, you will find a great "Amen" to this in your inner life. The power of Revelation 12:10 should be received by faith. Then we are to expect manifestations in the life, the circumstances and in the meetings. That is the new power for work in the church. May that be evident in your presbytery. May God fill all the presbytery with the spirit of prophecy.

The answer seemed so simple to him. Just turn to the Lord Jesus Christ for the power and for the gifts and for all the guidance churches needed to tackle difficult problems. Whether this meant anything at all to the ministers who heard or read the message is doubtful, for their thoughts were not his thoughts. Another letter was sent to R. M. Richards, in reply to an invitation to sit in at the Mountain Ash "Sasiwn" (Session). The reply was also printed in *Yr Efengylydd* (vol. xx), because it dealt with the problem of how to sense the presence of God:

> The saint should not be afraid of sensing God. In this experience you have the essence of revival fervour. That promise, "Lo I am with you always," stands unrevoked. Yet the gracious act of revealing Himself is progressive.

Next Evan Roberts considered the hard-pressed Apostle Paul and used this example to make a personal cry as well as a prophetic message to all who today lend the name of revivalist to any eloquent "gospeller" or "prophet" or "doer of wonders" who happens to be in the news:

> The care of the churches shall be given to him who has the Spirit of the Father. It is not learning that is needed here, but a limitless power to suffer and bear and enough sincerity to weep for the Church of Christ. My heart is in the church and the church is in my heart.

Evan Roberts did not know then that his heart's desire was soon to be satisfied and that he would bring back the spirit of revival. He spent 1925-1927 in Brighton and Southern England, but returned to Cardiff in 1927. A recently discovered letter to a Mrs. Enid Pugh provides evidence that he was still learning new lessons—this time about discernment and about prayer for healing.

214

When I was boarding in Brighton, the daughter of the house came home for an operation for tonsillitis. When I heard of it, I was instantly burdened with her state and I came to the conclusion that Death was hovering over her. I told her father—a man of much prayer—to pray about this. He, I fear, was sceptical about my being right. Later on, the operation was very successful and the daughter came home radiantly well. A few days later she called at the hospital and she was told by the Matron, "What a fright you gave us. Your heart stopped two or three times and we had to massage you. The kind of stuff he had given you did not suit your constitution. Had we known, we would have given you a different sleep-maker." I do not pretend to a gift of discernment but I must say, though it fell on me absolutely unsought, that I was really concerned at the time.

Roberts went to speak of a right to spiritual healing—which he certainly used in his little revival at Gorseinon. How he went to Gorseinon is another story.

Just after Christmas 1926, it became obvious that his father, Henry Roberts, was going downhill. During the spring and early summer of 1927 Evan travelled several times to Llanelly Cottage Hospital. He met some of his family and friends, and each time he was given a warm welcome, as if people were saying, "Come back. All is forgiven." One chapel persuaded him to give an address, and the Gorseinon and Loughor converts came along. How surprised they were to see a somewhat portly middle-aged gentleman whose broad, kindly face was quite unlike the old photographs. He had removed his wartime moustache and was clean-shaven once more. The eyes had lost their piercing gaze, but the voice was as clear and controlled as before. As soon as he began to speak, they knew that his message had lost none of its power. There was such intense feeling that an alert correspondent from the *Llanelli Mercury* sensed that a new drama was in the making:

> Shall we have a religious revival this year? That is the question that is heard recently in many places. What a blessing if one came. There is need for a spiritual visitation of God to our country. The churches are in a deplorable state in many places. As a result, the state of the people is low.

One year afterwards, the people knew God's answer—not a national awakening this time, but a time of refreshing for the faithful ones in and near Gorseinon and Loughor. The "Little Revival" was short-lived, yet it bore fruit.

22

The Little Revival
(1928-1930)

When Henry Roberts died in October 1928, his children were reunited at his funeral. Evan had been in and around Loughor for weeks. His sister, Mary, and her husband, Sidney Evans, had come home from their college at Cherrapunjee, India. His brother, the Rev. Daniel Roberts, came over from his Rhondda home.

During the actual funeral service, Evan Roberts did one of those unusual things for which people long remembered him. Sombre words and solemn tributes to the late Henry Roberts were given. Evan Roberts then interrupted the customary ritual as he came forward and started a long prayer whose theme was, "This is not a death but a resurrection. Let us bear witness to this truth." One of the eyewitnesses wrote:

> Something like electricity went through us. One felt that if he had gone on there would have been another revival there and then.

Some called it an unseemly display of emotion, others said pityingly that it showed that Evan had nervous problems.

But there were others present who described the whole happening as "a sign of the return of the old fire."

The deacons of Moriah took the opportunity to invite Evan Roberts to take part in some of the services which would commemorate the centenary of Moriah Chapel. News of this spread far and wide so that two hours before the meeting, the chapel was full. Visitors were pouring in and local people rushed in from work. A correspondent wrote:

> The aisles, the lobby and the stairs were chock-full of excited people. Another large crowd outside failed to catch a glimpse or hear the voice of the revivalist. The congregation waited with bated breath for a spectacular, soul-stirring revivalist sermon. But Evan Roberts remained calm and, in an attractive lucid style, he preached a sermon in Welsh, one far-reaching in its simple directness.
>
> The people from outside came into a vestry and sang hymns. That too was filled to capacity when it was announced that Evan Roberts would address the overflow meeting. They were ripe for a dramatic outburst and there were fervent interjections even as he began. But his coolness had a steadying influence. Scores of young people had come to see the one who is an honourable name on their parents' lips. He appeared robust and vigorous despite the silver creeping back from his temples. He was accompanied by Miss May Davies. He will participate again on Thursday afternoon and evening.

During this period, Evan visited his brother's church in the Rhondda and spoke to huge excited audiences. But he also went with Nantlais Williams to little fellowships and willingly spoke about the fight against materialism which was choking the churches. Once more his words, his poems, his brief but striking prayers, and above all his closeness to the Lord, made church leaders everywhere dream of another series of revival missions all over Wales. God, however, had other plans for him—on his own doorstep.

The humble instrument of the Holy Spirit was a middle-aged spinster named Mary Davies. Twenty-three years earlier she had travelled with four other girls, singing and reciting and testifying wherever the Lord took them. One girl returned to teaching, one married Richard Looker, the singer, one had a new career as an elocutionist and Mary stayed at home. Delicate and modest, she loved doing craftwork and painting while her sisters ran the post office. For many years she served quietly and gently the needs of other "children of the revival," and she prayed faithfully for God's work.

One autumn evening in 1928, she felt that God was commanding her to speak to a few godly people and ask them to come to her private room for prayer. Among these were Tom Walters of Moriah, Martin Jones of Bryn Hall and John Jenkins. Their first meeting was on 29 November 1928, and only three were present. As the numbers doubled, they used a large empty room below that "upper room" which Evan Roberts used on special occasions. There was such blessing in the meeting that it doubled and doubled again. Now Mary Davies felt herself commanded to write to Evan Roberts and ask him to come down for a few weeks.

He accepted the invitation. As soon as his telegram came into Gorseinon Post Office, one of the sisters left the counter and ran out into the street shouting the good news, "Evan Roberts is coming back." There was a surge of excitement and curiosity as the first meeting was called. Evan reminded them that he was only an instrument. "The Holy Spirit is the only source of spiritual life", he said. "It is not by might nor by power, but by MY Spirit, saith the Lord." Even at the first meeting, many backsliders from the 1904 revival were restored, and the blessing increased.

A week or two later, the whole gathering was moved to

the Moriah Chapel and many were convinced that the powers of revival had been restored. But sometimes there were upsets similar to those in 1905.

> Evan Roberts stood up and demanded that everything should stop because he was aware that there was a person in the meeting who was blocking the blessing. Then he went a bit further and declared that this person was guilty of disobedience It was impossible to restart the meeting until the ⁄ person stood up and confessed sin. After ⁄ ⁔⁔⁔ed, liberty was restored to the meeting. The ⁔⁔⁔ od at work.

At other times the powers made an impact on outsiders. One man drifted into a meeting and heard his wife and friends praying for him by name, as Evan Roberts urged them all to do. He found himself on his knees, pleading for forgiveness.

Although many of the prayer meetings had to be held in more spacious chapel rooms, the large room at the back of the Old Post Office continued to be the centrepoint where wonderful things happened. Evan Roberts always spent time in prayer and meditation before he came downstairs to the meeting place and he would not come if the atmosphere was wrong. One evening he sent for Mary and told her he would not come down because there were persons sitting in the room below who had a wrong spirit within them. Enquiries were made and it was discovered that two people had come to the meeting with the intention of opposing the work. They were asked to leave so that the blessing might come.

Many people in Gorseinon were present one day when two parents brought their little child to Evan's prayer room and asked him to baptise their child. As the revivalist began to pray, the room was flooded with a light and with a sense of the Spirit of God. The parents and family began to pray and praise. Soon they were joined by the people in the post office and then those outside the post office who had heard the loud praising. Shoppers in the High Street ran to join them and there was such a dense crowd that wagons and carts could not reach the crossroads. An urgent message was sent to the police station and a constable came along to clear the way for the traffic.

According to the testimony of Mr. Martin Jones of Gorseinon, Evan Roberts was now involved in healings, exorcisms and some prophesyings, but openly rebuked someone who tried to speak in tongues at one meeting. All through the 1904 revival he had avoided such things and usually told converts that although the gifts of the Spirit were scriptural, the children of the revival were not yet ready for them and would be easily deceived by false manifestations. But now twenty-five years had passed by. He felt able to lay hands on the Rev. Thomas Williams. He anointed him and then commanded the believers to claim his healing in the name of Christ. That minister recovered from a serious illness and went on preaching for twelve more years.

Martin Jones described an act of exorcism which he alone saw:

> I remember one of the persons under conviction— one made captive and bound by the devil totally. Evan prayed and commanded the devil to leave him. Soon I heard a legion leaving that man. He was rolling on the ground and the demons were doing him injury, but God had the victory and he was set totally free. He sang often of that victory at Calvary. He witnessed faithfully until he was called home to glory.

It was hardly surprising that some thought that Evan Roberts had become an Apostolic or Pentecostalist. The sense of wonder and awe that fell on people when in close contact with Evan Roberts can be accounted for in another way. Who can measure the dynamic effect of a truly spiritual man who has spent day after day in solitary communion with his Lord?

What if this man of enriched and heightened spirit is brought into the fellowship of men and women who have also loved the Lord and spent hours on their knees in prayer for the souls of those around them? And what if this spiritualised man and this praying band are then allowed to work alongside other groups who have long expected the Spirit to come and the blessing to fall? Need one be surprised when unusual things happen?

Among the little band of younger men who were privileged to have been especially blessed during those months was Haydn John, who heard the call of God and had a life-changing experience. On one occasion, John Roderick Davies, pioneer missionary and founder of the Brazilian Rural Bible Institute, was invited to join Evan Roberts in fasting and prayer for one of the post office sisters. Many years afterwards, John Roderick said, "I learned more about inward godliness during those three days and three nights than in an age of conferences, lectures and special meetings." Another man, Ben Davies, learned more from the hymns composed by the revivalist, which he wrote down. One was a prayer for the bending of the churches; another was a prayer for the fire to fall again from Calvary's altar.

All through 1929, Evan Roberts made every effort to prepare his people for the coming battle against the powers of darkness, and to safeguard them from all deceptions. Martin Jones said: "He was always in a spiritual battle against the principalities and powers of darkness in the world—and at war with the rulers of this age. He led our thoughts to the same position and set out things for us in order to pray against such evil powers." Some of the brief prayers which he gave to his "students" show what were his main concerns:

Fill us with Divine Spirit;
Fill us with Eternal Life.
Resurrection Life; Victorious Life.

Cast out sin in the whole of me.
O God, destroy it for Jesus' sake,
Take out our weakness and give us Holy Spirit
strength.
You shall be purified and lifted,
And shall sit in heavenly places.

Fill the world with the angels of God.
O God, release your spirit now and send
The good angels to drive out the evil ones.
O God, have the victory over Satan.
O God, remove all evil.
Give us the blessing of victory
Over temptation and sin.

Many of the prayers preserved so faithfully by Martin Jones and others sound like those he uttered in the sanctuary at Leicester. These prayer sentences were clearly intended for use by those involved in prayer warfare. Evan once told them: "A short prayer is as good as a long one. If God tells you after two words to stop, then STOP. God provides the words and not one of them will return void." The same idea appeared in a little homily on prayer which, it is said, was published as a pamphlet.

"There are many kinds of prayer," he wrote. "You pour out worship first, and then the flow ceases, and you get down to business. Going apart to pray may be just a prop. It should be a prayer LIFE, with prayer sentences pouring forth every day as you turn everything to prayer. Do not go on waiting for an opportunity to go to God. If you are in Christ, you are in God, so just pray where you are."

Healings, conversions and wonderfully answered prayers were the most talked of effects of the "Little Revival," but some would have said that the most enduring work was going

223

on in the little Bible classes where Evan expounded on "The Eternal Things of Heaven." There was no neglect of teaching ministry this time.

The first series was on Romans; then the books of Daniel and Revelation, which focused on the "Coming of the Messiah and Son of God." Evan was once more interested in Second Advent teachings by this time and actually prophesied to the students that "King George would be the last King of England before Christ returned."

He was still inclined to put prophetic messages and exhortations in place of expository teaching and he still had no body of doctrine to present. The last Bible school was devoted to Revelation, chapters two and three. The messages to the seven churches were applied to the spiritual condition of the many chapels and churches in Wales. He had given up hope of an instant national revival; he told the class that "Revival is not the goal. It is *a goal* but not *the goal*."

It must have been an unpleasant shock for him, when he revisited Gorseinon and Blaenannerch in 1931, that Evan Roberts found few signs of the revival's lasting influence. One year later he went into final retirement and vanished into the shadows of history. The new work at Gorseinon continued a little longer and bore more fruit in due course. However, this time there was no outward spread of revival fire to the other nations.

23

The Hidden Years
(1931-1937)

I n 1930, Evan Roberts was heading towards fame and influence once more—by 1931, he was tucked away in a Cardiff suburb and was almost a forgotten man. This time it was not nervous collapse nor the kind of burnout experienced by evangelists. It could have been an effect of entering his difficult fifties, but it was more like a reversion to the solitary life he had tasted before. His change of lifestyle coincided, oddly enough, with another collapse in that decade. The thousand nonconformist chapels of Welsh Wales, together with their language and culture and social life, began a serious decline as described by Ben Rees in *Chapels in the Valleys.* It was also the decade of the great "brain drain" from the depressed valleys, which robbed most chapels of their future preachers, youth leaders and teachers. The decline in spiritual vitality was often lamented by Evan Roberts in private letters. Throughout the thirties, he lost heart and could not believe another revival would begin.

There was no hint of this in the mid-months of 1930. Mr. Alun Gibbard mentions how Evan Roberts was addressing a great meeting in Caersalem, Llanelli, in the same week that

Dr. Lloyd Jones was preaching nearby. What a princely feast! One story suggested that Evan was in Llanelli again in August and spoke twice at events connected with the National Eisteddfod.

There were signs that he was being fully recognised by his Calvinist Methodist denomination. He was invited to take part in the Communion Service and in the Assembly's special "seiat" at their Mold Assembly. There was also talk of a new preaching mission to North Wales, but Evan Roberts replied: "My work is now confined to prayer and it is to such that I have devoted myself for twenty-five years. By preaching I can reach a few; by prayer I can reach the world, but people do not understand this."

When people challenged him to explain why he had been absent for so long, he told them that it was God who had sent him into exile in order to pray for the world. Now he was back in Wales, and everyone hoped for the flame to fall. He took part in Ammanford Convention's prayer meetings and the service to commemorate the great revival. There were signs of growing excitement on such Jubilee occasions.

A great multitude of ministers, lay leaders and humble members came from all over Wales and gave a royal welcome to Evan. The Rev. David Evans wrote: "If the multitude was occasionally too great even for the new chapel, the Lamb of God was occasionally too great for the multitude. I saw preachers unable to go on for weeping, and the Lord descending suddenly to take control of the meeting." People began to ask, "Is this the long-expected revival?" However, the Rev. Nantlais Williams and others turned their faces against all-night meetings, excited behaviour and people "taking their liberty" too far. Afterwards it was said that these restrictions had grieved the Spirit and quenched the revival.

It is possible that Evan Roberts began to distance himself because of the publicity which presented him everywhere as a prophet and "anointed of the Lord." He did not make his way to the annual "Cyfarfod Gweddi y Mynydd" (revival prayer conference), nor the Llandrindod or any other convention in the next three years.

An old convert named Dafydd Jones saw him walking the lanes alone in the Blaenannerch and Aberporth districts. Perhaps he expected to see a welcome meeting in those chapels, but there was none. In the early thirties, Evan Roberts remained in the company of Mr. and Mrs. Oswald Williams who vacationed in West Wales. When they lodged near the cathedral city of St. David's, they were invited to the home of Alun Morgan in Caerfarchell. They went with the family to an evening service where he was noticed and at once asked to address the congregation. Twenty years later, Mr. Morgan recalled: "I will never forget the lightning which came into his voice as he said, 'It has been announced that a prayer meeting will be held here tomorrow night. Take care, my friends, that it shall become a believing meeting.'"

During this same visit there was a touching incident. A Welsh lady begged to shake hands with Evan because, she said, "You were the means of saving my boy who was killed in the war." The story reminds us that a great number of revival converts were in the age group which fought the Great War, and that many were casualties either in body or in soul. During other holidays, Evan Roberts visited places associated with earlier revivalists, such as Dafydd Morgan of Cwmystwyth and Howell Harris of Trefecca. One year he was at Bronwydd near Cardigan and not far from the Mynydd, yet he again refused to attend the special revival prayer meeting in that quiet spot. He told the Rev. Tom Beynon: "I feel no great desire in me to cut across my holiday and go to the 'Feast.' In spiritual terms, there is neither a light nor a wind to show me the way or to drive me towards the Mountain." He promised to pray "that the Divine Spirit would penetrate through everything in the Memorial Festival." No one can remember ever seeing him there in later years.

He had developed a habit of writing single-verse poems to put on his letters and thank-you cards, and one of these was sent to Mr. and Mrs. Tom Beynon after a visit:

> *In tempest oft I find I am.*
> *Naught there but Thee to anchor me.*
> *The storm may rage; I will not fear.*
> *I know that Thou art very near.*
> *I will believe, I will believe in Thee.*

Evan Roberts could be found more frequently in the company of the Welsh bards and scholars. Some recall how he sat for hours listening to the literary adjudications or joining in the discussions among poets. He was in Fishguard for their Eisteddfod Week and was warmly welcomed by the Rev. J. T. Job who had once been deeply involved in revival events at Bethesda, Gwynedd. It may well have been at Fishguard that he met up with the bard "Dyfnallt" Owen, to whom he sent his Welsh poems later on. All this interest in Eisteddfodic events would have been regarded by loyal "children of the revival" as proof of serious backsliding. The most sympathetic of the old revival spokesmen was the Rev. Nantlais Williams, with whom Evan spent holidays at Porthcawl, where a former revival singer, Arthur Davies, held a pastorate. One of his English poems was composed at St. Hildas, Park Avenue, Porthcawl. It is a poem of hope:

> *The Day of God breaks on my soul,*
> *Scatters sweet fragrance rich and whole.*
> *Is there a better hour when I*
> *Can see His Temple in the sky.*
> *The Church of God, where shall she meet*
> *Her Lord, save at the Altar's seat.*
> *For her, sweet fellowship is found*
> *And all the Saviour's joys abound.*

After one of these holidays, Evan Roberts wrote a highly personal letter to Nantlais, enclosing a few verses. This letter reads like a prose poem and contains a number of philosophical statements of a solemn kind, which contrast with the occasional lighthearted bits. It is certainly not the product . of a broken-down or a broken-hearted man:

> The charm of the sea is in its movement. Let he who will sleep, its waves do not wait for either men's discords or for the musician's baton. It is you poets who tune in to the keynotes of its melodies. We landlubbers stub the toes of our feet against the stones at its edge. . . . There is no new way without its Calvary; no Pentecost without its persecutions. Neither is there fatherhood without the responsibility of the bent back. Gravestones are but the steps up which a new era ascends to its throne and its inheritance. . . . Ages of knowledge will turn into a mere candle for the generation which is nurtured in its righteousness. That is the story of Man. . . . A level balance is not to be had here. Tribulation and comfort— a cross and a crown. Many and warm regards.
>
> *Evan.*

Friendship with the literary circle had its rewards. In February 1931, the editor of *Y Goleuad* thanked him for poems called "Yr Hen Weddiwr" (Praying Veteran), and "Heddwch y Byd" (World Peace). Another peace poem was accepted by Prosser of the *Western Mail,* who undertook to publish it on the day when they officially opened the Temple of Peace in Cathays Park, Cardiff. This was a great honour. In the same period, Evan received a request from the Rev. W. O. Rowlands, the editor of *Trysorfa'r Plant,* who wanted an article for the children: "This letter is a kind of cry from Macedonia. We need to have that voice which was once audible on the walls of Zion." The poem was published in the *Reciter's Column* and may be the verses entitled, "Yr Ifanc Dewr," a call to be truly brave.

Evan Roberts had quite a flair for composing verses for special events in people's lives. One of these was a rather long poem sent to the wedding reception of his young pastor. He called it "literary confetti" intended to be scattered over them. One verse each is dedicated to the Moderator, the deacons, the jeweller who sold the emblem of endless love, to old friends and the grandma who cries, "Oh dear! aren't they both happy? God grant that it may last." Of course the poem ends on a more serious, tender note:

> *The Saviour whispered to their souls,*
> *Henceforth be man and wife,*
> *And keep your love for each alive*
> *Like burning coals—for life.*

The covering letter explained that such merriment was quite in order since the Creator himself had ordained marriage: "We can't expect [joy] to be absent because He is present. Since there is nothing like love to release humour, then He who made them must be pleased with our efforts to be merry, but NOT AT YOUR EXPENSE."

Evan Roberts was now far more at ease in social events than he had been in his twenties. The Rev. Emlyn Lewis praised his actions at an engagement party, and Mr. David Shepherd recalled very pleasant visits to his home. He was a welcome guest in the home of the Rev. Ferrier Hulme who had arranged his fiftieth birthday party in 1928. Some of the Welsh-speaking students in Cardiff liked visiting him and receiving encouragement. One sunny day in 1936 or 1937, Evan Roberts had a strange Irish visitor. A young, cheerful, brash cyclist stood on the doorstep, explained that he was cycling around Britain in order to promote a "revival prayer fellowship," and asked for support. This was J. Edwin Orr, who expected to meet a "venerable old man" and was surprised to see him so different.

In his book, *The Church Must Repent,* he wrote:

> We had a long talk discussing revival, the influence
> of prayer, the need of vision, and the prospect of a
> mighty awakening. As usual, Evan spoke of obedience.
> "Being wholly yielded," he said, "ensures that God will
> direct you all the day. Therefore one's task is to listen
> for the voice of God, and then obey. Vision is as
> desirable a gift as faith. I have seen men who had great
> faith, but who have never exercised it because of their
> lack of vision. I have seen others who had vision, but
> who never responded because of their lack of faith." The
> veteran warrior then promised to remember the Revival
> Fellowship in his own prayers.

Orr discovered that Evan Roberts was waiting for a sign.
"People ask me, my brother, if I see any signs of the revival
for whose coming we all pray. Now, as you travel about, you
may see the positive signs, but I am not so privileged just
now. I tell them that I see all the negative signs. The churches
seem to be at rock-bottom in their decline. I would compare
the state of the true church today with the state of the prodigal
son in the far country just before he went home to his father.
Mark you, he has not started for home yet, but he is utterly
fed-up. He won't be there much longer. So I predict of the
church as it is today." He did not know then that very soon
the darkness would deepen over the land.

One more thing is now known about those hidden, but
not unfruitful years, in Cardiff. After he had taken his daily
stroll from 52, Betws-y Coed Street, the home of Mr. and
Mrs. Oswald Williams, northwards to Llanishen Reservoir,
or southwards past the church and library to Roath Park, he
would come back to his desk in a room which had no view.
Then he would sit and pen the most tender and helpful letters
to those who needed help. He wrote to the Rev. Evan
Richards (Dakota) and the Rev. Ivor Pritchard (Ontario) who

thanked him for his timely prayer support and wondered how he knew so much about their need. Somehow Evan knew that a time of spiritual refreshment had come upon that church. A young minister in Milford Haven thanked him for a letter of encouragement which had been a means of grace and guidance during a long period of perplexity.

The young minister wrote: "You see more than the men who walk in and out among the people. Yours is the point of vantage above the battlefield. We plod and plough with downcast eyes. Most of us ministers have neglected exercising our wings." He added, "I have felt on more than one occasion that prayer is being offered for us by some who are not with us in the body."

In Evan's scrapbooks there are notes of the letters and poems of condolence sent to bereaved people, even in 1939-1941 when Evan Roberts himself was leaving the sunlit plain of his middle years and passing into some grim, dark valley of desolation.

1. To the mother of Gordon, crashed in the Egyptian Desert, 1940:

For out of Egypt shall a trumpet call
You to God's everlasting corps,
Out of whose ranks not one shall ever fall,
And, flying, know not danger any more.
Death aims to end the love with fire, but fails,
For love converts those ashes into flame
Out of whose glory love itself avails
And gives your Gordon an undying name.

2. To Bereaved Christian Parents:

There is an altar in the heart;
On which burnt sacrifice must lie,
When wit, nor grace, nor beauty's art
Redeem what God decrees to die.
There is an Altar by the Throne
Flaming with incense kindled prayer
Commingled with the martyrs' own
Who, crying, find no answer there.

There is an Altar shall combine
All love, faith, hope and riven soul
When Time shall burn with power Divine
And end the sacrificial scroll. Then shall all
Altars lie in One. . . . (Heb. 13:10-15)
And these ascend in glorious flame,
And sacrifice forever done,
And Altar but One IMMORTAL NAME.

3. To a widowed lady in need of consolation (January, 1941):

Why write now that Time has so worn away itself? Alas! crowds flock around the grave and gaze at the open wound, but few are they that stand by while the heart goes on aching. . . . You, dear friend, have no balm to heal the wound, nor as yet is there time to cover the scars. For what scars the human spirit can bear, God alone knows. I would speak comfortably to your ears, dinned as they are with so much of war, and so untuned to music now because of Death.

24

"Why Art Thou Cast Down, O My Soul"
(1938-1943)

The unseen world rained down its lead
For three long decades on my head.
Its thunders spoke with mighty crash,
When half a deluge caused a smash
And half my heart went limp with dread.
                                        (1940)

hat was this mysterious deluge which smashed upon Evan Roberts with such destructive force in his sixtieth year? Surely it was not the first signs of the disease for which he had consulted a specialist and attended the clinic of some doctor friend. Neither was it a flaring up of the old nervous trouble, although the scribbled diary entries and dozens of partly erased verses give that impression. Some lines are like those flashes which pierce the gloom of a furnace room when the doors of fiery ovens are briefly opened.

Many of the poem titles of this period suggest that his writing was a kind of therapy which gave free expression to a set of pain-causing feelings. Written between 1938 and

1942, his poems, "Maze," "Lost," "Prison," "Presentiments," "Malcontent," "Phantom Joy," "It Is Enough," and "Joy is Pain," are of this type. Others paint a bleak picture of humanity which is bowed down and seemingly accursed. There is a poem, "Prisoner at the Bar," in which mankind, including Evan himself, becomes in turn the transgressor, the accuser, the prosecutor, the jury, the judge and even the "hangman" who finally executes the dread sentence. In the saddest of these poems, Evan seems to be crying out "Why art thou cast down?" but is unable to continue the psalm.

One of the evident causes of this dangerous depression was the impact of a horrifying world-wide war, but there were other complex problems which would not go away. Just as in the wars of 1914-1918, Evan had gradually sunk into despair and weakness, so now in 1938-1943 his sensitive temperament felt the continuing anguish of a world where millions of women, children and old and helpless people were trapped. The seemingly unending pain, violence and hatred caused him to write in bitterness:

> Man, like the landscape, bears it brands.
> His forehead's beads show dire commands.

Picture him as an elderly, lonely bachelor sitting at his desk and reading daily stories of the horrors of war. Few of us in Britain can forget the horrified dismay felt when a sombre announcer reported the disaster to the *Prince of Wales* battleship and a cruiser, involving nearly two thousand men. And no elderly American reader could forget the agonising sensations of that day when the unbelievably dreadful facts about Pearl Harbour were read out on hourly bulletins. Evan Roberts could feel the same intense pain when he heard of tragedies involving just a few young lives. Therefore he wrote poems about a child killed in a bombing raid, or a young couple who had gone into some church as casual tourists and had been suddenly buried in the rubble.

Evan Roberts was not content to sit in mourning without looking for some answer. In a Welsh poem called "Ei Cherrigbedd" (Gravestone), he pleaded with God's people to return to the Law of God in the midst of this awful tumult, "lest faith grow cold and songs fall silent. People must go to the Altar of God and plead for a new outpouring."

In another poem, "Tangnefedd" (Peace), he sees the giant winds of fanaticism and violence whirling around mankind, but he also sees that the "Castle of Jesus" is glowing and that the great host of the Lord is drawing near.

Thirdly, there was the poetic vision of "Gwr y Wialen Haearn" (The Man with the Rod of Iron), who would overcome evil, remove all danger, guard all truth and bend all kingdoms to the will of God.

Lastly, "Bendith y Nos" depicts the grace of God coming down and healing the people. God will make the wilderness fruitful and reclothe the naked souls of men, he prophesied. Always this miracle of restoration and this victory depended upon the Cross which towers over the world.

> *How blest that there's only one Cross on this earth*
> *With its head above the clouds of this world.*
> *How blest there is but one church unspotted*
> *On the mountain of glory for ever.*
> *The Cross through all ages shall stand firm.*
> *Its wood nought shall rot till there comes*
> *The Church all-victorious from its campsites*
> *And the last of the lost in its hands.*

About a year after this, Evan saw men erecting new buildings on a bombed site and suddenly had a vision of God rebuilding too.

He who holds the stars in space
Shall fill again His holy place.
Let all who have a heart and will
Remember gold has unction still.
Oh! is it too much to believe
Another Temple we'll receive.

Evan's last word on this subject of national restoration was set into his longest and least revised poem called "The Song of the Seer." Behind it there was an urgent debate: "Would God remember mercy for a people who had done their best to break the covenant? IF they would now forsake their folly and return to the Lord, would the Lord God return to them?" There was also an urgent personal question behind the very first lines of the poem, "Oh! who has slain my ravens?" Had God deserted His prophet also and left him like a rope in a tug of war, stretched beyond measure? Did God intend him to go back as an effective messenger? The whole poem was a harsh picture of the people of Wales deserting, backsliding, defying God, laughing at the punishing rod and forgetting that dark side of the Covenant which decreed, even as Isaiah and Ezekiel had taught, that a people who would do such things are "lying in death." God's most righteous judgments must surely be enforced, he concluded. "The Lord of all nations will not rest—'til the nation lies down to cry". At the very last, the poet holds out a promise of forgiveness:

The Lord of all waters and ravens,
The Maker of all that is fine,
Will banish his wrath from the Heavens
And feed us with His bread and wine.
Jehovah is joy even now, sir.
His heart is a garden of Love.
His clouds shall be decked with a bow, sir,
And His song shall be the song of the Dove.

During those dark and bitter days, Evan Roberts sat in his room and refused to see visitors, such as Leith Samuel. When he was invited to an induction service at "Pembroke Terrace" Church in Cardiff, he sent back a very peculiar reply about the need for the new minister to bring back the sunrise and teach his people to walk in the light because of the "evil on the face of the earth, without any kind of lamp, its inhabitants sit beneath the power of a dark sceptre." There followed a bitter complaint about so-called leaders: "So many 'suns' have been seen in the moral world, which have been of no advantage for the feet of blind people. They felt their heat and enjoyed it greatly, but for them it was only half a sun. We ought not to suppose that any kind of knowledge will come without the coming of Light."

Gloomier still was the letter to the new minister, Mr. Mainwaring, wherein Evan bemoaned the loss of concern for the Sabbath Day, the consecrated temples and for the great apostles of the pulpit: "The power of Death has been pushed away into the future, its proper place according to the estimation of those who have 'mastered' the Unseen World. The Judgment yet to be has no more influence than a thunderstorm in paralysing Evil. The Bomb matters more than the Judgment Day. Heaven and Hell? The one does not attract, and the other does not terrify as they did in days of yore."

The last evidence of a saddened man is a private letter to David Shepherd of Gorseinon in December 1942. The young man had asked for guidance, and Evan gave him snippets of wisdom about how to be patient and adaptable, realistic and untroubled by temporary losses. Advising David to fight his own way out, Evan Roberts said three times over that he could not help him or "meddle" with him. He said nothing at all about praying and spoke slightingly about tears as just a sign of bafflement. Very surprisingly, he tells this earnest young man: "The only word I would have you receive from me is, 'Use your commonsense. Revelation tends to undermine it. Harness your intellectual powers and drive hard.' Your friend, Evan Roberts."

It is comforting to know that a subsequent letter to David Shepherd was more like his old self. Indeed this first letter sounds so unlike the man who saw visions and who wept over the churches and even more unlike the great intercessor and valued adviser of *The Overcomer* period. Surely some kind of personal declension had overtaken him. It is important to understand that it was not just reaction to war and social evils that brought him down, but a tragic mixture of personal loss, loneliness and failure.

Any man on the wrong side of sixty can feel he has no real purpose in his life. When Evan wrote such poems as "Doing Nothing," "Empty Hands," and "Gentleman Beggar," he was giving rein to his true feelings. He didn't want to be a sheltered lodger or a pensioner dependent on others' charity. In a Welsh poem he compared himself with a grasshopper who carries an ever-diminishing burden as it grows old. At first, he too can carry a full burden, then only a half sack, and at last only an empty sack because of ill health and weakness. The grimmest of these poems alludes to some bad experience in a hospital .

Sometimes he felt envy after visiting the home of a generous supporter. One morning after breakfast, he recorded his complaints in his notebook. (A year later he added a postscript condemning his envy as, "a sorry scavenger which creates an itch but brings no unguents.") This is what he wrote:

> What benefit do I receive from people's possessions at too great a distance for my senses to be aware. One friend has a good cellar; one owns a Rolls Royce; one has a study of his own; another has a cottage by the sea. One wallows in a chair by a fat fire, but I feel the cold. I am in digs—a non-paying guest—under many restrictions.

The house in Betws-y-Coed Road had disadvantages. Evan had to do his writing in a living room, not a study; and, secondly, the houses were built in a sunken lane so that it was impossible to have a view of the stream, the meadows and the tree-covered slopes of the hills that ring Llanishen. The Williamses moved in October 1941 to a more spacious house called Bucklands in Beulah Road, Rhiwbina, but Evan still felt trapped and cut off from his fellow men, who sat in cars and never conversed, and never opened their homes to him.

> *So slammed are doors that I can in no way enter*
> *To say, "How do you do," far less to sit*
> *At table where food, though scant, does hardly centre*
> *The mind at ease nor hold the scantiest wit.*
> *The world for these might crawl upon all fours*
> *Before they find a hand to open doors.*

Even greater is the bitterness behind this little parable of "Four Sorrow-Laden Men" who happen to meet at a crossroads:

> *Each carried shame; each face was set.*
> *Each told their tale of want and woe.*
> *Each sought of each comfort and help.*
> *As lions reach food for a whelp.*
> *Each sought in vain; All help was blank.*
> *Since there was none, they ate and drank.*

The last sorrow for him was the loss of creativity. Once he had dreamed of becoming a prophet, but now he was only, a "chaplain on a battlefield." He described his poems and scripts as "not rotten enough to engage hope, but not strong enough to give assurance of publication." A third poem grieved that he had lost the "spade" with which he used to dig up "silver coins of precious lore." And in "Someone Hereabouts" he savagely dismissed his "Blank verse and Blanker Muse." All that he had written recently was described as:

> *Fish uncaught; lines loose, and broken mesh.*
> *In shame I hide the creel and basket.*

In the end, that was just what he did; he scribbled in a notebook his decision to "fling to the sea what should be drowned and let my music find its pause." There were no more attempts at creativity for a long time.

Some would say: "How could such things come upon a man who had walked with God? Where was the victory he had preached about? Had he become a backslider?" Do we say this about Elijah mourning under his tree, or St. Paul in the midst of his stinging "thorns," or of despairing Henry Martyn, or John Bunyan in his personal "Slough of Despond," or Howell Harris who deserted his own "Settlement," or of poor, unbalanced Cowper? In Evan Roberts's case, it was still blessedly possible that the painful experience could turn into the kind of chastening which afterwards yields the peaceable fruit of righteousness. But first there had to be a reunion with his Lord and Saviour.

The first little sign of renewal can be seen in a poem drafted in July 1941 and completed later. The key verses in "Virtue Under Arms" describe the coming defeat of evil:

> *He whose challenge called to battle,*
> *He shall faint and flee.*
> *We shall triumph, says the Master...YEA, by me.*
> *Not by power, nor yet by armies*
> *Shall His work be done,*
> *But through spirit rich and mighty...By HIS SON.*

Another kind of personal hope and renewal glows from the Welsh poem, "Daeth yr Haul." In this picture, joy flows like a river through the meadows, calm winds return, songs are heard and all is gold purified by fire. "Why wonder that my heart is on fire since the Sun has entered in?" the poet shouts with joy.

Evan Roberts's last and finest testimony to what Christ did for him is given in the form of a parable about a man gathering stones in a harsh field—a common sight in Wales:

> He knelt at the broken furrow.
> And searched for the hidden stones.
> The hands made red in that burrow,
> Were they not the Master's own.
> The winds made this meadow so arid.
> The sun burnt that prison of clay.
> Where plough and ploughman now tarried,
> The stone of resistance's given way.
> He halts where MY furrow is broken.
> He kneels at MY bed of clay;
> And the hands made red are the token
> That the stones shall be gathered away.

Evan Roberts's crisis poems have been hidden until now, and some will wonder if anything worthwhile can come from such a story. Yet surely there is a priceless lesson to be learned. In the darkest days of war and confusion and loss; in the deepest shadows of poverty, loneliness, and fear; in the depth of spiritual defeat or dryness, a man who has known his God can say things which are a help and strength to others. And the good news is that whenever he is ready to cry, "Why art thou cast down O my soul, HOPE THOU IN GOD," he will be lifted up and set upon the Rock, and even given a new song. When those who read this story come to their juniper tree, they may hear Evan Roberts's aged voice saying,

> Lift your eyes; Look to your gracious Lord; let Him take the stones out of your barren heart and place you once more in a way of holiness and a field of fruitfulness.

25

Thine Age Shall Be Clearer Than the Noonday

hree long years after Evan Roberts entered those bitter months of perplexity and despair, he was free once more. The Lord had returned to him and taken away the stone and clay from his soul. Outward circumstances had also changed for the better. The worst of the war seemed to be over and there were fewer tragedies in the lives of people around him. Soon letters trickled in from old friends and from relatives. Best of all, he had at last learned how to be in all things content, especially after they had all had settled down in a larger house in Beulah Road, Rhiwbina. One quiet evening he sat at his desk once more, reading, copying and perhaps translating those comforting lines from Dr. T. Gwynn Jones's "Evening Hymn," which he intended to send to a widow.

When measured years and days must close,
When shades arise as darkness grows,
Come Thou, who knowest all, and guide.
Let sunshine fall at eventide.

The worlds high tumult fades and dies;
Sweet silence follows strident cries.
Thou, that ordainest all, abide,
Shine from Thy Throne at eventide.

There was no longer any likelihood or danger of becoming a public figure again, because the war years pulled a curtain across the past, and another generation had arisen who "knew not Joseph." Older men greeted him if he visited the few Welsh language chapels left in Cardiff, but the ministerial students at Cardiff Baptist College were hardly aware that he existed. Senior members of the Christian Union, who often walked past Beulah Road on their Saturday afternoon walks towards Caerphilly, had no idea that Evan Roberts lived nearby.

As Evan Roberts travelled over to Gorseinon, Neath and Maesteg to attend many funerals, he became aware that his own revival generation was thinning out swiftly. Just after the war, he went on visits to Miss May John the singer, Sidney Evans, his oldest fellow worker, and Richard Looker, his devoted admirer. Evan Roberts had his own special visiting cards, which were postcard poems, such as the one which was later engraved on the back of his memorial column in Loughor:

Dear Friend, ... God loves you.
Therefore seek Him diligently
Pray to Him earnestly.
Read His Word constantly.

In the post-war years, the Roberts family in Loughor and Neath, which had met and corresponded very rarely, began to draw together more positively. A great-niece shared that Evan began to visit her people at "The Bryn" and that: "To us girls he seemed like a distinguished English businessman, although he still talked to my mother in good Welsh. The twenty-year exile in Leicester had taken Uncle Evan out of Welsh life and culture too completely." She also confirmed that Evan had restored links with a family member, Davydd, who had never shown interest in his revival witness. Another lady recalled seeing Evan Roberts in the streets of Tredegar and sitting unnoticed in the pews of his brother Daniel's chapel.

Evan Roberts had regained much of his vitality and cheerfulness. He told Dyfnallt Owen in one letter that he could not understand the young students who were so worked up about their academic examinations, seeing that, in their real life "every grace and every virtue, every opportunity and every encounter with fellowmen is a hard moral examination. He could see exciting changes."

The veteran's life began to blossom in many ways. People from the United States and Canada sent substantial food parcels, for which he wrote personal letters of thanks. Welsh friends could not send food but they did send regular thank-offerings which supplemented his pension and the quarterly allowance from the Aged and Infirm Fund. When he received a small legacy, he sent off ten percent to the Talgarth Memorial Hospital.

He had begun to travel in England once more and was keen to buy better clothes. For a three-week stay in London, he took two suits, twenty shirts and eleven collars and ties. He was practical enough to check his funds, get his ration card and coupons and identity card, plus an emergency aid card for treatment.

Whatever his state of health, it didn't prevent him from enjoying life. The most exciting event in Evan Roberts's calendar was the annual visit to Mr. Sam Jenkins, who kept a guesthouse or residential hotel in Cartwright Gardens in the heart of London. His fare was paid for, his taxi or car from Paddington to the house arranged, and a series of outings planned. They visited old friends at Croydon and Tenterden and Mill Hill. He noted in his diary that Mrs. Davies of Mill Hill had given him bacon and eggs for breakfast, a good tea and haddock for supper. Sam Jenkins took him to theatres and choral concerts. Evan was thrilled with a concert in Kingsway Hall, a benefit for the Llandow Air Disaster Fund. No doubt, Sam Jenkins, who was precentor of Charing Cross Welsh Chapel, could get the best seats in the concert halls.

On 31 January 1951, Sam wrote to the *Western Mail* about how much he missed Evan: "I was hoping he would stay with me for at least a month, during which he would make his usual social round and would attend a few of the best concerts, for music was his great delight." In these years, Evan took new interest in public affairs and one person who met him at a funeral commented: "Evan Roberts had many shrewd things to say about men and affairs. I felt that, despite his enforced retirement, in no sense had he shut himself within himself."

News filtered through to the hundreds of ageing "children of the revival" that seventy-year-old Evan Roberts had been seen sitting in a theatre, standing in a sports ground and staying at a hotel. Many people were convinced that he was backsliding and more than a few wondered how he felt about spiritual things and about the dream of another awakening. They could have asked the members of his local church. Someone would drop into the house if he had been unable to go because of weakness. Whatever news they brought they could expect one question from Evan, "Did you meet the LORD tonight?"

In the letter to Dyfnallt, Evan showed he had not lost all memory of the revival. Even a rising wind would remind him of it:

> People heard the majesty, or was it the madness, of
> that wind. We sought to understand the best meaning of
> this strange sound and to interpret the world of the Spirit.
> . . . The wind took new fervours, the fire was satiated
> as it purified and consumed, the tongues found ears to
> hear even at midnight.

Yet when people began to talk about a fortieth year
anniversary meeting of the revival, and Evan was approached
by a Mr. Chester Morgan, his replies show little enthusiasm.
A letter dated 16 November 1944 compared the event with
a meeting of survivors from the forty-year Exodus from the
Wilderness. But Evan agreed that a Commemoration would
"enlighten the young people, refresh the old, and inspire the
faithful with new longings."

In later letters, he suggested transferring the affair to the
whole denomination; he refused to send a photographic block
of his profile, and he finally sent his excuses in April, 1945.

The reason for this coolness is clear enough in his letters.
He repeated his lament that "fear and reverence have lost
their throne and Faith has often been cast down. Neither the
pains of death nor the Judgment Day will grip and arrest
hearts as it did once." At this point he could write, "If there
is plenty of room to go back, there is plenty of need to go
forward." But his later letters offered no hope: "The things
of earth grow less and less and so does the earth itself until
there comes the Eternal fully in to take its place. That should
be your prayer as churches—for the Fullness to come."

The one contradiction to this picture is a scene
remembered by the Rev. R. Vivian Morgan of Pencoed, near
Bridgend. He happened to be preaching at "Bethel,"
Porthcawl, and was told by the lady of Chapel House that
Evan Roberts had been in the congregation, practically
unnoticed. Mr. Morgan had a time of fellowship with Evan
before the evening service and said that years afterwards he

remembered "the heavenly atmosphere so many years after the revival. In my evening service he sat beneath the pulpit. In the after-meeting he stood up in the big pew and spoke powerfully while we gazed at him."

In May 1949, Evan Roberts had to stay in bed all day for the first time. Some months later, he had to be treated in hospital again. He told Sam Jenkins that he was arranging to seek the advice of Sir Daniel Davies, the King's physician, who was a son of his old revival-time secretary, Mardy Davies. All correspondence in his notebooks stopped in September 1950 with one word: "ill"

That severe winter was his last—he was buried on 29 January 1951. At the age of seventy-two, he went to join the host of revival saints who had gone triumphantly before him. He was not buried in Cardiff, but in the family graveplot behind Moriah where he lies with his father, mother, sister and an unmarried brother. Some years later, a fund was raised by subscription and a memorial column was erected in front of Old Moriah.

The funeral itself was a Memorial Service conducted by Pastor Lunt of Moriah, the Rev. Geraint Nantlais Williams and the Rev. Lewis Mendus. Hundreds who loved and honoured Evan Roberts, but had lost sight of him for years, came now to sing his loved hymns such as "*Caersalem*" and "*Ton y Botel*," and his friend Sam sang a favourite revival song. Tributes were paid by a moderator, the Superintendent of the Forward Movement, the President of the Baptist Union of Wales, and by his veteran friend, the Rev. Nantlais Williams. With the small group of close relatives stood Mrs. Oswald Williams, that true sister in the Lord who had given him a home.

Of the many tributes to the revivalist, there was one in the *Western Mail* which showed great sensitivity and understanding:

He was a man who had experienced strange things. In his youth he had seemed to hold the nation in the palm of his hands. He endured strains and underwent great changes of opinion and outlook, but his religious convictions remained firm to the end.

The best way to end this story is by citing a little poem which Evan may have intended to be his last testimony:

Thanks be to God! His love is mine.
Heavens dazzling rays around me shine.
Freed through the Cross, the night is o'er.
Take, Lord, the glory evermore
                                        E. R.

Epilogue

Any attempt to measure Evan Roberts's influence on the Body of Christ has to take a middle way between respected leaders who have severely judged him, and equally godly men who have perhaps over-praised the one they called the "anointed of the Lord."

Evan Roberts has been judged several times for failing to undertake tasks, such as expository preaching and systematic theological instruction, for which he was totally untrained. Such work was not practicable during the tumults of the revival and was not even expected from him once he showed signs of breakdown. He had his own role as an exhorter.

Most church leaders were satisfied to know that his messages were doctrinally sound, usually derived from standard works. A college tutor said that Evan Roberts's weakness was that he had no framework of theology, philosophy, ethics or church history. What Evan Roberts had was a body of experience-based doctrine which he presented in words of fire. His themes were: assured salvation; baptism by the Holy Spirit; the "Real Presence of the Lord"; the need for full identification with Christ crucified; and the value of believing in Christ's victory and authority over the powers of evil.

His ethical principles were: consistency of life; sincerity of witness; faithfulness in stewardship; and constant resistance to temptations. His spiritual input during the revival was through ministering the gifts of the Spirit. His ministry after the revival was in the realm of intercessory prayer, communion with God, and continuous striving against the principalities and powers in high places. All these truths were given first of all to hundreds of revival converts, and then transmitted all over the world through the literature and conferences of *The Overcomers*.

Many of Evan Roberts's errors in handling meetings arose out of experimental methods which he soon dropped, such as the mobile worker teams inside chapels, the singing and reciting teams, the rather aggressive personal interrogations of whole audiences, and the substitution of unusual personal testimonies and messages for any kind of formal address. These things were not repeated in the third period of revival missions, so they must have been learning experiences. However, there were three or four serious incidents which seem to stem, oddly enough, out of the very same gifts which made him such a sensitive counsellor, exhorter and evangelist.

Is it so great a fault if sometimes the awareness of others' needs and distresses, or of other people's hypocrisies would confuse his judgment, overstrain his nerves and even reduce him to tears, silence and solitude? Only by the boundless grace of God could he be lifted again, restored and filled once more with power, so that he could exercise a lasting spiritual influence over the lives of hundreds. What then are the legacies of Evan Roberts?

The first spiritual legacy of Evan Roberts was that by acting in full obedience to the Holy Spirit, he released vital forces into chapels and churches of his day. Those notes of exultant praise and unrestrained love, joy and hope, which are heard so often today, were heard in the chapels for the first time from the mouths of those who had been set free from concealed sin, disobedience and barrenness. Some of the by-products were:

a. A continuing concern in many fellowships for giving maximum liberty to those who felt led to take part.

b. A welcome involvement in worship and in testimony (not teaching) of quite ordinary women and even children. This was new wine indeed for an age when both females and the young were so often told, "You should be seen not heard." Now the whole of Acts 2:18 came true and the Lord had His handmaidens as well as His menservants.

c. A new respect for the possibilities of supernatural happenings, such as visions, guidances, and discerning of spirits in private devotions and sometimes in public services. By 1928, this included prophesyings and healings.

d. A strong desire to offer direct praise TO the Holy Spirit as well as THROUGH the Holy Spirit. This principle was later modified by Evan Roberts but has continued to exert widespread influence.

e. A widespread use of the "altar call" in ways much more like its pure original form—not as friendly welcome or an invite to become members, but as a time for confession, a time for testimony and for solemn reconsecration.

The second spiritual legacy is the four principles of preparedness for Spirit-filling: Cleansing; Confession; Obedience; Public Witness. The reasons for that preparedness were crystallised in due course. There are twentieth-century movements which still commend a completely open confession of secret sins so that a cleansing prayer can be offered. There are many excellent Bible teachers who have continued to call on Christians to stand up, show their allegiance to Jesus and go out as witnesses. There are charismatic and other fellowships which have inherited his teaching not only to obey the Holy Spirit but to offer Him our love and praise. In our day, men like Harper, Wallis, and Kendrick have taught new attitudes of openness to the Holy Spirit. Not a few have gone on into places from which Evan drew back. Under the guidance of Mrs. Penn-Lewis he called on people to obey the One who sent the Spirit, and he advised converts and Christian workers not to cultivate "tongues" and to test all prophecies and visions.

Until very recent times, there have been chapels, halls and fellowships in Wales and Britain which have stayed faithful to this vision and to these principles. Some would say that they have received a new lease on life in the present times.

The third legacy comes from the long years at Leicester.

One great theme would totally possess his mind and heart for some time and inspire some fine writing. In 1904-1905, it was total obedience to the Holy Spirit; in 1906-1908, it was identification with Christ Crucified in order to share in His victory over sin; in 1909-1913, it was the laws of spiritual warfare; in 1913-1914, it was the Rapture of the Saints; in 1925-1930, it was Church renewal; in 1929, it was the pre-Rapture gifts of the Spirit.

Each theme seemed to match Evan Roberts's own experience and tasks so that everything else took second or last place. Sometimes this singleness gave power to the message; sometimes it caused problems when Scripture texts were wrongly used to support such ideas as: "prayerless churches can delay the Return of Christ"; "non-witnessing churches can hold up the Lord's final battle." In some cases Evan Roberts drew back, and this was especially true about his visionary experiences.

The fourth legacy is also from his Leicester period.

Instead of serving the spiritual needs of Welsh converts,

Evan found himself ministering first to those in England and Europe who wanted to be touched by revival fire and wanted to be God's dedicated servants. *The Overcomer* and the Workers' Conferences gave him access to hundreds of missionaries and workers all over the world. As for the ministry of intercession, who can ever measure its spiritual effects? These are recorded in eternity. However, there were several well-known mission pioneers of that era who said that Evan had taught them the secret of effectual intercessory prayer.

It was specifically for the workers that the unique *War on the Saints* was prepared. Opinions will always differ on the value of this book which Evan Roberts co-authored. It had a number of serious defects and unbalanced teachings, but it taught essential truths for this age:

a. Satan seeks to infiltrate many spiritual and evangelistic movements such as renewal and revival.

b. Christian churches need not only a spirit of discernment but a system or principles of discernment

c. Deliberate passivity of mind and body in any religious activity is treacherous and open to abuse.

d. By the blood of Jesus on the Cross, victory is always a certainty.

Once freed from its exaggerations, this unique book could continue to be a help and inspiration to new generations of Christian workers who also face the increasingly subtle forces of Satan and his agents. If it is, a new legacy may emerge from the "hidden years."

Can anything good come out of failure and isolation? Surely some priceless lessons can be learned from those long-lost poems and letters of the thirties and forties. Yes, in the darkest days of failure, confusion and bitterness and in the shadow of poverty, war and death, a man who "had been with Jesus" gave compassionate help and strength to others. Because he had walked with God, he was lifted up and set upon a Rock and given a new song to sing. And even in the long days of old age, as an irritated oyster creates pearls, so the suffering of this saint yielded the peaceable fruits of righteousness.

When any of us come to that place, may we hear the voice of men like Evan Roberts saying: "Lift up your eyes. Look to your Lord. Let Him take the stone out of your heart and put his winter sunshine in its place."

Appendix A

Two Addresses by Evan Roberts

1. A Gospel sermon preached in the tent at Llandrindod on Thursday evening the third week of August 1906.

(Author's note: I have translated this indirect speech reportage into direct speech exactly as Evan Roberts usually spoke.)

Sermon theme: "O Lamb of God, I Come."

Why should we follow the Lamb? You have asked the Lord to break you up and you have said that you want a broken, contrite heart. God's way to break you is by way of the Cross of Calvary. Will you take God's way? The disciples followed Him and they were counted as fools. Will you take that way? Are you willing to be private fools or public fools? Calvary was the place of the "Skull"—the place of failure in the eyes of the world, but of success from the standpoint of our God. It was there the Lord was crucified and His friends left Him. Will you take the way of the cross tonight and allow God to have His way? If you are willing, then life will flow out to the world. Are you willing to be conformed to His death—willing to be nothing, to have no reputation and to be fools for Christ's sake?

Jesus took the form of a servant and was made sin for us. Would you then take the place of a servant? God wants you to be humble. Oh! that the Spirit would reveal the Cross to you. The world is waiting to see the Christ—it is looking to the Church to see Christ there. What does the world see in the Church? Is it the self-centred life getting less and less, and the God-centred life growing day by day? Are you willing for the self-sacrifice, willing to be servants, willing to be nothing? For Christ to be all? Are you willing to let God do what He can do with a surrendered soul? If you intend to live the real Christian life, the world will take Christ. Real Christian life—not your ideas of what it is, but God's life in you.

Jesus can save and He does. He has blotted out the past and given us a new life. He is OUR Christ. Are we determined that Christ should have the utmost out of us? Do we crave to suffer and die for Christ? Jesus must see of the travail of His soul and be satisfied. So let us pour out our lives for the world. Let us be Godlike, because you can through Christ. Can you say tonight, "Oh Lamb of God, I come, and I will follow Thee?"

The world may scoff, but let it scoff. As long as God is smiling, that matters not. God is with us. Let the miser have his gold, but let us have Christ. HE is all that we want and you should want no more or less. HE is our Peace, our Saviour, our Guide and our all.

There is nothing in this world for the soul. You young men should not seek popularity but seek Christ—not ambition but Christ! Christ is sufficient. Christ is your friend and reveals the Father to us in such tenderness. So why not become real sons and daughters of God?

Oh, for Calvary to be revealed—the veil to be lifted. The

Cross can break all bonds and all one in Christ Jesus—of one mind, heart and one purpose for the glory of God. Are you willing for such a mighty movement to come? I have nothing but God, but God is enough for eternity. He is the Living God, the God who reigneth. The powers of darkness are strong, but "our God reigneth." Praise the Lord for the victory. Let us follow the Lamb—a broken heart for a broken heart. Oh Lamb of God, I come.

2. Same week at Llandrindod, Friday evening.

Sermon theme: "Love Your Enemies."

This is the command of Christ and we must follow the Master. Is this clear this very moment to every heart? God can make it clear and was willing to do so. Will you allow the Lord to make it clear? God is demanding that you should love your enemies. Calvary was the pattern. If anyone says he cannot love His enemies, let Him look to Calvary. There you will see God's love for He loved His enemies. When you see Christ on the Cross you will be willing to drop all things and follow Him step by step. You must not follow afar off but closely. Follow Him right to the Cross. Peter said, "I will die with Thee," but a few hours later he was far off. You must never rely on your own powers but on God's. You cannot love your enemies by yourselves but God's love in you can do this.

Will you flee or will you follow Christ to the Cross and be true to Him at every step? Will you follow Him to the Judgment Hall to be scoffed at and mocked? Will you be faithful to the Truth, the Light and to God? He is willing to fill you with His own love. If there is anything wrong in your hearts, then to the Cross with it. God is willing to make you like Himself. Can you pray for your enemies? If not, will you ask God to help you? God will never bless you if you ever oppress others and become taskmasters over His children. We are to be one in Him.

Do you love one another? Or are you too swift to see one another's faults and to magnify them and talk about them. Oh! DROP THAT! Ask God to help you to see the best in men. You must love ALL—the minister, the deacon, the rich and the poor. Do not love the environment but the soul. Friends may leave you but God never—just as flowers may fade but the life remains.

GOD, the source of all life, is willing to flood you with His pure life. The cry of every heart is for life—the world and also the Christian. Every man seeks life but the great majority seek in the wrong direction. Calvary is the way of life—the way of eternal life. Point the world towards Calvary not so much with words but by every act bearing the stamp of Calvary. It is not so much a case of seeing Christ and weeping as seeing Christ and having your wills bent by the Divine will. Calvary will be the song of Eternity so why not now?

The Holy Spirit is willing to reveal the Cross if we are willing to look. Satan has managed to veil the Cross and make people think it was something horrible when it was something glorious. Calvary was God's victory and when we gaze on Calvary we gaze upon God's deepest and highest victory. Drop everything and look at Calvary for there is life for a look at the Crucified One.

Jesus has saved not only the soul but the life. Are you willing for God to have the best out of you and to remove the worst out of you? He is willing to fill you and flood the world with His best, but He has to empty you first of everything which is contrary to His will. OH! glorious life of reckless abandonment to God. If you want to glorify God, you must be on the altar and then the flames will descend and God will be glorified through you. Does it matter what becomes of you if God is glorified? LOVE YOUR ENEMIES. LOVE ONE ANOTHER.

Appendix B

Letters Concerning Evan Roberts

1. Letter from Mrs. Jessie Penn-Lewis to the Rev. R. B. Jones concerning her position relative to certain revival matters, and Evan Roberts's health.—7 September, 1906

My Dear Son. (Can I call you anything else now?)

I do feel sorry I did not write more clearly to you. As the days go by I see that I really was in the mind of the Lord in asking you if you would come . . . I would not ask you unless I felt it really necessary. We are cut off here in this isolated country spot. It is impossible to get a breath from the outer world to help one to gauge the pulse of things. In the past it has served the Lord's purpose as I had mainly my desk-work to consider, but now that it is conflict and we need know something of the trend of things, I see it as a great hindrance.

I feel the situation is serious in Wales and, like me, you see we must be very sure of the Lord's leading every step. I could not speak to W. S. Jones and Owen Owen as freely as to you and I wanted to say things to you that I cannot put on paper. Evan Roberts cannot be left out of the situation for any step. . . .

I could give you a very great deal of the inside of things at Llandrindod which caused, or helped to cause, the added tension, etc. If Evan were able to grip the situation boldly, he could doubtless do much but:

(1) He is physically unable and the strain is too great and was too great at Llandrindod. It was a stiff battle of prayer in the background even to pull him through that week, and it nearly shattered me. None know what it meant for him to keep on his feet as the enemy raged on all hands. Happily my husband was with us and saw all the inside of things and his counsel was a great strength as to the course since then. He also saw through all that lay in opposition.

(2) If Evan was able now to throw himself into work that very course—nay, any course he took—would add to the tension. Possibly the Lord is keeping him still needing strength because the path is not clear. O. M. Owen wrote to say how good it would be if Evan could throw himself into the Convention movement, but that step is a serious one and needs weighing, and some aspects need explaining to you. . . . You will see therefore my object in asking you to come and meet him and have a couple of days. . . .

(3) I know too that my words at the "Breakfast" caused much antagonism. I was misunderstood. Some were really blessed but I heard that several, if not many, were angry and that it would take much to soften them. So I fear that I have unwittingly added to the difficulties. Then Evan Roberts's staying with us seems to be disliked; and this is easily explained.

At the back, centre and depths—the real core is the raging of hell against the Cross. I could give you a fair sketch of the adversary's tactics—not of flesh and blood but spirits. I nearly sank during that awful meeting and the Lord has since given me Jeremiah 12:5 about the ministers' attitude to me.

(4) We have a terrible fight before us but Evan Roberts must be "strong" ere he touches, for it will be no trifling battle. . . . My impression as to E. R. is that he really keeps in retirement until every trace of past strain has disappeared. Llandrindod showed that he is only just beginning to throw it off. It may be best that I keep from Wales for a time. . . . . Will you come? I call on you as a son in this hour of crisis, and Evan Roberts needs you too—but the Kingdom is the main need. For the sake of the Kingdom, I feel that you need to come.

2. 10 October, 1906. Letter of invitation.

Evan is maturing rapidly and is getting gloriously free in God. He is manifestly being prepared for service in Wales and I trust it will not be very long before the Lord will give him liberty to move about there. Then it will be seen what God has wrought in him. What God means by the Throne-Life is getting clearer and other souls are being drawn into the place of victory. (*the next paragraph is about moving to Leicester*) . . . Evan may be in Wales just then. You would rejoice to see how God is maturing him and how He uses him greatly in mighty burdens by prayer. The time here is fraught with great issues to the Kingdom and Eternity will reveal them.

3. August 1907. Letter of thanks sent from Davos in Switzerland.

I first want to tell you how God is with us and how Evan is progressing most rapidly in this rarefied air five thousand feet up in the Alps. From that day that you went to Leicester he has been steadily gaining and now he is able to think freely and God is pouring light in such a way that I can see the church, by Christmas, going to benefit greatly. I do not wonder that the adversary has raged and left unused no device from Hell to frustrate the coming power of God. And I knew that God was going to equip Evan here. We will come and tell you about all he has been through and the way God is giving him now to be able to dissect and define the entanglements by Satan in the supernatural sphere. I see God as training him as an expert for disentangling souls. . . . We are being specially trained for special work. . . . The great warfare of the past few months is the prelude to a great movement by God.

Appendix C

Letters from Evan Roberts to Friends

Letter A. An extract from his letter to Sidney Evans during his revival mission in Dowlais (see chapter 8)— 27 January 1905.

The Evil One often tempts me to speak my own words, but, PRAISE HIM, the Holy Spirit through His wisdom overcomes me, overcomes the world and the Devil in all his wiles. So He gives me words and ideas that answer to the needs of the crowd. This gives me trouble—I know not whether it troubles you.

I remember how in one meeting a "voice" said to me, "Cry out the word 'Judgment, Judgment!'" Praise be to the Spirit, I was prevented from doing so, else Mr. Self would have manifested himself at once.

Another thing. I thought it was necessary to make use at all times of these things I had from the Spirit. That is a mistake. He has plenty of variety. We must take care to be in His hands, body and soul . . . Yours in the bonds of love, Evan.

Letter B. To his friend, D. M. Phillips, from Carmarthen—9 October 1905.

Dear Phillips,

At last, behold a pen on paper. There is scarcely time to breathe in the mild atmosphere of the house of dear Mr. Wheldon, the Bank. I came here for a day only but, alas! Reuben has joined hands with Benjamin. It is a mistake for me to try and arrange and carry out my future. The people cannot understand why I do not move; and I fail to understand why I am staying! This I know—that I am moving swifter than ever—so swiftly that I cannot perceive myself moving. What a commotion there is in the tents. My soul is a kind of tabernacle, and self dwelling in innumerable tents around it. . . . Oh, some ceaseless moving continues! The "old man" and the pure heart enraging and getting furious for victory. . . .

Why shall I do next? Return to my strong castle or seek for another enemy? . . . I must move on because the voice of duty calls aloud. . . .

Letter C. To Nantlais Williams—1929/30. A parabolic sermon after declining the honour of being invited to take part in a Chapel Jubilee.

Thank you for the honour laid upon me by asking me to take part. I don't feel good that this is all in vain. It is good to yield to the wishes of the "saints" when one can. Though I cannot conform with your desires I am not distressed because I know you can get a better voice to address the people in this costly and holy place. In Wales there is a host of brave men faithful to Kingdom law, who have taken hold of the ploughshares and directed them toward the mark which is set before them, and have gone at it with a determination which flows out of their love for the work. Forgetting that which is behind they press towards the mark which they determined to reach at the beginning of their courses as preachers.

That which is buried is the strength and virtue of that which is visible. That is true in the world of Nature and in the world of Man. The bases of the skyscrapers are deep down in the clay; unless they go down they cannot go up. Even that cornstalk which trembles a few feet or more above the surface of the earth gives thanks for its positioning in the grainseeds which first went down into the darkness, coldness and moisture. If we see a mighty, tall, building we know it has sound foundations. If we see a field of wheat rejoicing in its glory, we remember how the field was a "cemetery" after it was trampled by the plough. That hand on the plough must work effectually and at a consistent depth and width between rows to ensure that not one bit is hardened and that the seed is not wasted. The really important thing is to break it up totally and deeply into the ground which is to receive it . . .

NOW, one of the perils in regard to Kingdom work is an expectation that the harvest will be speedy and "untimely." We are half-content to forget the laws of sowing and reaping. In its proper season we shall reap if we do not grow weary. *(Author's note: Here there was a personal word of encouragement to Nantlais.)*

Where are the multitudes which used to grow on the rich meadows of the precious Gospel? In Heaven, says the bard. The farmer will say, "That crop is the rickyard of Jesus and lies awaiting the great threshing on the Day of Judgment." That's true. You preachers of blessed Wales, lift your eyes and look upon the harvest which has already been safely gathered. Then you will remember and rejoice in your sweat behind the plough's handles. Sweet shall it be after the bitter work of pushing ahead past the obstacles which have challenged your strength.

Appendix D

Biographical Index

AWSTIN: T. Awstin Davies. Born, 1857. Died, 1934. Son of a Pontypridd minister. Became newspaper sub-editor; then a mining correspondent and full-time journalist. He was entirely responsible for the *Western Mail Revival Supplements*. He also took part in revival services. Later, became a supporter and eventual President of the National Eisteddfod Association.

CHADWICK, Samuel. Dynamic Founder and President of Cliff College, a Methodist seminary in the North of England.

DAVIES, Annie. A native of Maesteg, near Bridgend, in South Wales. A highly trained singer. She and her sister, Maggie, dedicated their gifts to revival work and travelled widely. (Further details in *Voices From the Revival,* Chapter 3.)

DAVIES, Rev. Mardy. A Presbyterian minister who volunteered to be Evan Roberts's secretary. He was the father of Sir Daniel Davies who was a physician to King George VI.

DAVIES, Mary. One of the five Gorseinon girls who offered in November 1904 to join a revival team to work with Evan Roberts. Travelled often with him before illness stopped her. Living in the Old Post Office, Gorseinon. Later played a vital part in the "Little Revival" of 1928-1930.

DAVIES, Roderick. Founder of the Brazilian Rural Bible Mission in Minas Geraes. Later founded the Ty Brazil home for retired missionaries and also did Rural Work in Dyfed.

EVANS, Florrie. Celebrated as the humble girl whose testimony—"I love Jesus"—challenged the minister and church at the commencement of the revival in Newquay, Dyfed. She later shared revival missions with her pastor, Joseph Jenkins.

EVANS, Sidney. Fellow student of Evan Roberts who was commissioned at Cardigan. Major revival figure in Gwent and the Swansea area. Later married Mary, who was Evan Roberts's sister. Went as a missionary to India and was Principal of Cherrapunjee College. Last ministry was in or near Gowerton. (Robert Ellis, *Living Echoes*)

EVANS, Rev. Young. Tutor at Trefecca Calvinist Methodist College near Talgarth in Powys. Sought to advise Evan Roberts on intellectual problems.

FRANCIS, Rev. Thomas. Loughor minister who became a friend and champion of Evan Roberts, was allowed to record his conversion and call. (*Western Mail Revival Supplement* 3). He became the editorial author of *Diwygiad a Diwygwyr*.

FRYER, Rev. A. T. Anglican clergyman who was a prominent member of a Society for Psychical Investigation. Made many detailed enquiries into revival phenomena.

FURSAC, Dr. Emil. Paris-based sociologist/psychologist who investigated Evan and others closely. Author of *Un Mouvemente Mystique dans Pays de Galle.*

HUMPHREYS, Morgan. A Professional journalist linked with Welsh and English newspapers in North Wales. Made important contributions to the *Cyfrol Goffa Diwygiad,* and to a later B.B.C. programme—mainly because he was always with the revivalist in North Wales Missions.

HULME, Rev. Ferrier. Methodist minister who was profoundly touched by the revival and ever afterwards befriended Evan Roberts. Held circuit pastorates in Gloucesterr, Stroud, and Bristol, 1920-1940.

JENKINS, Rev. Joseph. See Eifion Evans's book and *Cyfrol Goffar Diwygiad.* His diaries are in the CMA collection.

JENKINS, Sam. A Llanelli-born furnaceman who became a famed Gospel singer in the Revival. Eventually moved to London and ran a Commercial Hotel. Evan's last close friend.

JONES, Rhys Bevan. Famed minister from the Lower Rhondda. Founder and Principal of the Porth Bible Training Institute. Leading post-Revival expositor, Convention speaker and author. (See *Kings Champions,* last chapter, for details.)

JONES, Martin. Gorseinon workman and chapel deacon whose vital and unique testimonies of the 1929 revival were fortunately recorded in or about 1954.

JOSHUA, Seth. Pontypool-born rough diamond who became an evangelist sponsored by the Presbyterian Forward Movement. Instrumental in the conversion and consecration of both Sidney Evans and Evan Roberts in October 1904.

LEWIS, Elvet (ELFED). Deeply influenced by the revival, he became a princely preacher, poet, hymnist, and author of *With Christ Among the Miners*.

PENN-LEWIS, Jessie. Extraordinary writer and expositor who was active in the Keswick movement, then founded *The Overcomer Testimony* and exercised a world wide ministry. Neath-born, but was wed to the City Treasurer of Leicester. Orthodox Quaker linkages. Died in London in 1927

MATTHEWS, David. Native of Aberdare, Glamorganshire. Widely travelled evangelist and singer-composer (*Matthews' Mission Melodies*). Author of *I Saw the Welsh Revival*, Moody Press.

MEYER, Dr. F. B. Major figure in revival meetings and conventions for many years. Bible teacher and author. Ministry at Leicester. A Free Church Council statesman.

MORGAN, Rev. Vyrnwy. Anglican clergyman. Author of *The Revival in Wales* which argues that it had no lasting effect.

ORR, Dr. J. Edwin. Author of seven major books, such as *The Church Must Repent*. International consultant on world revival history. His research records were deposited at Los Angeles.

PHILLIPS, David M. Presbyterian minister in the Rhondda Valley. First biographer of Evan Roberts (1907), he also wrote three other books of which *Dynamic Preaching* is inspiring and undeservedly forgotten.

PRICE, Rev. Peter. Minister in Dowlais near Merthyr. Scholarly man who was bitterly opposed to Evan Roberts's work.

PRITCHARD, Rev. Ivor. Welsh pastor at Hamilton in Ontario, Canada, he wrote to Evan when a local revival began.

REES, Annie Mary. Elocutionist and evangelist who sometimes assisted Evan Roberts. (See *Voices from the Revival.*)

ROBERTS, Daniel. Brother of Evan, he too was caught up in the revival work. Became a Presbyterian minister.

ROBERTS, Mary. Younger sister of Evan. Joined his revival work

SHEPHERD, David. Gorseinon. Semi-retired evangelist who has recently restored Evan Roberts's chapels, Pisgah and Old Moriah—now open for visits by overseas parties.

STEAD, William T. Journalist and moral crusader. Wrote about the revival. On board the TITANIC when it sank in April 1912.

WILLIAMS, Rev. Dr. John. Native of Brynsiencyn in Anglesey who became pastor of Princess Road Welsh Chapel, Liverpool. Made Chairman of the Liverpool Revival Committee.

WILLIAMS, J. C. Born at Neath to a North Walian minister. Born-again at Skewen. Founder and administrator of the Prayer Watch, but spent some time in Baltic countries.

WILLIAMS, Rev. Thomas Charles. Welsh Presbyterian minister who became the President of the Anglesey Association. First to welcome Evan Roberts back after his long exile.

WILLIAMS, Rev. Nantlais. Pastor of Bethany Welsh Calvinist Methodist Church, Ammanford. Founder of Ammanford Convention. Hymnist and poet. Editor of *Yr Efengylydd* and other magazines. Became an elder statesman of his denomination but never gave up his friendship and admiration for Evan.

Appendix E

Suggested Readings

THE MAIN REVIVAL: CHAPTERS 1-12

Charles Clark	*Pioneers of Revival*
Brynmor Jones	*The King's Champions*
Brynmor Jones	*Voices from the Revival* (1993)
R. B. Jones	*Rent Heaven*
D. M. Phillips	*Evan Roberts—Great Revivalist*
J. T. Rees	*Evan Roberts—His Life and Work*
David Matthews	*I Saw the Welsh Revival*
Chile Pine	*The Revival of the Welshman's Soul*
Dr. Fursac	*Un Mouvement Mystique Contemporaine*
Jessie Penn-Lewis	*The Awakening in Wales*
Elvet Lewis	*With Christ Among the Miners*
Gomer Roberts	*Cyfrol Goffar Diwygiad*
Francis	*Diwygiad a Diwygwyr*
R. Ellis	*Living Echoes*
Eifion Evans	*The Welsh Revival of 1904*
Holyoake	*The Afterglow* pp. 1-19 (1907)
W. T. Stead	*The Revival in the West*
J. Stewart	*Invasion of Wales by the Holy Spirit.*

| A. Morris | *Newscuttings of the Welsh Revival* |
| *Western Mail* | Revival Supplements 1-5 (Awstin) |

THE REVIVAL MISSIONS: CHAPTERS 12-16

Y Glorian	April & May 1905; Jan 1906
Negesydd	April & May 1905; Jan 1906
Baptist Times	23 May 1905; 12 & 26
	December 1906
The Cambrian News	March 1905
Cardigan & Teifiside Advertiser	March 1905
Western Mail	Revival Supplement 6

BOOKS:

Gomer Roberts	*Cyfrol Goffar Diwygiad.*
D. M. Phillips	*Evan Roberts—Great Revivalist*
	(pp. 379-404)
G. Hughes	*The Evan Roberts Liverpool Mission*

THE LEICESTER PERIOD: CHAPTERS 17-21

Mary Garrad	*Jessie Penn-Lewis*
Evan Roberts & Mrs. Penn-Lewis	
	War on the Saints (1912)
The Overcomer	1909-1924
The Life of Faith	1906, 1908, 1911, 1919
Yr Efengylydd	Volumes 1-3, 1908-1910
ibid.	Volumes 18, 20, 21
	(Messages of Evan Roberts)

THE LAST BLESSING AND THE LAST YEARS: CHAPTERS 22-25

| Edwin Orr | One chapter in each *Can God* and |
| | *The Church Must Repent.* |

Alun Gibbeard	Essay in *Cylchgrawn Efengylaidd,* 1980
Y Goleuad	Articles on 14 February 1951; 16 May 1951; 18 May 1990
Western Mail	Obituaries and Tributes; January & February 1951

Calvinist Methodist Archives (National Library of Wales) Letter-books, diaries, and poems of Evan Roberts.

We commend to your interest the companion volume:

Voices From The Revival

This is an invaluable presentation (Anthology)
of 120 eyewitness reports and testimonies collected,
arranged, and interpreted by the Welsh author of
An Instrument of Revival, Brynmor Pierce Jones.

TOPIC:
    Revival.

SOURCES:
    Praise; Prayer; Witness; Outreach;
    Opposition to Revival; Community Impact;
    and a remarkable collection of conversion/
    consecration stories.

OBTAINABLE FROM:
    The Evangelical Press of Wales
    Bryntirion, Bridgend
    Wales

                    or

    Bridge Publishing & Distribution
    2500 Hamilton Blvd.
    South Plainfield, NJ 07080

Other quality books by Bridge Publishing:

AZUSA STREET

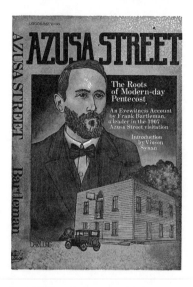

In the early 1900s, the name "Azusa Street" became synonymous with the Holy Spirit's renewal in America. What began in a Los Angeles barn became a powerhouse and streaked across America like fire.

Now from the pen of John Bartleman, an early leader of the movement, we have an eyewitness account of the "latter rain"--when Pentecost moved from California to Maine and back!

PP: 268
PRICE: $7.95
ISBN: 0-88270-355-2

AZUSA STREET AND BEYOND

Here, in one volume, is the story of the explosive growth of the Pentecostal movement in this century. Leaders from every phase of this dynamic work of God express their own views about Pentecostalism's history, theology, practice, and future.

What was it like to be at Azusa Street? What were the motivating beliefs that propelled Pentecostals into worldwide expansion? Will Pentecostalism survive another century?

PP: 245
PRICE: $7.95
ISBN: 0-88270-607-1

HOWELL HARRIS:
HIS OWN STORY

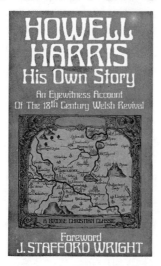

Howell Harris was brought up to regard the Nonconformists as "a perverted and dangerously erroneous set of people"—hardly a promising start for a man who was to play a major role in the Welsh Revival.

Yet in these extracts from his writings and diaries, we can read the thoughts of Howell Harris before, during, and after his own conversion. We can see God breaking through the barriers separating "church and chapel" and discover Christians of different denominations preparing the country for revival.

PP: 92
PRICE: $3.95
ISBN: 1-85030-004-6

We commend to your interest the companion volume:

Voices From The Revival

This is an invaluable presentation (Anthology) of 120 eyewitness reports and testimonies collected, arranged, and interpreted by the Welsh author of *Instrument of Revival*, Brynmor Pierce Jones.

TOPIC:
  Revival.

SOURCES:
  Praise; Prayer; Witness; Outreach;
  Opposition to Revival; Community Impact;
  and a remarkable collection of conversion/
  consecration stories.

OBTAINABLE FROM:
  The Evangelical Press of Wales
  Bryntirion, Bridgend
  Wales

          and/or

  Bridge Publishing & Distribution
  2500 Hamilton Blvd.
  South Plainfield, NJ 07080